SUCCESS
AND HOW HE WON IT

From the German of E. Werner

E. Werner

Hawk Press

Published by

Hawk Press
4836/24, Ansari Road, Daryaganj
New Delhi – 110 002
Phones: +91-11-23278618, +91-11-43667199
E-mail: thehawkpress@gmail.com
www.thehawkpress.com

CONTENTS

Chapter I	1
Chapter II	6
Chapter III	13
Chapter IV	20
Chapter V	28
Chapter VI	35
Chapter VII	41
Chapter VIII	51
Chapter IX	56
Chapter X	64
Chapter XI	75
Chapter XII	89
Chapter XIII	98
Chapter XIV	107
Chapter XV	121
Chapter XVI	131
Chapter XVII	142
Chapter XVIII	156
Chapter XIX	167
Chapter XX	179
Chapter XXI	185

Chapter XXII   193

Chapter XXIII   209

Chapter XXIV   226

Chapter XXV   241

Chapter XXVI   265

CHAPTER I

It was growing late in the afternoon, yet the principal church of the capital was still densely filled. From the numbers present, the beautiful floral decorations of the altar, and the long line of handsome equipages waiting without, it was evident that the ceremony about to be celebrated had awakened interest and sympathy far and wide.

As usual on such occasions, when the sacredness of the place forbids any distinct utterance of curiosity, or other feeling, the spectators found vent for the restlessness of expectation by whispering, and the gathering together of heads in little groups, and by an eager attention to all that was going on in the neighbourhood of the vestry. A general exclamation of satisfaction was heard when its doors opened, and, as the first tones of the organ pealed forth, the wedding party appeared.

A numerous and brilliant company thronged round the bridal pair at the altar. Rich uniforms, heavy velvet and satin dresses, airy fabrics of lace, flowers and diamonds waved and rustled confusedly in a truly dazzling splendour. The aristocracy of birth, and the aristocracy of finance, represented each by its most distinguished members, had met, as it seemed, to enhance the prestige of the marriage ceremony.

To the right of the bride, first among the guests, stood a tall and stately officer, whose uniform and various orders bore witness to a long military career. His bearing was simple and dignified, suited to the solemnity of the occasion, and yet it seemed as though, behind the set gravity of the features, there lurked a something at variance with so joyful an event. His look was singularly gloomy as it rested on the young couple, and, when he turned from them and glanced through the crowded church, an expression of suppressed pain, or anger, passed over the proud face, and the firmly-closed lips trembled slightly.

Opposite him, and next to the bridegroom, stood a gentleman in plain clothes, also advanced in years, and also, as it appeared, closely related to the young people; but neither his lavish display of brilliants in watch, rings and pin, nor the extreme self-importance of his bearing, could procure for him a shade of that distinction which his opposite neighbour possessed in so eminent a degree. His whole appearance was decidedly ordinary, not to say vulgar, and even the unconcealed triumph now illumining his countenance could set no other impress on it.

The triumph was, indeed, great with which he gazed on the bridal pair, and he looked down the aisle on the closely-packed rows of chairs and on all the bright assembly, with the satisfaction of one, who, after long striving, sees and welcomes the fulfilment of his aims and hopes; clearly, no shadow troubled his gladness at the event now to be solemnised.

But of all present, these two men alone appeared to take a deep interest in what was passing; least of all were the principal actors moved. The most unsympathising of the guests, the greatest stranger, could hardly have shown a more complete indifference to the solemn act about to be performed than these two, who, in a few minutes, would be for ever united.

The bride was about nineteen, and of undeniable beauty, but around her there seemed to reign a sort of icy chill, which ill became the hour and the place. The light from the altar-candles played on the thick folds of her white satin dress, shone in the diamonds of her costly ornaments; but it fell on a face which, with the beauty of marble, seemed for the time being at least--a time when the most frigid calm might naturally yield and kindle--to have acquired also a statue-like coldness and fixity.

The flaxen hue of the heavy tresses, on which her myrtle wreath rested, contrasted strangely with the well-marked eyebrows, and dark, almost black eyes, uplifted to the priest but once or twice during the entire ceremony. The pale, regular features, shaded on either side by her flowing veil, bore that distinctive mark of breeding which birth, and birth alone, can give. Indeed this high-bred air was the chief characteristic of her appearance; it showed itself not only in her delicate and noble features, but was so plainly stamped on her carriage and entire being, that all other qualities, some, perhaps, striking even deeper root, were by it overshadowed and held in the background.

A young lady fitted only, it would seem, for the higher spheres of life, never to be brought in contact with those possible men and things which, perchance, may exist in its lower phases. Yet, in spite of all this, something in the dark eyes betrayed more energy and character than are usually found in a lady of fashion, and possibly the present hour was one to call such energy and such strength of nature to the front. As the ceremony proceeded, the gentleman in uniform to her right, and three younger officers who stood behind him, gazed, ever more intently, ever more anxiously, at her face; it remained, however, calm and impassible as it had been from the first.

The bridegroom at her side was a young man of about eight-and-twenty, one of those not very uncommon individuals who seem expressly created for the gilded surroundings of a salon, who there alone find their significance, obtain their triumphs and pass their lives. Blamelessly correct in mien and toilette, his whole being seemed to denote the extremity of languor. His features, fine and agreeable in themselves, bore an expression of apathy so complete, of so boundless an indifference to all and everything, that they lost their charm for the observer. He had led his bride to the altar with the air of a man leading a lady to the place destined for her in any ordinary assembly, and he now stood by her, and held her hand, in precisely the same apathetic fashion. Neither the importance of the step he was about to take, nor the beauty of the woman he was there to wed, seemed to make the slightest impression on him.

The priest's discourse came to an end and he proceeded to the actual marriage service. Loud and clear his voice rang through the church, as he asked Arthur Berkow and the Baroness Eugénie Maria Anna von Windeg-Babenau if they consented to take each other for man and wife.

Again the officer's face twitched nervously, and he darted a look almost of hatred across to the other side. Next minute the double "yes" was spoken, and one of the oldest, proudest of aristocratic names had been exchanged for the simple, plebeian Berkow.

Hardly was the service over and the last word of the concluding benediction uttered, when the gentleman wearing the handsome brilliants pressed hastily forwards, evidently intending to embrace the newly-married lady with much ostentation. Before, however, he could carry out his project, the officer stepped between them; quickly, as though claiming an indisputable right to be first, he took the young bride in his arms; but the lips which touched her forehead were cold, and his face, as he bent over her, remained hidden a few seconds from all around. When he raised it, his expression had changed to one of calm and quiet dignity.

"Courage, father, it had to be!"

These words, intelligible to him alone, were breathed so low as to be barely audible, but they gave him back his self-command. Again he pressed his daughter to him with a wistful tenderness, which had in it something like a prayer for pardon. Then he left her free, giving her over to the now inevitable embrace of the other, who had waited with visible impatience, and would no longer be deprived of his right to salute "his dear daughter-in-law."

She certainly made no attempt to withdraw herself from him, for the eyes of the whole church were upon her. Standing motionless, with no shade of disturbance on her beautiful face, she only raised her eyes to him; but in her look there was a haughtiness so unapproachable, so icy a repulse of that which could not be openly refused, that she made herself understood even here.

Somewhat disconcerted, her father-in-law changed his vehement demonstration of affection to an attitude of respectful politeness, and the embrace, which immediately followed, was in reality little more than a form, his arms touching nothing more substantial than the flowing drapery of her bridal veil. The new relation's assurance, though certainly far from small, had yet not held its ground before that glance.

Young Berkow made things easier for his father-in-law. Something passed between them which looked like shaking hands, but, in truth, his white kid gloves hardly came into contact with those of the Baron. It seemed, however, fully to suffice them both; he then offered his arm to his young wife and led her away. The bride's satin train rustled over the marble steps and down the aisle as the two passed out, followed by the guests in gay procession. Shortly afterwards the carriages outside were heard to drive away one by one.

The church was soon emptied. Some pressed to the doors to see the departing visitors once more; some hastened out to give vent to all their important observations and reflections with regard to the toilette, bearing and appearance of the young couple and those nearly connected with them. In less than ten minutes the vast place was empty and deserted; only the evening glow shone through the tall windows and flooded the altar and great altar-piece with its crimson light, so that the figures on the old golden background seemed quickened into life.

Fanned by a current of air, the candles flared unsteadily, and the flowers, lying crushed and trampled under foot on the ground, where they had been so prodigally strewn, breathed forth their dying odours. What better end could the poor flowers serve amid such a blaze of jewels, on so high a festival as this, when the daughter of an old baronial house had been given in marriage to the son of the city millionaire?

The carriages had already reached the Windeg mansion, and life and movement were beginning to circulate through the gaily lighted rooms. In the principal salon, radiantly illuminated by countless wax-lights, the young bride stood leaning on her husband's arm, cold, beautiful and haughty, as she had stood at the altar an hour before, and received the congratulations of the eager friends pressing round her with their good wishes.

Had she really set the seal on her own happiness by that "yes" she had so lately spoken?--the dark shadow still resting on her father's brow might perhaps have given the fitting answer.

CHAPTER II

"Well, thank Heaven, we are in order at last! but it was high time, for they may be here in another quarter of an hour. I have given the people up on the hill full instructions; as soon as the carriage is visible on the heights, the first salute is to be given."

"Why, my dear Director, you are all fire and excitement to-day!"

"Keep some of your strength for the important moment of the reception."

"Indeed, your present position as Master of the Ceremonies and Lord High Chamberlain" ...

"Spare your pleasantries, gentlemen!" said the Director with some vexation in his tone. "I wish one of you had been honoured with this confounded post. I have had enough of it!"

The entire staff of officials connected with the great Berkow mines was assembled in full dress at the foot of the terrace running before the château. Built in the style of an elegant and modern villa with a handsome façade, great plate-glass windows and a fine entrance, the house produced a striking effect, which was still further heightened by the tasteful gardens surrounding it on all sides, and looking specially beautiful to-day in their fête-like dress.

The conservatories had evidently been stripped of their richest treasures for the decoration of the steps, balconies and terraces. The rarest and most precious plants, so seldom brought in contact with the outer air, unfolded here their wealth of colour, and perfumed the air with their sweet scents. On the broad lawns stood fountains, throwing high into the air their sparkling waters, and round them, most carefully cultivated, bloomed all the native beauties of spring in her first awakening. At the chief entrance a lofty triumphal arch was reared, all decked with flags and garlands, and the great gates, thrown wide open, were also twined with flowers.

"I have had enough of it!" repeated the Director, stepping up to the other gentlemen. "Herr Berkow demands the most brilliant reception possible, and thinks he has done everything when he gives us unlimited credit. As to the good-will of the people, he never takes that into account. Well and good, if we had the working men of twenty years ago to deal with! When, for once in a way, there came an off-day then, any kind of a holiday with a dance in the evening, one need never be anxious about the way they would cheer; but now--what with passive indifference on the one hand, and open hostility on the other, they were very near refusing to give any reception at all to their young master and his bride. If you go back to town to-morrow, Herr Schäffer, it would do no harm, in your report of our festive doings, to let a hint drop of the state of things. It seems they either do not, or will not, know of it there."

"That I certainly shall not!" returned the other. "Do you care to listen to our respected governor's very polite language when he has to hear of anything unpleasant? As for me, I prefer at such times to retire to the greatest possible distance from his august person."

The others laughed; it hardly seemed as though the absent master were held in much veneration among them.

"So he really has brought about the grand marriage," began the chief engineer. "He has given himself trouble enough about it. It will be some compensation for that patent of nobility which has been hitherto so persistently denied him, and for which, above all else, his soul yearns. He has, at least, the triumph of seeing that the noble old houses feel no prejudice against him as a plain commoner. The Windegs are willing to ally themselves with him."

Herr Schäffer shrugged his shoulders. "They had no choice left. The embarrassed state of the family affairs is no secret in the city. I doubt if it has been an easy thing to the proud Baron to give up his daughter on such a speculation. The Windegs have always been, not only among the oldest, but also among the haughtiest of the aristocracy; but even pride must bend to a bitter necessity."

"One thing is certain, this grand connection will cost us a famous sum of money," said the Director. "The Baron is sure to have made his conditions. Besides, I really do not see the object of all these sacrifices. I could understand it, if they were made with a view to buying rank and a title for a daughter, but Herr Arthur will be just as plebeian as before, in spite of his wife's ancient lineage."

"Do you think so? I would wager not. They will grant to the husband of a Baroness Windeg-Babenau, to the Baron's son-in-law, all that his father has striven for in vain; and, as for the latter, in his daughter-in-law's salon, nothing can hinder him from meeting all the people who have hitherto held him at a respectful distance. Don't tell me! The governor knows well enough what this marriage will bring him in, and so he can afford to pay something for the cost of it."

One of the officials, a fair young man with a tight-fitting dress-coat and irreproachable gloves, here thought fit to put in an observation.

"For my part, I don't understand why the newly-married pair should make their wedding trip to our solitudes, and not rather to the land of poetry, to Italy" ....

The chief-engineer laughed out loud.

"What an idea, Wilberg! Poetry in a match like this, between money and a title! Besides, wedding tours to Italy have become so general that they probably appear vulgar to Herr Berkow. At such times the aristocracy retire to their estates, and we must be aristocratic before everything."

"I fear there is another and a deeper reason," said the Director. "They suspect that the young fellow would continue in Rome, or Naples, the same sort of life he has led in the capital for the last few years, and it is high time to put an end to it. His expenditure latterly might be reckoned by tens of thousands! Most springs may be exhausted, and Herr Arthur was in the right way for trying this little experiment on his father."

Schäffer's thin lips curled sarcastically.

"His father has always encouraged him in it; he only reaps what he has sown! Perhaps you are right It will be easier for him to get used to the yoke up here in these wilds, and to learn to obey his wife. I am only afraid she may not fulfil her mission with much enthusiasm. It certainly is not a very enviable one."

"Do you think she has been forced to marry him?" asked Wilberg eagerly.

"Nonsense--forced! the thing is not done in a tragic way now-a-days. She has simply yielded to reasonable advice, and to a clear insight into the position of affairs. I have no doubt this marriage of convenience will turn out tolerably well. They do mostly."

The fair Herr Wilberg, who clearly had a leaning to the tragical, shook his head with a melancholy air.

"It may be--not! If, in the heart of the young wife, true love should awake later, if another .... Good heavens, Hartmann! cannot you lead your men farther off. You are covering us with a perfect cloud of dust, you and your regiment!"

The young miner, to whom these words were addressed, and who was passing at the head of about fifty of his comrades, gave a contemptuous glance at the carefully appointed dress of the speaker, and another at the sandy carriage-road, where the miners' heavy shoes certainly had raised some dust.

"Right about face!" he cried, and the column wheeled round with almost military precision, taking the direction indicated.

"What a bear that Hartmann is!" said Wilberg, fanning the dust from his coat with his handkerchief. "Not a word of excuse for his awkwardness! 'Right about face!' in a tone of command, like a general at the head of his troops. And then he takes so much upon himself! If his father had not put in his word, he would have forbidden the girl Martha to recite my poem composed for the bride's reception, my poem--which I" ....

"Have already read aloud to everybody," finished the chief-engineer in an undertone to the Director. "If only it were a little shorter! but he is right; it was audacious of Hartmann to wish to forbid it. You should not have posted him and his people just on this spot; there is no sort of welcome to be looked for from them. They are the most rebellious fellows on the whole works."

The Director shrugged his shoulders. "Yes, but then they are the finest men. I have stationed all the others in the village and on the road, the élite of our people ought to be at the chief entrance, the post of honour. On an occasion like this, one wishes to make a show of one's belongings."

The young miner, who was thus being discussed, had, in the meantime, stationed his comrades round the triumphal arch and placed himself at their head. The Director was right; they were fine fellows, but they were all surpassed by their leader, who towered high above them. He had a powerful, well-knit frame, this Hartmann, and he looked to full advantage in his dark miner's dress. His face would hardly have been called handsome, if judged by the strict laws of symmetry. The brow might have seemed too low, the lips too full, the lines not noble enough; but those sharply-cut and well-marked features were certainly no ordinary ones.

The light curly hair lay thick on the broad massive forehead, and a wavy brown beard encircled the lower part of the face, the manly bronze of which did not betray that it was so often deprived of air and sunshine. His parted lips had a defiant look, and in the rather sombre expression of his blue eyes lay a something which can hardly be defined, but which impressed itself at once on ordinary minds, and was respected by them, as the sure token of a superior mind. His whole appearance was that of energy incarnate, and however little sympathy his stiff, unbending bearing might excite, it yet commanded attention at the first glance.

An older man who, although wearing the miner's dress, did not appear to belong to the working-men, drew near now, accompanied by a young girl, and came close up to the group.

"Good day to you. Here we are ready to take our part. How do things go, Ulric? Are you all in order?"

Ulric assented shortly, while the others returned the old man's greeting with a hearty, "Good day, Manager Hartmann!" and the looks of most of them turned on his young companion.

The girl was about twenty and very comely. She wore the holiday costume peculiar to the locality, and it became her well. Rather below the middle height, her head hardly reached to the gigantic Hartmann's shoulder; her fresh young face, with its blooming cheeks and clear blue eyes, a little sunburnt and crowned with thick dark plaits, had strength in it as well as attractiveness. She had made a movement, as if to offer her hand to the young man, but he stood with his arms folded, and she let it fall quickly. The Manager noticed this, and looked sharply at them both.

"We are out of humour because we could not have our own way for once?" he asked. "Never mind, Ulric, it does not happen often, but when you push matters too far, your father must speak a word of authority."

"If I had anything to say about Martha, I should certainly have spoken out pretty plainly," declared Ulric decidedly, and a dark look fell upon the splendid bouquet in the girl's hand, which certainly owed its origin to a hothouse.

"I believe you," said the old man equably; "it would be exactly like you. For the present, however, she is my niece and has to conform to my wishes. But what is the matter with your arch up there? The great flag-staff is drooping; you must bind it up more firmly, or the whole concern will be tumbling down, wreaths and all."

Ulric, to whom this warning was specially addressed, looked up indifferently at the wreaths in danger, but made no attempt to come to their rescue.

"Don't you hear?" repeated his father impatiently.

"I thought I was hired to work in the mine, and not here at a triumphal arch. Is not it enough that we should have to mount guard in this place? Let those who built the thing set it to rights again."

"Can't you forget the old tune for one day?" cried the old man angrily. "Well then, one of you go up and see to it."

The miners all looked at Ulric, waiting for a sign of assent from him. As none came, they did not stir; one man only made a move, as though he would respond to the summons; the young leader turned silently and looked at him. It was but a single glance from the imperious blue eyes, but it had the effect of command. The man stepped back at once, and no other hand was raised to help.

"I wish it would fall on your obstinate heads," cried the Manager hotly, as he mounted with quite youthful activity and tied up the flag-staff himself. "Perhaps that would teach you how to behave on such a day as this. You have spoilt Lawrence already amongst you; he used to be worth something, but now he only does what his lord and master Ulric directs."

"Ought we to be so overjoyed that a new set of fine masters is coming?" said Ulric in a low tone. "I should have thought we had had enough of the old!"

The Manager, still busy with the flag, luckily did not hear this speech; but the young girl, who had stood silent on one side, turned hastily and cast an anxious look upwards.

"Ulric, for my sake!"

At this injunction the defiant young miner held his peace, but his features did not soften by a shade. The girl remained standing before him; she seemed to hesitate, having something to say and not liking to say it. At last she spoke in a low tone, half questioning, half entreating.

"So you really will not come to the fête this evening?"

"No."

"Ulric!" ...

"Let me be, Martha, you know I can't bear your dancing nonsense."

Martha stepped back quickly, her red lips pouting, and a glistening tear in her eyes which sprang even more from anger than from wounded feeling at his unfriendly reply. Ulric either did not notice it, or did not care; indeed, he seemed to trouble himself but little about her. Without wasting another word, the girl turned her back on him, and crossed over to the other side.

The eyes of the young fellow, who just before had been willing to help with the flag, followed her intently. Evidently he would have given much that the invitation should have been addressed to him. He, assuredly, would not have rejected it so cavalierly.

In the meantime, the Manager had come down, and was reviewing his work with much satisfaction, when the first volley burst forth from the hill opposite, followed, at short intervals, by another and another. As was natural, these signs that the expected visitors were approaching at last, produced some excitement. The gentlemen assembled out yonder became suddenly animated.

The Director hurriedly inspected all the preparations for the last time; the chief-engineer and Herr Schäffer buttoned their gloves, and Wilberg rushed over to Martha, probably to ask, for the twentieth time, whether she were sure she knew his verses, and would not endanger his triumph as a poet by inopportune shyness. Even the miners betrayed some interest in the young and, as it was said, beautiful bride of their future master. More than one drew in his belt, and pressed his hat more firmly on his head. Ulric alone stood quite unmoved, erect and disdainful as before, and did not even cast a glance over at the other side.

But the reception, prepared with so much thought and care, was to turn out differently from what had been hoped and expected. A cry of horror from the Manager, who was now standing outside the great arch, drew all eyes in that direction, and what they saw was certainly terrible enough.

CHAPTER III

Down the steep road which led from the village, came, or rather flew, a carriage, the horses of which, startled probably by the salutes fired, had shaken off all control, and were careering wildly down the hill. The carriage rocked to and fro on the uneven ground, and was in imminent danger, either of being thrown down the precipitous incline to the right, or of being dashed to pieces against the great trees which bordered the road on the other side. The coachman seemed to have lost all presence of mind. He had let fall the reins, and was clinging desperately to his seat, while from the hill behind, the gunners, prevented by the trees from seeing the accident they had brought about, crashed forth report after report, spurring the terrified animals on and on in their mad course. What the fearful issue must be, was only too plainly visible. At the bridge below a catastrophe would be inevitable.

The people assembled before the house did what crowds mostly do on such occasions. They screamed, ran helplessly hither and thither, but it occurred to no one to give that practical help which was so urgently needed. In that moment upon which everything depended, not one, even among the miners, had the courage, or the quick wit, to rush forwards. Yes, there was a single exception, one man who preserved his self-possession! To take in the whole danger at a glance, to thrust aside his father and comrades, and to spring out from among them, was for Ulric the work of an instant.

In three bounds he had reached the bridge; a scream of horror from Martha rang out after him--too late! He had already thrown himself before the horses and had grasped the reins. High in the air reared the affrighted creatures, but instead of stopping, they set out with fresh fury, dragging him along with them. Any other man must have been thrown to the ground and trampled under foot, but Ulric, by his giant strength, succeeded, at last, in getting the mastery. A tremendous pull at the reins, on which he had never slackened his hold, made one of the horses stagger and lose its footing. It fell, and in its fall, dragged the other down with it. The carriage stopped.

Ulric went up to the door, confidently expecting to find its occupants, or at least the lady, in a swoon. According to his notions, that was the usual condition of fine ladies and gentlemen who found themselves exposed to any danger; but here, when, if ever, a fainting-fit might have been justifiable, there was absolutely nothing of the sort. The lady stood upright in the carriage, holding to the back seat with both hands, her eyes, fixed and dilated, still intent on the chasm before her, where the journey would, probably, next minute have come to a frightful end; but no sound, no cry of alarm, escaped her firmly closed lips. Ready, if it came to the worst, to risk springing out, an attempt which, however, would certainly have proved fatal, she had looked death in the face silently and without shrinking, with how thorough a sense of the peril incurred, her countenance showed.

Ulric seized her quickly and lifted her out, for the horses struggling on the ground, and striving wildly to free themselves, were still dangerous. It only took a few seconds to carry her over the bridge; but, during these few seconds, the dark eyes were fixed steadfastly on the man who, with such disregard of his own life, had almost thrown himself under her horses' feet. Perhaps it was all too unusual a sensation for the young miner to bear in his arms a burden clothed in silken sheen, to feel waving round him, fluttering over his shoulder, a gauzy white veil, for as his eyes rested on the beautiful pale face which had made so brave a stand in the moment of danger, a bewildered look passed over his features, and he set down his charge hastily almost roughly, in a place of security.

Eugénie still trembled slightly, and she drew a long breath of relief, but there was no other sign of the terrible alarm she must have undergone.

"I--I thank you. Pray look to Herr Berkow!"

Ulric, already turning to leave her, stopped with a shock of surprise. "Look to Herr Berkow," the young wife had said, at a time when most women would have called in anguish on their husband's name, and she had said it quite coolly and quietly. A dim notion of that which the gentlemen on the terrace had so freely discussed, dawned on the young man as he turned and went to look after "Herr Berkow."

This time there was, however, no need of his assistance. Arthur Berkow had got out of the carriage and crossed the bridge alone. The passive indifference of his nature had not belied itself during this critical time. When the danger had come upon them so unexpectedly, and his wife moved, as if about to spring out, he had laid his hand on her arm, and said in a low tone:

"Sit still, Eugénie; you are lost if you attempt to jump."

Then no further word was spoken. While Eugénie stood erect in the carriage, looking out for help, and resolved, at the last moment, to risk a spring, Arthur remained motionless in his place; as they neared the bridge, he just passed his hand over his eyes, and he would probably have allowed himself to be dashed to pieces with the carriage, if assistance had not been forthcoming at that decisive moment.

He now stood near the parapet of the bridge, perhaps a thought paler than usual, but perfectly steady, and without a trace of emotion; whether he had felt none, or whether he had already mastered it, Ulric was forced to confess to himself that such equanimity was, at least, something out of the common. The young heir had a moment ago looked Death full in the face, and now he stood, calmly scrutinising, as some curious phenomenon, the man whose energy had rescued him from mortal peril.

That help, which was no longer needed, poured in now on all sides. Twenty hands were busy raising the horses and helping down the coachman, still half stupefied with fright. The entire swarm of officials pressed round the young couple, giving utterance to their regrets, their sympathy, their profound sorrow. They fairly exhausted themselves with questions and offers of assistance, wondering how the accident could possibly have happened, ascribing it alternately to the report of the guns, to the driver and to the horses. Arthur stood a few minutes passive, and let the stream flow over him. Then he stayed it with a gesture.

"Enough, gentlemen, pray! You see we are both unhurt. Let us now go on to the house."

He offered his arm to his wife to lead her away, but Eugénie stood still and looked around.

"And our deliverer? I hope he has not been injured?"

"Ah yes, true!" said the Director, somewhat ashamed. "We had nearly forgotten that. It was Hartmann who stopped the horses. Hartmann, where are you?"

There was no answer to his call, but Wilberg, who, in his admiration for the romantic deed, quite forgot his old grudge against the doer, cried eagerly:

"He is standing out there yonder!" and rushed across to the young miner.

When the gentlemen had hastened up, Ulric had at once retreated, and he was now standing with his back turned to them, and leaning against a tree.

"Hartmann, you must come.... Good heavens! what is the matter with you? Where does all this blood come from?"

Ulric was visibly struggling against an attack of faintness, yet his face flushed angrily as the other made an attempt to support him. Indignant that he should be thought capable of such weakness, he raised himself hastily, and pressed his clenched hand still more firmly to his bleeding forehead.

"It is nothing--nothing but a scratch. If I had only a handkerchief!"

Wilberg was about to produce his, when suddenly a silk dress rustled close by him. Young Lady Berkow stood by his side, and, without speaking, held out her own little one, trimmed with costly lace.

The Baroness Windeg could never have been called upon to offer practical help to a wounded man, or she would have said to herself that this tiny embroidered morsel of cambric was ill-qualified to stanch such a stream of blood as now poured forth, the thick masses of light hair having, for a time, impeded the flow. Ulric must have known better how useless it was, yet he stretched out his hand for the proffered help.

"Thanks, my lady, but that will not serve us much," said the Manager, who had come up, and now laid his arm round his son's shoulder. "Keep still, Ulric!" and he drew out his own strong linen handkerchief, and applied it to what appeared to be a deep wound in the head.

"Is it dangerous?" languidly asked Arthur Berkow, coming over to the spot accompanied by the other gentlemen.

With one push Ulric freed himself from his father, and he stood erect, his blue eyes gleaming more darkly than ever, as he answered roughly:

"Not in the least. Nobody need trouble themselves about it, I can take care of myself."

The words had a disrespectful sound, but the recent service he had rendered was too great for any one to find fault with them. Herr Berkow seemed relieved that the answer spared him any further trouble about the business.

"I will send the doctor to him," said he, in his quiet indifferent way, "and we will reserve our thanks for another time. At present, there seems to be assistance enough. Will you not come, Eugénie?"

His wife took the arm he offered her, but she turned her head once again, as if to assure herself that the required succour was really there. It seemed as though she did not quite approve of the way her husband treated the matter.

"Our whole reception is a failure!" said Wilberg to the chief-engineer a few minutes later, as, quite dispirited, he joined the others in escorting the proprietor's son and his bride to the house.

"And your poem into the bargain!" joked the person addressed. "Who can think now of flowers and verses? Really, for any one who believes in omens, this first home-coming can hardly be called promising. Deadly peril, wounds and bloodshed! there is something romantic in it, just in your style, Wilberg. You should write a ballad about it, only this time you would have no choice but to take Hartmann for your hero."

"And what a bear he is after all!" said Wilberg excitedly. "Might he not have said a word of thanks to Lady Berkow when she offered him her own handkerchief? And then he replied to Herr Arthur in such an ill-mannered way. But the fellow has the strength of a giant! when I asked him why, for goodness sake, he had not put a bandage on sooner, he answered curtly that he had not noticed the wound at first. What do you say to that? He gets a blow on the head which would have stretched one of us senseless, and he first tames the horses, carries the lady away from the carriage, and only awakes to the fact that he is wounded when the blood rushes down in a stream. I should like to see any one else who could do it!"

The miners had gathered round their comrade in the meantime, and much dissatisfaction was expressed among them at the way their future master had behaved to him. It seemed to give them great offence that he should have, for the time being at least, eluded all expression of gratitude. Many dark looks, many cutting remarks passed; even the Manager wrinkled his brow, and, for a wonder, uttered no word in Arthur's defence.

He was still trying to stanch the blood, and was actively aided therein by Martha, whose face betrayed anxiety so unmistakable that it must have struck even Ulric, had not his eyes been turned in quite a different direction. Long and gloomily he gazed after the party which had just left him. Clearly his thoughts were taken up by something far other than the pain of his wound.

As the old man was placing a temporary bandage on his son's bleeding brow, he noticed that Ulric still held the lace handkerchief in his hand.

"That cobweb," said he, with unusual bitterness, "that embroidered cobweb would have been a great deal of use to us! Give it to Martha, Ulric, she can restore it to her ladyship."

Ulric looked down at the dainty little thing which lay so softly between his fingers; as Martha stretched out her hand for it, he raised it quickly and pressed it to his wound, staining the delicate lace a deep red.

"What are you about?" said his father, half-astonished, half-angry. "Are you going to stop up a hole in your head an inch deep with that thing? I should think we had handkerchiefs enough of our own."

"Yes, yes, I did not think what I was doing," returned Ulric shortly. "Let it be, Martha, it is spoilt now any way!" and, so saying, he thrust it into his blouse.

The girl's hands, which had been so busy, fell down idly all at once, and she stood by while the Manager adjusted and secured the bandage. Her eyes were fixed wonderingly on Ulric's face. Why had he been in such a hurry to spoil the pretty thing? Was it because he did not want to give it back?

The young miner certainly possessed no special aptitude for the rôle of a sick man. He had shown himself very impatient of the services rendered him, and it had needed all his father's authority to induce him to submit to them. Now he stood up and declared emphatically that it was enough, and that he must be left in peace.

"Let him alone, an obstinate fellow!" said the Manager. "You know well there is nothing to be done with him. We shall hear what the doctor says. You are a pretty sort of hero, Ulric! You would not lend a helping hand with the arch built in honour of the family; on no account, it would be demeaning yourself! but you can throw yourself under the horses' feet when they are running away with the said family, without one thought for the old father who has nobody in the world but his son to look to! You don't mind doing that! Ah! that is being what you call 'logical' in your new-fangled speech. Now, you lads who follow your lord and master in everything, it will do no harm this time if you take example by him."

With these words, through which, spite of their disguise of assumed grumbling, the pride he felt in his son and his tender love for him showed all too plainly, the old man seized Ulric's arm and led him away.

CHAPTER IV

Evening was drawing on. The festivities on the Berkow estates had been participated in by the bridal pair, and, so far at least, had attained their end. After the happy termination of that perilous incident which had so nearly compromised the whole proceedings, the original programme had been strictly adhered to. The young couple, everywhere in requisition during the afternoon, found themselves at last at home, and left to each other's company. Herr Schäffer had just taken his leave, he was to return to the elder Herr Berkow in the city the following morning; and the servant, who had been busy with the arrangements of the tea-table, now disappeared in his turn.

The lamp on the table shed its clear mild light on the pale blue draperies and costly furniture of the little salon, which, like all the other rooms in the house, had been newly and splendidly decorated for the reception of the new mistress, and formed part of the suite appropriated to her use. The silk curtains, closely drawn, shut from it the outer world; flowers filled the stands and vases, perfuming the air, and on a table before a little sofa stood the silver tea-service ready for use. In spite of all the splendour, it was a perfect little picture of domestic comfort.

So far, at least, as the boudoir itself was concerned; but the newly married couple hardly seemed as yet to appreciate its home-like charm. The bride, still in full dress, stood in the middle of the room musing, and holding in her hand the bouquet which Wilberg, in Martha's stead, had had the happiness of offering her. The scent from the orange-blossoms engrossed her attention so completely, that she had none left for her husband, and he certainly made no very vigorous claim upon it. Scarcely had the door closed behind the footman, when he sank into an armchair with an air of exhaustion.

"It is enough to kill one, this making a show of one's self for ever! Is not it, Eugénie? They have not granted us a minute's respite since yesterday at noon. First the ceremony, then the dinner, then a most fatiguing journey by rail and post, which went on all through the night and forenoon of to-day, then the tragic episode; here again a reception, presentation of officials, dinner.... My father did not remember evidently, when he sketched out the programme, that we possess anything like nerves. I own that mine are completely unstrung!"

His wife turned her head and cast a very contemptuous glance at the man, who, in his first tête-à-tête with her, could talk of his nerves. Eugénie did not appear to have much knowledge of such ailments; not a trace of fatigue was to be seen on her fair face.

"Have you heard whether young Hartmann's wound is dangerous?" asked she by way of answer.

Arthur had exerted himself to make an exceptionally long speech; he seemed surprised that it had obtained so little notice.

"Schäffer says it is nothing," he returned indifferently; "he has spoken to the doctor, I think. By the by, we shall have to make the young fellow some sort of recognition. I shall commission the Director to see about it."

"Ought you not rather to take the matter into your own hands?"

"I? No, pray spare me that! I hear he is not a common miner after all, but the son of the manager, a deputy, or something of the kind. How can I tell whether money, or a present, or what would be the proper thing to give him? The Director will manage it admirably."

He let his head sink into the cushions again. Eugénie answered nothing; she sat down on the sofa and leaned her head on her hand. After the pause of a minute or so, it seemed, however, to occur to Herr Arthur that he owed his young wife some attention, and that he could not possibly remain silent and buried in his arm-chair during the entire hour the tea-drinking would be supposed to last. It cost him an effort, but he made the sacrifice and actually rose to his feet. Going over to his wife, he seated himself by her side, took her hand and even went so far as to attempt passing his arm round her. But it was only an attempt. With a quick movement, Eugénie drew her hand out of his and retreated from him, casting a glance at him like that which, yesterday in church, had so spoiled his father's first embrace. There was the same cold haughty repulse in her look which said better than any words: "I am not to be approached by you, or any like you."

But this high disdainful manner, so imposing to the father, proved less so when employed towards the son, probably because the latter was no longer to be awed by anything. He appeared neither intimidated nor disconcerted at this evident show of repugnance, but merely looked up with some faint surprise.

"Is that disagreeable to you, Eugénie?"

"It is new to me at least. You have hitherto spared me such marks of affection."

The young man was too apathetic to feel all the bitter meaning of these words. He took them as a reproach.

"Hitherto? Well, yes, etiquette was rather severely maintained in your father's house. During the whole two months of our engagement, I had not once the happiness of seeing you alone. The continual presence of your father or your brothers laid a restraint upon us which, now we are together quietly for the first time, may well be laid aside."

Eugénie retreated still farther.

"Well then, now that we are quietly alone together, I declare that such tender demonstrations, made just to satisfy appearances, and in which the heart has no share, are positively distasteful to me. I release you once for all from any such obligations."

The surprise in Arthur's face became a little more marked now; so far, however, he was not really roused.

"You seem to be in rather a peculiar humour to-day. Appearances! Heart! Really, Eugénie, I should not have expected to find such romantic illusions in you of all people."

An expression of deep bitterness passed over her features.

"I took leave of all illusions in life when I promised you my hand. You and your father were bent on uniting your name with that of Windeg, which is old and noble. You thought, by doing so, you would obtain those honours and that society from which you had hitherto been shut out. Well, you have gained your end. For the future, I must sign myself Eugénie Berkow!"

She laid a most contemptuous stress on the last word. Arthur had risen; he seemed to understand at last that this was something more than a bride's caprice, called forth, possibly, by his negligence during the journey.

"You certainly do not seem to like the name much. Until to-day, I had no idea that, in taking it, you had yielded to constraint from your family, but I begin to think"----

"No one has constrained me!" interrupted Eugénie. "No one has even persuaded me. What I did, I did voluntarily, with full consciousness of what I was undertaking. It was hard enough for them at home that I should be sacrificed for their sakes."

Arthur shrugged his shoulders; it was plain from the expression of his face that the conversation was beginning to weary him.

"I really do not understand how you can speak in such a tragic tone about a simple family arrangement. If my father, in making it, had other objects in view, I suppose the Baron's motives were not of a very romantic nature either, only he, probably, had still more cogent reasons for approving of a marriage by which he certainly was not the loser."

Eugénie started up, her eyes flashed, and a hasty movement of her arm threw the fragrant bouquet to the ground.

"And you dare to say that to me? After what occurred before your suit was accepted? I thought, at least, you would blush for it, if indeed you are still capable of blushing."

The young man's languid, half-closed eyes opened suddenly, large and full; there came a gleam into them, like a sudden spark shooting up from beneath dead ashes, but his voice retained its quiet matter-of-fact tone.

"First of all, I must beg of you to be a little clearer. I feel myself quite unable to make out these enigmatic speeches."

Eugénie crossed her arms with a rapid movement; her bosom heaved tumultuously.

"You know, as well as I do, that we were on the brink of ruin. Whose the fault may have been, I cannot and will not decide. It is easy to throw stones at one who is struggling with adversity. When a man has inherited estates overburdened with debt, when he has to maintain the repute of an old name, to keep up a position in society, and to assure his children's future, he cannot amass money as you do in your industrial world. You have always had gold to throw away, your every wish has been forestalled, every whim gratified. I have tasted all the misery of an existence, which, wearing of necessity the outward mask of splendour, was every day, every hour, drawing nearer inevitable ruin. Perhaps we might yet have escaped, if we had not fallen precisely into Berkow's nets. He fairly forced his help on us at first, forced it upon us until he had got everything into his hands, until we, pursued, entrapped, despairing, literally knew not which way to turn. Then he came and claimed my hand for his son as the sole price of deliverance. Rather than offer me up, my father would have braved the worst, but I would not see him sacrificed, his whole career destroyed, I would not have my brother's future blighted, our name dishonoured, so I gave my consent. Not one of my family knew what it cost me!--but, if I sold myself, I can answer for it to God, and to my conscience. You, who lent yourself to be the tool of your father's base designs, have no right to reproach me; my motives were at least nobler than yours!"

She paused, overcome by her emotion. Her husband still stood motionless before her; there was the same slight pallor on his face as had been visible at noon, when the danger was just overpast, but his eyes were veiled once more.

"I regret that you did not make these disclosures to me before our marriage," said he, slowly.

"Why?"

"Because you would not then have incurred the humiliation of signing yourself Eugénie Berkow."

The young wife was silent.

"I had not the slightest suspicion of these--these manipulations on my father's part," continued Arthur, "for my habit is in no way to interfere with his business concerns. He said to me one day, that if I chose to sue for the hand of Baron Windeg's daughter, my proposal would be accepted. I agreed to the plan, and I was formally presented to you, our betrothal following a few days later. That is my share of the business."

Eugénie turned away.

"I would rather have had a plain avowal of your complicity than this fable," she said coldly.

Again the man's eyes opened wide, and again that strange light gleamed in them, ready to kindle into flame, but ever anew quenched by the ashes.

"It seems I stand so high in my wife's estimation, that my words do not even find credence with her?" said he, this time with a decided touch of bitterness.

Eugénie's fair face expressed the most sovereign contempt, as she turned it towards her husband, and she answered slightingly:

"You really must excuse me, Arthur, for not meeting you in a spirit of perfect confidence. Until the day you entered our house for the first time on an errand I understood but too well--until then, I had known you only through the city gossip, and it"----

"Drew no flattering portrait of me? That I can well believe. Will you not have the goodness to tell me what people were pleased to say of me in town?"

She raised her large eyes and looked him steadily in the face.

"People said that Arthur Berkow only made so princely a display, only threw away thousands upon thousands, in order to buy the favour of the young nobility and the right to associate with them, hoping that his own humble birth would thus be forgotten. People said that in the wild, dissipated doings of a certain set, he was the wildest, the most dissipated of all. As to some of the other reports, it would ill become me as a woman to pronounce upon them."

Arthur's hand still rested on the back of the armchair on which he was leaning; during the last few seconds it had buried itself involuntarily deeper and deeper in the silken cushions.

"And you naturally do not think it worth while to attempt to reclaim this lost sinner, on whom sentence has been passed without appeal?"

"No."

She spoke this 'No' in a freezing tone. The young man's face twitched a little as he drew himself up quickly.

"You are more than sincere! Never mind, it is an advantage to know exactly on what footing we are to be together, for together we must remain for a time, at all events. The step we took yesterday cannot be recalled immediately, without exposing us both to ridicule. If you provoked this scene with a view to showing me, that though my presumption had won your hand, yet I must learn to hold myself at a respectful distance from the Baroness Windeg--and I fear this was your sole object--you have gained your end, but"----here Arthur relapsed into his old languid manner, "but I beg of you, let this be the first and last conversation of the kind between us. I detest everything which resembles a scene; my nerves really will not bear them, and it is always possible to regulate one's life without any such useless excitement. And now I think I shall best meet your wishes by leaving you alone. Allow me to wish you good evening."

He took up from the sideboard a silver candelabra, in which lights were burning, and left the room. Outside the threshold he stopped a moment and turned to look back. The gleam in his eyes was no longer faint, it blazed up for one second clear and bright; then all grew dull and lifeless once more, but the candles flared unsteadily as he crossed the anteroom, possibly from the current of air, or was it because the hand which carried them shook a little?

Eugénie remained alone. She drew a deep breath of relief as the portière fell behind her husband. As though needing some fresh air after so painful a scene, she drew the curtains back, half opened the window, and, stepping on to the balcony, looked out at the balmy spring evening. The stars shone faintly through the thin transparent clouds which veiled the heavens, and the landscape without looked indistinct and shadowy, for the deep twilight had already fallen, clothing it on all sides with its dusky garment The flowers on the terrace below filled the air with their fragrance, and the low splash of the fountains came refreshingly to the ear. Peace and rest were everywhere--everywhere but in the heart of the young wife, who, to-day, for the first time, had crossed the threshold of her new home.

It was over at last, the dumb torturing struggle of the last two months, through which she had been supported by the pain and by the ardour of the fight itself. For heroic natures there is something grand in the idea of giving up one's whole future for others, of buying their salvation with the happiness of one's own life, of sacrificing one's self in their stead to an inexorable destiny. But now when the sacrifice was made, when deliverance had been secured, when there was nothing left to fight for, and nothing to overcome, now all the romantic glamour, which filial love had hitherto woven round Eugénie's resolve, faded away, and she began to feel deeply the cold desolation of the life before her.

The breezy, balmy air of the spring evening seemed to stir in its depths all the long-repressed anguish of this young soul, which had demanded its share of love and happiness from life, and which had been so cruelly robbed of its lawful due. She was young and beautiful, more beautiful than most, she was of a noble old race; and the proud daughter of the Windegs had ever adorned the hero of her youthful dreams with all the brilliant chivalry of her forefathers. That he should be her equal in name and rank was a thing never questioned .... and now? Had the husband, who had been forced upon her, possessed that energy and strength of character which she prized above everything in a man, she might, perhaps, have forgiven him his plebeian birth; but this weakling, whom she had despised before she had known him----Had the insults, which she, with fullest intent, had heaped upon him, and which would have stung any other man to fury, even roused him from his apathetic indifference? Had this apathy of his been shaken even for one moment by the open expression of her contempt? Another, a stranger, must throw himself before the maddened animals this morning, at the risk of being trampled to death by them.

Before Eugénie's mental vision rose the face of her deliverer with its defiant blue eyes and bleeding forehead. Her husband did not even know whether this man's wound were dangerous, whether it might not prove mortal, yet both he and she must have perished but for that energetic, lightning-like deed.

She sank back into a seat and hid her face in her hands. All that she had suffered and fought against for months pressed in on her now with tenfold power, and found utterance in the one despairing cry, "My God! my God! how shall I bear this life?"

CHAPTER V

Herr Berkow's very extensive mining works lay at some distance from the capital, in one of the remoter provinces. The neighbouring country offered no great attractions. Hills, and nothing but hills; for miles around only the uniform dark green of the pines, which clothed alike the heights and valleys; buried in their midst occasional villages and hamlets, and, here and there, a farm or a country-house. But the soil up in these parts could not yield much. The treasures of the land lay hidden under the earth, and therefore was it that all the life and activity of the neighbourhood congregated to the Berkow estates, where operations on a magnificent scale were carried on for bringing these treasures forth to the light of day.

The estates were rather isolated and cut off from the great lines of communication, for the nearest town was some miles distant; but the great labyrinth of buildings, store and dwelling houses, which had sprung up in these quiet valleys, with all their busy life and movement, formed almost a town in itself. Every appliance which industry or science could suggest, every assistance which machinery and men's hands could afford, was here brought into play to wring its treasures from the reluctant earth. A perfect host of officials, of engineers, inspectors, and superintendents, all under the control of the Director, formed a colony apart, and the men, to be counted by several thousands, only a small minority of whom could be lodged on the spot, lived in the adjacent villages.

The undertaking which, from a very insignificant beginning, had only been raised by the present proprietor to the vast proportions it had now attained, seemed almost too great for the means of any private individual. A gigantic capital was indeed needed to keep it on foot; it was by far the most important enterprise of the sort in the province, and took the lead, therefore, in its branch of industry. This settlement with its unlimited forces of machinery and hand labour, with its establishments and dwelling-houses, with its officials and working-men, formed a state in itself, and its master was as sovereign a lord as any ruler of a small principality.

It was somewhat surprising that a man at the head of such an undertaking should have hitherto failed to obtain a distinction for which he had striven, and which had been granted to others who had done less for the industry of the country. But whenever the decision on such matters emanates directly from a very high quarter, the character and conduct of the candidate for honours come into question. It was so here. Berkow enjoyed but little sympathy in the leading circles of society; there were so many dark spots in his past life, which his riches could veil, but not altogether efface. He had certainly never come into open conflict with the law, but he had often enough drawn very near those confines where the law's action makes itself felt. It was even averred by many that his operations in the distant province, on however grand a scale they might be, were yet not altogether exemplary.

Much was said of an unscrupulous system of working, which aimed only at increasing the proprietor's wealth, and took no heed of the ill or well being of those human agents impressed into its service, of arbitrary encroachments on the part of the officials, of a low ferment of discontent among the hands. But, after all, these were only reports, the settlement itself lay too far off for them to be verified; on the other hand, the fact remained certain that it proved an almost inexhaustible source of wealth to its owner.

Every one was forced, indeed, to confess that this man's perseverance, tenacity, and industrial genius, were at least equal to his unscrupulousness. Sprung originally from a very low condition, tossed hither and thither by the waves of life, he had at last succeeded in gaining a point of vantage, and now for some years had enjoyed the undisputed position of a millionaire. In fact, fortune had latterly seemed to follow in his footsteps; each time he put her to the test, she remained faithful to him, and the most precarious transaction, the most hazardous speculation, would invariably succeed if his hand were but at the helm.

Berkow had become a widower early in life, and had never re-married. To his restless mind, always bent upon the chances of gain, home-ties seemed more of a chain than a consolation. His only son and heir had been brought up in the capital, and nothing had been spared for his education in the way of tutors, professors, visits to the University, and home and foreign travel. But as for any peculiar preparation for his calling as the future head and leader of a great industrial enterprise, such a thing was not thought of.

Herr Arthur showed a decided distaste for learning anything beyond the usual fashionable curriculum, and his father was much too weak, and much too vain of the brilliant rôle his son was playing--to support which he himself cheerfully paid--ever to insist upon a more thorough course of study. If it came to the worst, there were always capable men enough to be had whose technical and commercial knowledge could be secured at a high salary. So the young heir came but once a year to his possessions in the far-off province, while his father, though he took up his residence occasionally in the capital, still retained the superintendence of the whole concern.

The young couple had not been specially favoured by the weather during their visit to the country. The sun showed itself but rarely this spring-time; after many rainy days it shone out at last, however, as if to greet the Sunday. The shafts were empty and the works at rest; but in spite of the Sabbath calm and the smiling sunshine, something of the gloomy monotonous character of the country seemed to weigh on the whole colony.

No attempt at embellishment, no attention to the convenience of the inhabitants, was noticeable in the buildings connected with the industry of the place, or in the dwelling-houses; they were all constructed on a strictly utilitarian principle. That a due sense of the beautiful was not wanting to the proprietor, his own house sufficiently attested. Care had been taken to build it at a suitable distance from the works, and so that it should command a full view over the wooded hills. Within and without it was fitted up and decorated in so luxurious a style as to be almost princely, and with its balconies, terraces and flower gardens, it looked like an oasis of fragrance and poetry lying in the midst of this busy region.

In the immediate neighbourhood of the shafts stood the cottage of Hartmann, the Manager. Its appearance plainly showed that the occupant enjoyed a position of peculiar privilege, and so indeed it was. In his youth the sturdy miner had married a girl in the service of the late Frau Berkow, and a special favourite of her mistress. Even after her marriage the young woman preserved something of her old relations with her former employers, and so it came to pass that her husband was favoured and preferred in every way, advanced from post to post, and finally even promoted to be working-manager. These relations and these favours ceased, it is true, at Frau Berkow's death; the widower was not the man to trouble himself about former members of his household, and when Hartmann's wife also died shortly afterwards, the old connection came altogether to an end.

But from that time forth, the Manager had cherished a strong devotion to the Berkow family, to whose support he owed his present position so devoid of care, whereas, without it, he would probably, like so many of his comrades, never have got beyond the laborious, poorly-paid work in the mines. Several years ago he had brought home his sister's orphan-child, Martha Ewers, and now she admirably filled the place of mistress of his house. As for the fulfilment of his secret desire that she and his son should come together as man and wife, there seemed so far but small prospect of it.

On this particular Sunday morning, the cottage, formerly so peaceful, had been the scene of one of those excited discussions which unhappily had ceased to be uncommon between father and son. The Manager, standing in the middle of the room, was declaiming violently at Ulric, who had just returned from the Director's house, and now leaned, silent and morose, against the door. Martha stood a little apart, watching the strife with unconcealed anxiety.

"Was such a thing ever heard of!" stormed the old man. "Have you not enemies enough up yonder, that you must set to work to hunt up more? A sum of money is offered to my gentleman there, large enough to begin housekeeping upon, and he sets his obstinate head against it, and says 'No!' without more ado! But what do you care about housekeeping and the like? Much you think of taking a wife! To bury yourself in your newspapers when you come home from work; to sit up half the night over your books, and stuff your head full of that new-fangled nonsense which an honest miner has no need to know anything about; to play the lord and master among your mates, so that soon we shall not have to ask the Director, but Herr Ulric Hartmann, what is to be done upon the works--that is all that pleases you. And when, for once in a way, we are reminded that, after all, we are nothing more as yet than a Deputy, then we talk of 'not taking payment,' and throw it back in our employers' faces. I should think if any one ever really earned money, it was you that day."

Ulric had listened in silence so far, but at the last few words he stamped his foot angrily.

"Once for all, I will have nothing to do with the set up there. I have told them that I want no payment for my 'courageous act,' which they make such a fuss about, and I'll take none, so there's an end of it."

The Manager's anger flamed out again; he was just beginning a still sharper remonstrance when Martha interrupted him.

"Let him be, uncle," said she shortly; "he is right."

The old man, quite disconcerted at this unlooked-for interference, stared at her open-mouthed.

"Oh! he is right, is he?" he repeated grimly. "I might have been sure you would take his part!"

"Ulric is angry that they should have tried to pay their debt through the Director, without giving themselves any further trouble about the matter," continued the girl firmly, "and it was not seemly. If Herr Berkow had spoken to him himself, and said just one word of thanks ... But he indeed! he troubles himself about nothing on earth. He always looks as if he were half asleep, and as if it cost him the most dreadful effort even to look at one; and when, for a wonder, he is not really asleep, he lies all day long on a sofa and stares at the ceiling" ...

"Let the young master alone!" broke in the Manager hastily. "All that lies at his father's door. From his childhood, Herr Berkow has given way to all his wishes, and encouraged him in his faults. He used to tell him constantly how rich he would be one day, and to send away the tutors and servants if they would not obey the youngster. Later on, when he grew older, he was only to associate with counts and barons. Money was handed over to him in heaps, and the madder his way of life was, the better his father was pleased. How could a young lad like that keep his own goodness of heart? For a good heart he had, young Arthur, as to that no one shall say me nay! I ought to know, for I have ridden him often on my knee--and he had some feeling too. I remember well when he had to go away to town after his mother's death, how he clung to me and cried bitterly, so that they could not get him away, though Herr Berkow was begging, and coaxing, and promising him everything in the world. I had to carry him to the carriage myself. No doubt, when he had been in the city a while with all those bonnes and masters, it was different; next time he just gave me his hand, and since then he has always grown prouder and cooler, until now"----an expression of pain passed over the old man's face, but he shook off the weakness quickly, and went on. "Well! it does not matter much to me, but I do not like to hear you rail at him, whenever you get a chance, especially Ulric, who has a downright hatred to him. If that obstinate fellow had had as much of his own way, and some thousands to spend into the bargain, I should like to know what he would have grown into! Nothing good, that is certain."

"Perhaps something worse, father," said Ulric, curtly, "but he would not have grown into a milksop like that, you may take my word for it."

The conversation, which again seemed taking a critical turn, was now fortunately brought to an end. There came a knock at the door, and a servant, in the rich and somewhat over-decorated livery of the Berkow family, entered without waiting for an invitation, and greeted the Manager with a "Good-day."

"Her ladyship sent me over. I am to tell your Ulric--oh! there you are, Hartmann! Her ladyship wishes to speak to you; I am to say she will expect you over there at seven o'clock sharp."

"Me?"

"Ulric?"

These two exclamations were uttered by the old man and his son, in a tone of equal surprise; as to Martha, she stood looking at the man in blank astonishment. He continued equably:

"There must have been something up between you and the Director, Hartmann. He was with her ladyship quite early to-day, though, in a usual way, she does not trouble herself about the gentlemen's business matters, and I was sent off to you at full speed. There is plenty to do up at the house, I assure you; all the gentlemen from the works are invited to dinner, and there are all sorts of grandees coming out from the town too.... But I have not a moment's time. Be punctual, seven o'clock, just after dinner."

The man seemed really in a hurry; he nodded shortly, by way of adieu to all present, and went.

"There!" burst forth the Manager. "They know already of your ridiculous refusal up there. Now look to yourself to find a way of settling the business."

"Shall you go, Ulric?" quickly and eagerly asked Martha, who had remained silent so far.

"What are you thinking of, child?" scolded her uncle. "Do you suppose he can say no again, when the mistress sends expressly for him. But you and he would both be capable of it, really!"

Martha did not attend to this speech. She drew nearer her cousin, and laid her hand on his arm.

"Shall you go?" she repeated in a low tone.

Ulric stood looking darkly at the ground, as though a struggle were going on within him. Presently he threw back his head hastily.

"Certainly I shall. I should be glad to know what her ladyship can be pleased to want with me now, after passing a whole week without once taking the trouble to inquire"----

He stopped short, as if he felt he had said too much. Martha's hand slid from his arm, and she stepped back, but the Manager said with a sigh,

"Well, Heaven save us, if you go behaving in that way up yonder! To make things worse, old Berkow came down yesterday evening. If you two get together, your time here as Deputy is over, and mine as Manager will not be long. I know the master well!"

A contemptuous expression played about the young man's lips.

"Make your mind easy, father. They know how fond you are of the 'family,' and what trouble your unnatural son causes you. He won't even bow down to his betters! No one will quarrel with you, and I"---- here Ulric drew himself up to his full height, in defiant self-assertion, "I shall stay on here for a time, at least. They dare not send me away, they are far too much afraid of me."

He turned his back on his father, pushed open the door, and walked out. The Manager clapped his hands together, and was about to send another thundering reproof after his rebellious son, but Martha stopped him, by again, and still more decidedly this time, taking Ulric's part. Tired of the strife at last, the old man caught hold of his pipe, and prepared to go out likewise.

"Hark ye, Martha," said he, turning round in the doorway. "I can see this by you. There is no rebel living but can be over-matched. You have found your master in Ulric, and he will find his, too, as sure as my name is Gotthold Hartmann!"

CHAPTER VI

Meanwhile preparations were being made up at the great house for the grand dinner which was to take place that day. Servants ran up and down stairs, cooks and maids bustled about the kitchens and pantries. There was everywhere something to be attended to, some alteration to be made, and the whole house offered that appearance of busy unrest which usually precedes a festivity.

The quiet reigning in young Berkow's rooms seemed even greater by the contrast. The curtains were let down, the portières closed, and in the adjoining apartments, the servants glided noiselessly about over the thick carpets, putting everything in order. Their master was accustomed to dream away the greater part of the day, lying at full length on his sofa, and he did not care to be disturbed by even the slightest noise.

The young heir lay, with half-closed eyes, stretched on a divan. He held a book in his hand, which he was, or rather had been, reading, for the same page had remained long open before him; probably he had found the trouble of turning the leaves too great. Presently, the book fell from his negligent hold, and slipped from his long delicate fingers on to the floor. It would not have been a great exertion to stoop and pick it up, still less to call for that purpose the busy servants near at hand, but he did neither. The book lay on the carpet, and Arthur passed the next quarter of an hour without changing his position or moving in the slightest degree. His face showed sufficiently that he was not meditating on what he had read, he was not even day-dreaming; he was simply feeling himself unutterably bored.

The somewhat ruthless opening of a door which led from the corridor into the neighbouring room, and the sound of a loud imperious voice within, put an end to this interesting state of things. The elder Berkow asked if his son were still there, and, on receiving a reply in the affirmative, he sent the servant away, pushed back the heavy portières, and entered the inner room. His countenance was flushed as though from vexation or anger, and the cloud resting on his brow grew darker as he caught sight of Arthur.

"So you are still lying on that sofa, just as you were three hours ago!"

Arthur was not accustomed, it seemed, to show his father even the outward forms of respect. He had taken no notice of his entrance, and it did not now occur to him to modify the extreme negligence of his attitude.

The lines on his father's brow grew deeper still.

"Your apathy and indolence really begin to pass belief. It is even worse here than in town. I hoped you would conform to my wishes, and take some interest in the success of a concern which was started solely on your account, but"----

"Good Heavens, sir!" said the young man, "you do not want me to trouble myself about workmen and machinery and such things, do you? I never have done so, and I can't, for my life, comprehend why you should have sent us here of all places. I am nearly bored to death in this wilderness."

He spoke languidly, but quite in the tone of a spoilt darling, accustomed everywhere, and under all circumstances, to see his caprices taken into account, and to whom even the suggestion of anything unpleasant was an offence. Something must have happened, however, to irritate his father too much for him to yield this time, as was his custom. He shrugged his shoulders impatiently.

"I am pretty well used to your being bored to death in every place and in all company, whilst I have to bear all the care and burden alone. Just now, worries are coming in upon me on all sides. It cost sacrifices enough to free the Windegs from their obligations, and here I find nothing but vexation and disagreeables without end. I have had a meeting this morning of all the superior officials with the Director at their head, and I was forced to listen to complaints, and nothing but complaints. Extensive repairs in the shafts--increase of wages--new ventilators. Nonsense! as if I had time and money for that now!"

Arthur listened without any show of sympathy; if his face expressed anything, it was the desire he felt that his father would go away. But the latter was not so obliging; he began to pace up and down the room.

"This comes of trusting to one's agents and their reports! For the last six months I have not been here in person, and everything is going to the deuce. They talk of a ferment of discontent among the hands, of grave symptoms and danger threatening, as if they had not full authority to draw the reins as tight as they choose. A certain Hartmann is pointed out to me as chief agitator. He is looked upon by the other miners as a sort of Messiah, and he is secretly stirring up the whole works to revolt. When I ask why, in Heaven's name, they have not sent the fellow about his business long ago, what answer do I get? They dare not! So far, he has given no grounds for dissatisfaction on the score of his work, and his comrades fairly worship him. There would be a strike on the works if he were sent away without sufficient motive. I took the liberty of telling these gentlemen that they were a set of timid hares, and that I would take the thing into hand myself. The shafts will remain as they are, and as to the question of wages, not an iota of difference shall be made in them. The least attempt at a rising will be met with the utmost severity, and I shall dismiss the plotter-in-chief myself this very day."

"You can't do that, sir!" said Arthur suddenly, half raising himself on the sofa.

Berkow stood still in surprise.

"Why not?"

"Because it was precisely this Hartmann who stopped our horses and saved us from certain death."

His father uttered an exclamation of suppressed wrath.

"The devil! it must just be that fellow! No, then, certainly we cannot send him off at a minute's notice, we must wait for an opportunity. By the by, Arthur," with a displeased look at his son, "it was rather too bad that I should have to hear of that accident from a stranger. You did not think it worth while to write a syllable to me about it."

"Why should I?" returned the young man, resting his head wearily on his hand. "The thing was happily over, and, besides, they have nearly worn the life out of us up here with their sympathy, their congratulations, their questions, and their palaver about it. I do not think one's life is so valuable it is worth making such a fuss about its being saved."

"You don't think it is?" said the father, looking keenly at him. "I should have thought, as you were only married the day before"----

Arthur answered only with a shrug. Berkow's eyes rested on him with a still more searching gaze.

"As we are on the subject--what is all this between you and your wife?" asked he, all at once, without anything by way of preface.

"Between me and my wife?" repeated Arthur, as though trying to remember who was meant.

"Yes, between you two. I expect to take by surprise a newly-married pair in their honeymoon, and I find a state of things here which I should never have supposed possible. You ride out alone, and she drives alone. You never go near each other's rooms, and when you are together, you have not half-a-dozen words to say to one another. What does it all mean?"

The younger man had risen now, and was standing opposite his father, but he had not thrown off his sleepy look.

"You seem to have mastered the details thoroughly, sir," said he. "You could hardly have learnt them all in the half-hour we spent together yesterday evening. Have you been questioning the servants?"

"Arthur!" Berkow's anger was breaking forth, but the habit of indulgence towards his son made him overlook this great offence. He forced himself to be calm.

"It appears you are not accustomed up here to the fashionable way of doing things," continued Arthur, quite undisturbed. "Now, in regard to this, we are eminently aristocratic. You know, sir, you are so fond of all that is aristocratic!"

"Leave your jests!" said Berkow, impatiently. "Is it your pleasure, too, that your wife should allow herself to ignore you in a way which is already the talk of the whole place?"

"I leave her free, that is, to do as she likes, just as I intend to do myself."

Berkow started up from his seat

"This is really going too far! Arthur, you are"----

"Not like you, sir!" interrupted the young man. "I, at least, should never have forced a girl into giving her consent by threatening her with her father's recognisances."

The colour faded suddenly from Berkow's face, and he stepped back involuntarily, asking in an unsteady voice,

"What--what do you mean?"

Arthur drew himself up erect, and some animation came into his eyes as he fixed them on his father.

"Baron Windeg was ruined, that every one knew. Who ruined him?"

"How should I know?" asked Berkow, ironically. "His extravagance, his love of playing the grand seigneur when he was head over ears in debt, was cause enough. He would have been lost without my help."

"Indeed? So you had no ulterior object in view when you gave him your help? The Baron was never offered the alternative of surrendering his daughter, or of preparing to meet the worst? He decided voluntarily upon this marriage?"

Berkow laughed, but his laughter was forced.

"Of course. Who has been telling you anything to the contrary?" But, in spite of his tone of assurance, his look fell. This man had probably never yet lowered his eyes when reproached with an unscrupulous act, but he could not meet his son's gaze on this occasion. A bitter expression passed over the young man's face; if he had had any doubt hitherto, he knew enough now.

After the pause of a second, he renewed the conversation.

"You know that I never had any inclination for marrying, that I only yielded to your incessant persuasion. Eugénie Windeg was as indifferent to me as any other woman. I did not even know her, but she was not the first who had been willing to give up her old name in exchange for wealth. At least, that was how I interpreted her consent, and that of her father. You never thought fit to inform me of that which preceded and followed my proposal. I had to hear of the barter that had been made of us both from Eugénie's mouth. We will let that be. The thing is done, and cannot be undone; but you can understand now that I shall avoid exposing myself to fresh humiliations. I have no wish to stand a second time before my wife, as I had to do the other evening, while she poured out all her contempt for me and my father, and I--I could but listen in silence."

Berkow had been dumb so far, and had half turned away, but at these last words he looked round at his son quickly with some astonishment.

"I should not have believed that anything could irritate you so much," said he slowly.

"Irritate? Me? You are mistaken, we did not reach the pitch of irritation. My lady-wife deigned from the first to mount on the high pedestal of her exalted virtues and of her noble descent, and I, who, in both respects, am equally unworthy, preferred to admire her only from a distance. I should seriously advise you to do the same, that is, if ever you attain to the happiness of her society."

He threw himself down on the sofa again with an air of contemptuous indifference, but even in his sneer there was a touch of that irritation his father had noticed. Berkow shook his head, but the subject was too embarrassing, and the rôle he played towards his son in this business too painful for him not to seize the first opportunity of putting an end to the discussion.

"We will talk it over again at a fitting time," said he, taking out his watch hastily. "Let us have done for to-day. There are yet two good hours before the people arrive; I am going over to the upper works. You will not come with me?"

"No," said Arthur, relapsing into indolence.

Berkow made no attempt to use his authority. Perhaps, after such an interview, the refusal was not disagreeable to him. He went away, leaving the young man alone once more, and, with the renewed stillness, all the latter's apathy seemed to return to him.

While the first bright spring day smiled on the world without, while the woods lay bathed in sunshine, and the sweet scent of the pines rose up from the hills, Arthur Berkow lay within in the darkened room, where the curtains were so carefully lowered, the portières so closely drawn, as though he alone were not created to enjoy the free mountain air and the bright light of day. The air was too keen for him, the sun too dazzling. It blinded him to look out, and he said to himself that his nervous system was shaken beyond all description. The young heir, who had at his disposal all that life and this world can give, thought, as he had often thought before, that after all both the world and life are horribly empty, and that it is assuredly not worth while to have been born at all.

CHAPTER VII

The state dinner, prepared with lavish expense and on a most luxurious scale, was over at last. It had procured for Berkow one special triumph, independently of the pleasure he must have felt at seeing how numerous were the guests around him. The nobility of the neighbouring town, and its leading personages in particular, had always been exclusive to the last degree. No member of it had condescended as yet to enter the house of a parvenu, whose equivocal antecedents still shut him out from the highest circles of society; but the invitations bearing the name of Eugénie Berkow, née Baroness Windeg, had been universally accepted. She was, and would ever remain, a scion of one of the most ancient and noble houses of the land.

No one could or would wound her by a refusal, more especially as it had not remained a secret how she had been forced into this union. But, if the bride were to be met with fullest esteem and sympathy, her father-in-law, in whose house the dinner was given, could not possibly be treated otherwise than with politeness, and so this too came to pass.

Berkow was jubilant; he knew well that this was only the prelude to what must happen in the capital next winter. The Baroness Windeg would certainly not be allowed to fall out of her sphere because she had sacrificed herself to filial love. She would now, as hitherto, be looked on as an equal in spite of the plebeian name she bore. And touching this name, too, the object for which he had so long striven lay now, as he hoped, almost within his grasp.

But if, on the one hand, the ambitious millionaire felt that he owed his daughter-in-law some thanks, notwithstanding that she had on this day more than ever assumed the airs of a princess, and had held herself completely aloof from him and his, the behaviour of his son, on the other hand, surprised as much as it angered him. Arthur, who had been in the habit of associating exclusively with people of rank, seemed all at once to have lost all taste for such company. He was so extremely cool in his politeness towards his distinguished guests, he even maintained so studied a reserve towards the officers of the garrison, with whom, on previous visits, he had always been on a familiar footing, that he more than once approached those bounds which a host cannot overstep without giving offence. Berkow could not understand this new whim. What could possess his son? Did he want to show his opposition to his wife by thus obviously avoiding her guests?

Those gentlemen from the town, who had ladies under their escort, started early on their return-journey, for the long rains had made the roads almost impracticable, and a drive of several hours in the darkness was not a thing to be desired. This gave the mistress of the house liberty to withdraw, and Eugénie at once availed herself of it, leaving the reception-rooms and retiring to her own private apartments, while her husband and his father stayed with the remaining visitors.

At the appointed hour, Ulric Hartmann made his appearance. Since his early childhood, since Frau Berkow's death, when his parents' relations with the great house had altogether ceased, he had not been within its walls. Indeed, the master's château, with its surrounding terraces and gardens, was to the whole working-population a closed Eldorado, into which even the officials only gained occasional access when called thither by some weighty matter of business, or by a special invitation. The young man walked through the lofty hall, lined on each side by flowering plants, up the carpeted stairs, and through the well-lighted corridors, until in one of the latter, he was received by the servant who had brought him the message in the morning. The man showed him into a room, saying:

"Her ladyship will be here directly," and, with this observation, shut the door and left him alone.

Ulric looked round the large handsomely decorated ante-room, the first of a long suite of apartments, all of which were now completely empty. The guests were still assembled in the distant dining-room which looked out on the garden, but the emptiness and stillness of this part of the house made its splendour yet more impressive. The portières were all drawn back, and Ulric could see through the long suite of handsome rooms, each one of which seemed to surpass the others in beauty.

The thick, dark-coloured velvet of the carpets drank in the light, so to speak; but it shone all the brighter on the richly gilt decorations of the walls and doors, on the silk and satin furniture, in the tall mirrors which reached to the ceiling and cast forth the reflection of it in a thousand brilliant rays, yes, even on the waxed floors bright and smooth as glass; it set off to fuller advantage those pictures, statues and priceless vases with which the salons were so profusely ornamented. All that wealth and luxury can give was here brought together, and the effect was one which might well dazzle an eye accustomed to obscurity, and most at home in the dark mazes of the mine.

But the sight, though it would certainly have been confusing to any of his comrades, appeared to make no impression on Ulric. His look glanced darkly through the sparkling vista, but there was no admiration to be traced in it. Each costly thing which drew his attention seemed to rouse up within him a feeling of enmity, and he suddenly turned his back on the glittering perspective, and gave a little vehement stamp with his foot on finding that there were no signs of any one as yet. Ulric Hartmann, clearly, was not the man to wait patiently in an anteroom until such time as he could be conveniently received.

At last something rustled behind him; he turned round and took a step back involuntarily, for a few paces from him, just under the great chandelier, stood Eugénie Berkow. Up to this time he had seen her but once, on the day he had carried her from the carriage, and she then wore a travelling-dress of dark silk, whilst her face was shaded by her hat and veil. Of that meeting he had preserved only one remembrance, that of the great dark eyes which had scanned his countenance so closely.

Now--ah yes, indeed! this was an apparition very different from any that had hitherto come within the young miner's sphere of vision. Over the white silk dress flowed a delicate white lace, which waved like a cloudlet round her tall and slender figure. Into these airy folds some roses seemed to have been wafted, and a wreath of roses encircled her blonde head, the shining tresses of which rivalled in their soft brilliancy the pearls about her neck and arms. The blaze of the wax-lights fell full on this lovely picture so fitly framed by its surroundings. As she stood there, it seemed as though nothing ought to approach her which had anything in common with the ordinary life of this work-a-day world.

But although Eugénie's whole appearance might betoken the high-born lady of fashion, that being the rôle which she had this evening exclusively played--her eyes showed plainly that she could be something else too. They lighted up now with a glad expression, as she caught sight of the young man, and she went up to him with quiet friendliness.

"I am pleased that you came when I sent for you. I wanted to speak to you to clear up a misunderstanding. Come with me."

She opened one of the side doors, and entered the adjoining room, followed by Ulric. It was her own boudoir, and separated her apartments beyond from the suite before mentioned--but what a contrast it was to the latter! Here only a mellowed light streamed from the lamp over the tender blue draperies and hangings. The foot, bold enough there to tread, sank silently into the yielding carpet, and the caressing air was warm and balmy with the scent of flowers.

Ulric stood on the threshold as if spell-bound, though he was in general but little used to fits of shyness. Here all was so different to the dazzling rooms he had left, so much more beautiful, so dreamily still. The wrath with which he had looked on all that splendour had gone out from him; in its place there stirred a something which he could not define, a something born of the gentler influences now so strangely surrounding him. But in the next minute a hot anger at this weakness burned up within him, he drew back instinctively as from some vaguely-felt danger, and his whole being rose up in inflexible hostility to this atmosphere of beauty and fragrance with all its seductive charm.

Eugénie stopped, noticing with some surprise that the miner was not following her. She took a seat near the door, and her eyes scrutinised his face narrowly. The curly light hair entirely covered the still fresh scar, and the wound, which might well have proved dangerous to another man, had had but little effect on this powerful frame. Eugénie sought for some trace of past suffering, but found none. Her first question related, however, to his injury.

"So you have quite recovered? Does the wound really give you no pain now?"

"No, my lady, it was not worth speaking about."

Eugénie did not appear to remark the short ungracious tone of the answer. She continued, speaking with the same kindness.

"I heard, certainly, from the Director's mouth on the very next day that there was nothing to be apprehended, or we should have had you more thoroughly cared for. After his second visit to you, the Director assured me again that there was no question of any danger, and Herr Wilberg, whom I sent to your house on the day after the accident, brought me the same report."

At the first words of her little speech Ulric had raised his eyes and fixed them on her face. His moody brow cleared slowly, and his voice had a gentler sound as he answered,

"I did not know, my lady, that you had troubled yourself so much about it. Herr Wilberg did not tell me he came from you, or"----

"Or you would have been rather more friendly to him," concluded Eugénie, a little reproachfully. "He complained of the brusque way in which you treated him that evening, yet he was so full of sympathy for you, and offered with such cheerful alacrity to procure me the news I wished for. What do you object to in Herr Wilberg?"

"Nothing--but he plays on the guitar and writes poetry."

"That does not seem to be any special advantage in your eyes," said she, half-jesting; "and I hardly think you would be guilty of it, if you were to change places with him. But we will leave that! It was for something else I sent for you. I hear," she played in rather an embarrassed way with her fan, "I hear from the Director that you have declined a mark of our gratitude, which he was commissioned to offer you from us."

"Yes," Ulric assented briefly, without adding one word to soften the harsh monosyllable.

"I am sorry if the offer, or the way in which it was made, has offended you. Herr Berkow,"--a faint flush overspread Eugénie's face as she uttered the untruth--"Herr Berkow certainly intended personally to express to you his thanks and mine. He was prevented from doing so, and therefore begged the Director to represent him. It would grieve me much if you were to see in that any proof of ingratitude or indifference on our part towards our deliverer. We both know how deeply we are in your debt, and you would hardly now refuse me too, if I were to beg you to receive from my hands"----

Ulric started up; the happy influence of her first words had been quite destroyed by the close of her speech. His face had grown pale, when he guessed what was her object, and he broke out recklessly,

"Let that matter be, my lady. If you offer me money, you too, I shall wish I had let the carriage go over with all that was in it!"

Eugénie was a little startled by this outbreak of that savage wildness for which Ulric Hartmann was feared by every one about the works. Such a look and such a tone had certainly never been addressed to Baron Windegs daughter; it was indeed the first time she had been brought in contact with one belonging to the working classes. She rose offended.

"I do not wish to impose my thanks upon you. If the expression of them displeases you so much, I regret that I should have called you hither."

She turned away and was about to leave the room, but the movement brought Ulric to his senses. He took one hasty step forwards.

"My lady--I--forgive me! I would not vex you for the world!"

Eugénie was struck by the passionate, remorseful tone. She stopped and looked at him, seeking in his face for the key to his strange conduct; but his vehement cry for pardon had disarmed her.

"You would not vex me?" she repeated, "but you do not mind how much you hurt other people's feelings by your ungracious ways? The Director's, for instance, and Herr Wilberg's?"

"No, I do not," returned Ulric, "no more than they would mind hurting mine, if the case were reversed. There is no talk of friendliness between the officials and us."

"No?" asked Eugénie in surprise. "I did not know that the officials and the hands were on such bad terms, and Herr Berkow cannot suspect it either, or he would assuredly have tried to mediate."

"Herr Berkow," said Ulric, sharply, "has cared during the last twenty years for every possible thing on the works, except for the welfare of the hands employed, and so it will go on, until we begin caring a little about him, and then--oh, my lady! I was forgetting that you are his son's wife. Forgive me!"

She was silent, a little confounded by his reckless plain-speaking. What she now heard was, in truth, only what had often before been hinted in her presence about her father-in-law, but the terrible bitterness of these words made her feel all the depth of the gulf which lay between him and his subordinates. Whoever brought an accusation against Berkow was sure beforehand of having his daughter-in-law's sympathy. Eugénie had herself had bitter proof of his unscrupulousness, but she was sensible that, as his son's wife, she ought not to make this evident. If she noticed Hartmann's last speech at all, it must be to reprove him, and she preferred to let it pass.

"So you will not accept any mark of our gratitude, not even from my hands?" she began again, waiving the dangerous subject. "Well, then, I can do nothing but tender my thanks to the man who saved me from certain death. Will you reject them, too? I thank you, Hartmann!"

She held out her hand to him. It lay only a few seconds, white and delicate as a flower, in the miner's strong work-hardened palm, but its touch sent a quiver through him. All the bitterness went out of his face, the threatening look from his eyes; the defiant head was bent over her outstretched hand, and his features bore an expression of gentleness and submissiveness, which none of his superiors could ever boast of having seen on Ulric Hartmann's countenance.

"Oh, you are giving audience here, Eugénie, and to one of our people!"

Berkow's voice sounded behind them, as he opened the door at this moment, and came in, accompanied by his son. Eugénie drew back her hand and Ulric stood up erect. As those tones met his ear, he resumed his characteristic attitude of silent hostility, which became even more marked, as Arthur exclaimed, with a sharpness, oddly contrasting with his habitual languid manner,

"Hartmann, how do you come here?"

"Hartmann?" repeated Berkow, attracted by the name, and going up nearer. "Oh, here we have our friend the agitator, who"----

"Who stopped our horses when they were running away in their mad fright, and who was injured himself in saving our lives!" put in Eugénie, quietly, but very decidedly.

"Ah, yes!" said Berkow, disconcerted by this reminder, and by his daughter-in-law's resolute look. "Yes, indeed, I heard of it, and the Director was telling me that you and Arthur had already given a proof of your sense of the obligation. The young man has come, no doubt, to express his thanks. I hope you were satisfied, Hartmann?"

The cloud rolled back on Ulric's brow blacker and more menacing than ever, and the reply, which hovered on his lips, would probably have brought down on him the most serious consequences. Eugénie stepped up to her protégé and touched him lightly on the arm with her fan. The miner understood the warning; he looked at her, saw the unconcealed anxiety in her eyes, and his hatred and defiance gave way once more. He answered quietly, almost coldly:

"Certainly, Herr Berkow, I am satisfied with her ladyship's thanks."

"I am glad of it," said Berkow, shortly.

Ulric turned to Eugénie.

"I can go now, my lady?"

She bowed her head in silent assent. She saw but too plainly what constraint the man had to put on himself in order to remain quiet. With one slight movement of the head directed to the master and his son, a salutation evidently bestowed with much reluctance, he left the room.

"Well, I must confess that your protégé has not very good manners," remarked Berkow, with a sneer. "He takes leave in rather an off-hand way, and does not wait to be dismissed. But there, how can such people learn the proper way to behave! Arthur, you seem to find something remarkably interesting in this Hartmann. I hope you have looked after him long enough?"

Arthur's eyes had indeed followed the miner with an intent gaze, and they were still fixed on the door he had closed behind him. The young man's eyebrows were drawn together slightly, and his lips firmly set. At his father's remark, he turned round.

The latter went up to his daughter-in-law, with a great show of politeness.

"I regret, Eugénie, that your complete ignorance of the state of things here should have led you to an act of excessive condescension. You, naturally, could have no idea of the part that fellow plays among his comrades, but he should, on no account, have been permitted to come to this house, much less to enter your boudoir, even under the pretext of returning thanks for a present."

The lady had seated herself, but there was a look on her face which made it seem advisable to her father-in-law to remain standing, instead of taking a place at her side as he at first intended. She compelled him too "to admire her only from a distance."

"I see they have only told you half the story," she answered, coolly. "May I ask when you last spoke to the Director?"

"This morning, when I learned from him that he had been commissioned to hand over to Hartmann a sum, which I, by the way, consider much too large. It is quite a fortune to such people! But I do not wish to lay any restrictions on you and Arthur, if you think it right to show your gratitude in this exaggerated way."

"So you do not know that the young man has refused the money altogether?"

"Re--refused?" cried Berkow, starting back.

"Refused?" repeated Arthur. "Why?"

"Probably because it offended him to be put off with a sum of money offered through a third person, while those whom he had saved did not think it worth their while to add even a word of thanks. I have made good this latter negligence, but I could not persuade him to accept the smallest thing. It does not seem as though the Director had managed the matter so 'admirably.'"

Arthur bit his lip. He knew these words were meant for him, though they were spoken to his father.

"It appears, then, you sent for him yourself?" he asked.

"Certainly."

"I wish you had left it undone," said Berkow, somewhat irritated. "This Hartmann is pointed out to me on all sides as the chief promoter of that revolutionary spirit which I am about to meet with the utmost severity. I see now that too much has not been said about him. If this fellow dares to refuse such a sum, because it has not been paid to him with all the ceremony his mightiness demands, he may well be capable of anything. I must remind you, Eugénie, that there are certain considerations my daughter-in-law must keep in mind even when she is giving a proof of her kind feeling."

The old contemptuous look played about Eugénie's lips. Remembering the compulsion to which she had been subjected, she felt but little disposed to yield to her father-in-law's wishes, and the bitter thought of it rising within her made her overlook the real justice of what he said.

"I am sorry, Herr Berkow," she answered, icily, "that other considerations must have weight with me besides any your daughter-in-law may be bound to regard. This was an exceptional case, and you must allow me to act on my own judgment in such matters both now and for the future."

She was again every inch the Baroness Windeg, as she thus recalled the plebeian millionaire to his place; but whether the cause of dispute had angered him too much, or whether the wine, which had flowed so freely at dinner, had produced some little effect on him, he did not this time show her the same boundless respect, but answered with some heat,

"Really? Well, then, I shall thank you to remember,"----but he got no further in his speech, for Arthur, who had remained in the background so far, taking no part in the conversation, stood up all at once at his wife's side, and said quietly,

"I must beg you, sir, to put an end to this unpleasant discussion.--I have left Eugénie unlimited freedom of action, and I do not wish that any one else should attempt to restrain it."

Berkow looked at his son as though he had not heard aright. He was accustomed to see Arthur display the most passive indifference on all occasions, great and small, and was as much surprised by his son's interference as by this open championship.

"You seem to have quite gone over to the opposition to-day," he returned in a jesting tone. "I shall do well to beat a retreat before such combined forces, particularly as I have some business matters to attend to still. I hope I may find you rather less disposed to quarrel to-morrow, Eugénie; and you, Arthur, somewhat more tractable than you have shown yourself to-day. I wish you both a good evening."

CHAPTER VIII

When Berkow left the room in suppressed wrath, he had probably no idea of the embarrassment his sudden departure would cause to the two who remained behind, an embarrassment they had not felt since the evening of their arrival, for never since then had they been alone together. They had met only in the presence of strangers, or at table when the servants were in constant attendance, and this unexpected tête-à-tête seemed equally unwelcome to both. Arthur, no doubt, felt that he could not exactly follow on his father's heels; he must at least address a few words to his wife first, but several seconds passed before he made up his mind what to say, and when at last he was about to speak, Eugénie forestalled him.

"You need not have come to my assistance," said she coldly. "I should have been able to vindicate my independence and hold my own against your father."

"I do not in the least doubt your independent spirit," answered Arthur in the same cool tone, "but I have misgivings as to my father's delicacy. He was about to bring up a subject, the remembrance of which I wished to spare both you and myself. That was the sole object of my interference."

She was silent and leaned back in her seat, while her husband, standing by the table, took up the fan that was lying there and examined its arabesques with an appearance of much interest. A second and more uncomfortable pause ensued, until at last he began again:

"As to this business with Hartmann, I really do admire the self-abnegation you have shown in it. You, of all people, must feel a strong antipathy to persons of his class."

Eugénie opened her large eyes wide, and looked at him sternly.

"I feel an antipathy to nothing but to weakness and vulgarity. I respect any one who has energy thoroughly to fill his place in the world, whether that place be a high or a lowly one."

There was a hard ring in her voice. Arthur's hand, still playing with the fan, moved rather nervously, and there was a slight quiver about his lips. He started a little when she spoke of weakness and vulgarity, though the expression of his face was as indifferent as ever.

"A most elevated view of the matter," said he carelessly. "But I am afraid you would modify it in some degree, if you were to be brought in nearer contact with the rough wild sort of life which often obtains in the lowly places."

"But this young miner is something out of the common," declared Eugénie decidedly. "He may be wild and untamed, like one of Nature's elements which grow to be a danger when not properly directed. I did not find him rough."

She had involuntarily spoken with some warmth. The latent, half-stifled fire in Arthur's eyes gleamed out again, as he fixed them on her.

"You appear to exercise a marvellous degree of authority over this 'wild untamed element of Nature.' It was on the point of breaking out in an unseemly manner before my father. You had but to raise your fan, and the angry lion became as gentle as a lamb." Here the said fan was so violently opened and closed by the young man's slender white fingers that the costly toy was in serious danger, while he went on half mocking. "And in what a knightly manner he bent over your hand! If we had not come in, I believe he would have ventured to kiss it like a real preux chevalier."

Eugénie rose hastily. "I fear, Arthur, this man may force from you and your father something more than a mere sneer, and I do not know whether Herr Berkow does wisely to drive his people into an opposition, which is constantly growing, and the consequences of which may one day recoil on his own head."

Her husband's gaze was riveted on her as she stood before him, and yet her rustling silks and airy laces, her roses and soft pearls, were nothing new to him, any more than the proud and beautiful head with its dark indignant eyes. Perhaps he was struck by her earnest championship of her protégé. He preserved the same careless, half-mocking tone in which he had spoken hitherto, but it concealed a feeling of suppressed irritation, and the fan he held in his hands met with decided ill-luck. The delicately carved ivory was broken in two as he flung, rather than threw, it on to a chair.

"Our deliverer has been reading you a lecture on socialism, I am sorry I missed it. But this Hartmann is certainly remarkable in one way. He has accomplished that which nothing had hitherto achieved, he has actually led us into a lively conversation. But the interest of this theme must be pretty well exhausted by this time, do not you think so?"

The entrance of a servant with a message brought the conversation to an end. Arthur availed himself of the pretext to depart, taking leave of his wife in the cold, ceremonious manner which marked all their intercourse. Hardly had the servant closed the door and left her alone, when Eugénie began to pace up and down the room in evident agitation. She was revolted at the coldness and heartlessness shown about Ulric's brave deed, but it was not that alone which made her steps so hasty and drove the angry colour to her cheeks.

Why could she not meet her husband with that thorough contempt she found so easy towards his father? Was it possible he could be worthy of better things? There was something in Arthur's boundless indolence which parried every blow, and even gave him at times a secret superiority over the proud, passionate woman, carried away but too often by her warmth of temper. On that first evening when, with terrible candour, she had disclosed to him the truth, he must have felt himself a deeply humiliated man; to-day, when she had shown him how falsely he had judged his deliverer and hers, the wrong was clearly on his side; and yet on both occasions he had confronted her with a dignity which was not crushed and annihilated by her contempt.

She would not recognise this, would not confess to herself how it wounded her that never, since the explanation between them, had he made the slightest attempt to temper the coldness of their relations, even by a word. She would certainly have repulsed any such attempt with all the disdainful pride at her command, but that she should never be called on to do so, that he should never take the trouble to go one step beyond that which appearances absolutely required, vexed her in spite of herself.

Eugénie was prompt with her love as with her hate, and her feeling towards her husband had been of a decided nature even before she gave him her hand--but it was not possible to look down on him from a lofty eminence, as she could look down on his father. She felt that vaguely, though she could give no account to herself of what had compelled this feeling within her.

Arthur, going through the corridors, met the Director and the chief-engineer who had been detained to confer on some business matter with Berkow and were now about to leave the house. The young heir stopped all at once.

"May I ask, sir, why Hartmann's refusal to take the money offered him was immediately communicated to Lady Eugénie and to her alone? Why did I hear nothing of it?" asked he sharply.

"Well," said the Director rather confused, "I really did not know you attached any importance to it, Herr Berkow. You declined all personal interference in the matter so decidedly, and her ladyship showed from the first so much interest in it, that I thought myself bound"----

"Oh, indeed!" interrupted Arthur, with the same nervous little twitch about his lips. "Well, her ladyship's wishes should be complied with certainly, but I must beg of you, in all such matters of business"--he laid an emphasis on the last word--"not quite to overlook me another time. I expressly desire that I may be the first to be acquainted with them in future."

So saying, he left the astonished officials, passing on to his own rooms. The Director looked at his colleague.

"What do you say to that?"

The chief-engineer laughed. "Signs and wonders are to be seen! Herr Arthur begins to take an interest in matters of business! Herr Arthur desires to be acquainted with them! Such a thing has never happened before since I have known him."

"But this is not a business matter at all," said the Director irritably. "It is a mere private transaction, and I can guess how it has been. Hartmann has behaved to the lady in that delightfully amiable manner of his we know so well. I thought it was rather odd that she should send for him. Fancy him in a drawing-room, with his savage reckless ways! He is quite capable of telling her what he told me this morning in the office: he does not want any payment, and he did not risk his life for the sake of money. The lady has been indignant at his insolence and her husband also, and now there will be some nice pleasant things for me to hear from Herr Berkow, because I allowed the interview to take place."

"Well, it will be the first time Herr Arthur has ever been indignant at anything that concerns his wife," said the other indifferently, as they went down the steps. "It seems to me that the glacier-temperature about this married couple is extending gradually to all around them. You feel the ice in the air directly you come near them, does it not strike you?"

"It struck me that Lady Eugénie looked admirably handsome. She was rather cool, certainly, but still admirably handsome!"

The chief-engineer made a comic little grimace expressive of horror.

"For Heaven's sake, do not adopt Wilberg's style! You are getting on into the fifties, you know. Talking of Wilberg, he is already head over ears in romantic adoration, but I doubt whether he, or his inevitable verses, will excite much jealousy in high quarters. Herr Arthur seems as little inclined to worship his wife as she to be worshipped. Marriages of convenience are made up every day, it is true, but I can't help having a sort of feeling about this one, as if it could not take quite the usual course, as if beneath all the ice there lay something like a volcano, which will burst out one fine day with thunder and lightning, and give us a bit of an earthquake and a catastrophe on a small scale. That would certainly 'shed some poetry on the arid steppes of our everyday life,' as Wilberg would observe, supposing always the eruption spared him and his guitar. But here we are below, good night!"

CHAPTER IX

More than a month had passed since the festivities. Herr Berkow, coming down "to surprise his children," as he said, had scarcely found the pleasure he had hoped for in his visit, which was certainly rather premature. He had gone back to the city after a few days to settle the arrears of business awaiting him there, and now he was expected to return to the château, for a second and, this time, for a longer stay.

Nothing was changed in the life of the young people; it was, if anything, more divided, colder, more "aristocratic" than at first. On both sides the end of the honeymoon was looked forward to with considerable longing; it had been arranged that they should stay in their country retreat until such time as the fine summer weather should make a longer journey desirable. They would return from their travels in the autumn, and definitively take up their residence in the capital, where their future abode had already been prepared for them by Berkow with much lavish expenditure.

The morning shift was just finished, and Ulric Hartmann was on his way back to his father's house. He had been obliged to moderate his usual swift pace, for at his side walked Herr Wilberg, also going home from his office. This gentleman had been lucky enough to catch Ulric up, and had attached himself to him. It was rather surprising to see one of the officials on such familiar terms with the Deputy Hartmann, who enjoyed but little sympathy among his superiors; still more surprising was it that such familiarity should come from Herr Wilberg, unless indeed the old saying that "extremes meet" be taken as an explanation.

There was, however, another reason here. The chief-engineer little knew what his jokes had brought about, but his laughing hints as to the subject-matter for a ballad had, unfortunately, fallen on a too receptive soil. Wilberg had made up his mind to treat the subject poetically, but he was still in doubt as to whether the masterpiece should be in the form of a ballad, an epic, or a drama. At present one thing only was settled, namely, that it should unite in itself the combined excellences of all three styles.

Unhappily for Ulric, his energetic and courageous act had awakened in the future author's mind the notion that the miner was exactly fitted for a hero of tragedy, and Wilberg now dogged his footsteps perpetually, in order to study this most interesting character. When Ulric further took it into his head to refuse the considerable sum offered him with a disdainful pride which abashed even the Director, the romantic halo about him grew so strong in the poet's eyes that nothing could shake or diminish his admiration, not even the inconsiderate rudeness of the object of it, nor the cutting remarks of those in authority, who hardly approved of such an intimacy.

Ulric could not be said to meet him half-way, or in any manner to facilitate his "studies;" he tried often impatiently to shake off the company thus forced upon him, as one tries to free one's self from a troublesome fly, but it availed him little. Herr Wilberg was determined to see in him a hero, a rough, wild, undisciplined sort of hero, it is true, but still a hero; and the more this view of him was justified by his behaviour, so much the better pleased was the would-be author, who only studied him the more closely for each such fresh development of character.

At last the young miner shrugged his shoulders, and resigned himself to the inevitable. Custom did its work, and there grew up at length between the two a sort of familiarity, not over respectful on Ulric's part.

The wind was still blowing rather cold from the north. Herr Wilberg prudently buttoned up his coat, and tied the ends of his thick woollen scarf carefully together, as he said with a sigh,

"What a lucky fellow you are, Hartmann, with your health and strength of iron! You can go up and down the shafts from heat to cold, and come out afterwards into this biting wind, whilst I have to protect myself from every variation of temperature. And I get so nervous, so shaken, so irritable! That is the way when the spirit gains too great dominion over the body. Yes, Hartmann, it is the press of thought and feeling that does it!"

"I think, Herr Wilberg, it is more likely your everlasting tea-drinking that is the cause of it," replied Ulric, with a rather compassionate glance at his weakly little companion. "If you go on swallowing that hot, thin stuff morning and evening, you will never get strong."

Wilberg glanced up aloft at his adviser with a look of infinite superiority.

"You do not understand, Hartmann. I could not possibly bear such a heavy diet as yours. My constitution would not stand it, besides, tea is of great service to the mental faculties. It quickens me, it stimulates me when the day's work is done, and when in the quiet eventide the Muses draw near"----

"You mean, when you are making your verses," interrupted Ulric, drily. "So that is what the tea is for? Well, they are just what I should expect from it."

It was fortunate that the poet was just then busy trying to fix in his memory a rhyme which had come into his mind. He hardly heard the insulting remark, but turned to his companion next minute in quite a friendly way.

"I have something to beg of you, Hartmann, to desire, to demand!" said he, reaching his climax in well-graduated tones. "Something which you must agree to, no matter at what cost. You are in possession of an article which is perfectly worthless to you, but which would make me the happiest mortal under the sun. You must give it up to me."

"What must I give up to you?" carelessly asked Ulric, who, as usual, when Wilberg was talking, had only half listened.

Herr Wilberg blushed, sighed, looked down, sighed a second time, and, after these preliminaries, thought fit to proceed to speech.

"You remember the day when you came to her ladyship's rescue! Ah, Hartmann, what a pity it is you should have no adequate conception of the poetry involved in such a situation! If I had been in your place! But we will leave that. She offered you her handkerchief when she saw you were bleeding. You kept it in your hand, while the others were looking to your wound. Good Heavens! you cannot possibly have forgotten such a circumstance as that!"

"Well, what do you want with the handkerchief?" asked Ulric, suddenly attentive.

"I wish to possess it," murmured Wilberg, casting down his eyes with a melancholy air. "Ask from me what you will, but let me have that precious souvenir of the woman I adore!"

"You!" cried Ulric, in a tone which made the other spring back and look anxiously round to see that no one was by.

"Don't shout like that, Hartmann! You need not be so horrified because I say I adore the future proprietor's wife. It is something far different from what you are accustomed to consider as love. It is--but you do not know what a platonic affection means."

"No, I don't," returned the miner, shortly, increasing his pace, and evidently desirous of breaking off the conversation.

"You cannot possibly understand it," declared Wilberg, with much self-satisfaction, "for you cannot, and never will, rise to that pure elevation of feeling of which only highly-cultivated minds are capable, that feeling which, without a hope, without a desire, can content itself with adoring in silence from afar. Or what do you think a man should do else, if he loves a woman who belongs to another?"

"Overcome his love," said Ulric, in a low voice, "or"----

"Or?"

"Strike the other man down."

Herr Wilberg beat a hasty retreat to the other side of the road, where he remained standing transfixed with horror.

"What brutality! What appalling principles! So you would seal your love by assault and murder? You are a man to be feared, Hartmann! And you can say such a thing as that with the tone, the look of .... Her ladyship was right when she said you were like one of Nature's untamed elements which"----

"Who said so?" broke in Ulric, looking at him darkly.

"Her ladyship. 'A wild untamed element,' she said, and the description was most striking, most apt, Hartmann"-- The young man ventured a little nearer his companion, but timidly still, and approaching him by degrees. "Hartmann, I could forgive you everything, even what you said just now, but the one thing I cannot forgive is your conduct to her. Have you alone no eyes for her beauty and grace, which disarm the very roughest of your comrades, that you should avoid the sight of her, as if it would bring you ill-luck? If her carriage appears in the distance, you turn round and get out of the way; if she rides by, you step into the house nearest at hand, and I warrant, you make that long round every day past the Director's house, for no other reason than that you might meet her once at the park-gates and be obliged to take off your cap to her. Oh, this stubborn, bitter class-hatred, which spares not even women! I repeat it to you, Hartmann, you are a man greatly to be feared."

Ulric was silent. Contrary to his wont, he submitted to these reproaches without answering a syllable, and by so doing, he strengthened Wilberg in the delusion that his arguments had at last produced some effect. Encouraged by this, he began again,

"But to return to the real matter in hand. The pocket-handkerchief"----

"How should I know where the thing is?" interrupted Ulric, roughly. "It is lost, or Martha may have given it back. How should I know!"

Wilberg was just going to launch out into indignation at the indifference with which an object, in his eyes of such priceless worth, was treated, when he suddenly perceived Martha standing before her uncle's house. He shot down on her like a hawk, and began to question her as to where the said handkerchief might be hidden, whether she had really given it back, or whether, within the range of possibility, it might yet be found.

The girl seemed not quite to understand him at first; when she found out what it was all about her face darkened perceptibly.

"The handkerchief is there still," she said, decidedly. "I thought to do well one day when I took it out and washed the stains from it, but Ulric raved like a madman, because I had even touched the thing. He has got it in his chest."

"Oh! so it was only a pretext for refusing me?" said Wilberg, with a reproachful look at Ulric, who had listened with suppressed anger, and who answered almost with a sneer:

"Make up your mind to it, Herr Wilberg, the handkerchief is not for you."

"And why not, may I ask?"

"Because I mean to keep it," said Ulric, laconically.

"But, Hartmann"----

"When I once say no, I mean it. You might know that, Herr Wilberg."

Wilberg lifted his hands and eyes towards Heaven, as though calling on it to witness the offence done him; but suddenly his arms fell down inert, and he drew himself up quickly, as a voice said behind Martha,

"Can you not inform me, my dear .... Ah, Herr Wilberg! I am interrupting a most animated conversation."

The person addressed stood speechless, overcome at least as much by despair as by delight at this unexpected meeting; for the distressing consciousness was on him, that he, who hitherto had only confronted her ladyship in the faultless attire of full-dress, must now stand before her, arrayed in a blue paletot and green comforter, to say nothing of a nose tipped by the cutting wind with a most unbecoming red. He knew how unfavourable this combination of colour must be to him; not an hour ago he had vowed to himself that he would exchange the green comforter for one of a more flattering hue, and now a mischievous chance had brought him before the eyes of his ideal!

Herr Wilberg wished himself deep down in the shafts, and yet retained sufficient power of thought to be irritated at Hartmann, who, with all the dust of his daily work upon him, stood like a statue, and moved never a muscle.

Eugénie had come along the road which led by the Manager's house, and seeing at first only the young girl, had entered the garden unnoticed. Her last question remained a moment unanswered, for both men were silent.

At last Martha spoke. She had cast a rapid glance at her cousin, when the lady appeared on the scene so unexpectedly; now she turned quickly to her.

"We were just speaking of the lace handkerchief your ladyship gave for a bandage, and which has never been returned."

"Ah, yes, my handkerchief," said Eugénie, indifferently. "I had quite forgotten it, but since you have kept it so carefully, child, you can give it me back."

"I did not keep it; Ulric has it." Martha gave him another look, dark and scrutinising as the first, and even Eugénie turned with some surprise to the young man who had greeted her neither by word nor gesture.

"Well, you then, Hartmann! Or do you not wish to restore it?"

Wilberg was growing more and more exasperated at Ulric's "shameful behaviour," for he stood there motionless with knitted brows and lips firmly closed, and just the same look of stubborn resistance on his face as that with which he had armed himself on entering her boudoir. One could see plainly that he was struggling with himself to keep down the hatred he felt for his master's young wife! This time his better nature conquered.

Herr Wilberg noticed that, at the first sound of that voice addressing itself to him, he started, as though pricked with shame at his own conduct, that a flush rose to his brow, and that his attitude lost something of its defiant hostility. The sermon so lately delivered had certainly had some effect, else how should this stiff-necked Hartmann, whose will was of iron, and who was to be moved neither by fear nor favour, have yielded in silent obedience to a simple question, have turned to the house, and, after the lapse of a few minutes, come back holding the handkerchief?

"Here it is, my lady."

Eugénie took the morsel of cambric, seeming to attach very little importance to it.

"And now, Herr Wilberg, as I have met you here, perhaps you can best give me the information I want. It is the first time I have come by this road, and I find that the bridge which leads to the park is closed by a gate. Can it be opened, or must I go back all round by the works again?"

She pointed to a bridge at a little distance from them. It crossed a wide ditch, which bordered the park on this side, and it was closed by means of an iron gate.

Herr Wilberg was in despair. The gate was securely fastened; it was done to keep the work-people, whose dwellings lay for the most part about here, out of the park, but the gardener had the key; Wilberg would hasten, would fly to fetch it, if only her ladyship could bear to wait until ....

"Oh no," broke in Eugénie, rather impatiently. "You would have twice to make the round which I want to avoid. I would rather go back."

Wilberg would not hear of it. He begged and entreated the lady to grant him the happiness of this one small service. His pretty little speech was brought to an abrupt conclusion by the sound of a loud crack.

Ulric had gone up to the gate and seized it with both hands. He shook the iron rails with such force that the bolts and locks creaked again. Finding that it did not give way promptly, his features contracted angrily, he gave one violent thrust at it with his foot, and so made an end of all resistance. The fastenings, which were not in the best condition, yielded; the gate flew open.

"Good Heavens! Hartmann, what are you about?" cried Wilberg, terrified. "You are spoiling the lock. What will Herr Berkow say?"

Ulric gave him no answer. He pushed the gate quite back and turned quickly round.

"The way is open, my lady."

Eugénie did not look half so shocked as the young clerk. She even laughed, as she proceeded towards the path so vigorously cleared for her.

"Thank you, Hartmann. Do not make yourself uneasy as to the spoilt lock, Herr Wilberg; I will take the responsibility on myself. But, as the gate is open now, will you not take the shorter cut through the park?"

What a proposal! Herr Wilberg did not hasten, he rushed, he flew to the lady's side, racking his brain even in this hurried moment to find an interesting and striking theme on which to discourse; but he was obliged to begin with a very prosaic one, for Eugénie, turning her head once more, looked curiously after the enigmatic being who had puzzled her so much once before, as though she would again try to read the riddle of his character with her grave meditative eyes. "That Hartmann has the strength and the fury of an old Berserker. He crashes down locks and bolts without more ado, just to"----

"Just to make my way easy," continued Eugénie, with a touch of irony, as she looked at her companion. "You would not have been guilty of such a forcible act of politeness?"

Wilberg protested against even the supposition of such a thing. Her ladyship could not believe for a moment that he would have laid violent hands on other people's property, and that too in her presence; no, most assuredly he would not.... But she listened to his protestations with marked abstraction, and in spite of all the pains he took to interest her, he could not succeed in fully gaining her attention once during their walk through the park.

CHAPTER X

Hartmann pulled to the gate again and returned slowly to the house. He stood at the entrance watching the two figures until they disappeared down one of the park avenues.

"I thought, when you said no, you meant it, Ulric?"

The young man turned round and scowled at Martha standing by his side.

"What is it to you?" said he, roughly.

"To me? nothing. Don't frown like that, Ulric. You are angry with me because I reminded my lady of the handkerchief; but it belonged to her, and what could you do with that soft, white little thing? You could not even touch it when you came home from work, and I am sure you have looked at it often enough!"

There was a slight but unmistakable touch of irony in the girl's voice, and Ulric must have noticed it, for he exclaimed hastily:

"Let me be! I will have none of your sneers and your spying. I tell you, Martha"----

"Now, now, what is to do out there? Are you two quarrelling?" interrupted the Manager, as he joined them at the door.

Ulric turned away with a muttered exclamation of anger, but he did not seem inclined to continue the discussion. Martha, without answering her uncle, hurried past him into the house.

"What is the matter with the girl?" asked the old man, looking after her wonderingly, "and what were you two about? Have you been giving her hard words again?"

Ulric threw himself sullenly down on the bench.

"I am not going to be taught what I should do or leave undone, least of all by Martha."

"Well, well," said his father quietly, "she is very sure not to do anything to vex you."

"Why should not she vex me as well as any one else?"

The Manager looked at his son and shrugged his shoulders.

"Why, boy, have you no eyes in your head, or will you not see it? It is true, you never did care about the girls, and, after all, it is no wonder if you understand nothing about them."

"What is there for me to understand?" asked Ulric, growing attentive.

His father took his pipe out of his mouth and blew a cloud of smoke slowly into the air.

"That Martha cares for you," he answered laconically.

"Martha? For me?"

"I do believe he did not know it," said the Manager, in unfeigned astonishment. "His old father has to tell him such a thing as that! But that is the way when people fill their heads with all sorts of nonsense, which only confuses them! Goodness knows, Ulric, it is time you gave up all the other folly and took a good managing wife who would bring you to a better way of thinking."

Ulric was still gazing over at the park, and his eyes were fixed and gloomy as before.

"You are right, father," said he slowly. "It is time."

The old man nearly let his pipe fall in his surprise.

"My lad," he said, "that is the first reasonable word I have heard from you. Have you come to your senses at last? Yes, it is time indeed. You could have kept a wife long ago, and where could you find a prettier, a better, or a cleverer than Martha? I need not tell you how happy it would make me for you two to come together. Think it over, Ulric."

The young man sprang up and began pacing rapidly to and fro.

"Perhaps it would be best. There must be an end of this, there must! I felt that to-day again ... and the sooner the better!"

"What has come to you? There must be an end of what?"

"Nothing, father, nothing. But you are right; when once I have a wife, I shall know I belong to her, and my thoughts too. So you think Martha cares for me?"

"Go in and ask her!" cried the Manager laughing. "Do you think that I should have the girl in the house still if she cared for any one else! She does not want for suitors. I know plenty who would be glad of her, and there is Lawrence who has been trying to win her for ever so long, he has never got her to say 'yes' yet. She will say it to-day for you, if you choose; trust me for that."

Ulric listened with eager attention; but in spite of his father's flattering assurance, there was not much joy or satisfaction to be seen in his face. He looked as though he were trying forcibly to keep down some rebellious feeling which would not let him make up his mind, and there was something wild and almost convulsive in his manner, as, a sudden determination burning up within him, he turned at last to the old man and said:

"Well, if you think I shall not be refused, I ... I will go and speak to Martha."

"Now, at once?" asked the Manager in surprise. "But, Ulric, a man cannot go courting all in a minute like that, when a quarter of an hour before he had no notion of such a thing. Think over the matter first."

Ulric moved impatiently. "What is the good of waiting? I must know where I am. Let me go in, father."

The old man shook his head, but he was far too much afraid that his son would repent him of his hasty resolve to offer any very serious opposition. In the joy of his heart he cared little if the long-wished-for union were brought about in a somewhat unusual manner. He determined to stay quietly outside, so that the young people within could settle the business at their ease, for he knew Ulric well enough to be aware that any inopportune interference on his part would spoil everything.

In the meantime the young man had crossed the passage rapidly, as if he neither could nor would grant himself one moment for reflection. He opened the door of the room they commonly used, and saw Martha sitting at the table. Her hands, usually so busy, lay idle in her lap. She did not look up as he entered, and seemed not to notice that he came and stood quite close to her chair. He could see quite plainly that she had been crying.

"Do you bear me ill-will, Martha, because I was out of temper just now? I am sorry for it. Why do you look at me so?"

"Because it is the first time you ever were sorry for it. You never cared before how I took your ill-temper. Let it be so still."

Her tone was cold and meant as a repulse, but Ulric did not allow himself to be intimidated by it. His father's revelations must really have had some powerful effect on his stubborn nature, for his voice was unusually gentle as he replied.

"I know I am a great deal worse than the others, but I can't help it. You must take me as I am; perhaps you will be able to make something better of me."

At his first word the girl had looked up surprised, and she must have seen something strange in his face, for she moved hastily as if to rise. Ulric held her fast.

"Stay here, Martha, I want to talk to you. I want to ask you ... Well, I am not one for many words, and between us they are not needed. We are first cousins, we have lived together for years in the same house. You know best whether you can care for me at all, and you must know too that I have always been fond of you in spite of all our quarrels. Will you be my wife, Martha?"

The wooing was abrupt, brusque and stormy, as became the suitor's nature.

He drew a long breath, as if with these decisive words a weight had fallen from him. Martha still sat motionless before him. Her blooming colour had faded, had changed to a deep pallor, but she neither trembled nor hesitated as she uttered a low half-stifled "No."

Ulric thought he had not heard aright. "You will not?"

"No, Ulric, I will not!" repeated the girl resolutely, though almost under her breath.

The young man drew himself up offended.

"Well then, I might have spared my words. My father has been mistaken and so have I. No offence, Martha."

Wounded in his pride by the curt refusal he had met with, he was about to leave the room at once, but a look at Martha arrested him. She had risen and was grasping the chair with both hands, as though needing its support. No word of reply or of explanation came from her lips, but they trembled so and there was such an expression of unspoken pain in her white face that Ulric began to feel his father might be right after all.

"I thought you cared for me, Martha," he said, with some slight reproach in his tone.

She turned hastily from him and hid her face in her hands, but he caught a sound like that of a sob repressed with difficulty.

"I might have known I was too savage, too rough for you. You are afraid, you think I might grow worse after the marriage. You will have a better husband in Lawrence. He will let you have your own way in everything."

The girl shook her head and slowly turned her face to him again.

"I am not afraid of you, though you are often a bit rough and wild. I know you can't help it, and I would have taken you as you were, ay, gladly, perhaps! But I will not take you as you are now, Ulric, as you have been ever since .... ever since the young mistress came home."

Ulric started, and a flaming blush spread over his face. He wished to break out in wrath, to bid her be silent, but he could not bring his lips to frame a syllable.

"Uncle thinks you care for no one because your head is taken up with other things," continued Martha, more and more excitedly. "Yes, indeed, quite other things! You have never given me a thought, and now you come all at once and want me to be your wife. You want some one to help drive away your thoughts, Ulric, don't you? and the first one who comes is good enough for that. Even I am good enough for that! But things are not so bad with me yet that I should be put to such a use. If I cared for you more than for the whole world beside, if it were to cost me my life to part from you, I would rather have Lawrence, I would rather have any one now than you!"

This passionate outbreak, contrasting with the girl's usually quiet demeanour, might have shown Ulric what deep root he had taken in her heart. Perhaps he did feel it, but the cloud still rested on his brow and the flush on his face grew deeper with every word. He gave her no answer, but, as she now broke out into loud weeping, stood at her side quite dumb, making no attempt to comfort or to calm her.

Some minutes passed in torturing silence. Martha lay with her head and arms resting on the table. Nothing was to be heard but the sound of her convulsive sobs and the monotonous ticking of the old clock against the wall.

At length Ulric stooped down to her. His voice was not so hard as it had been, but it was scarcely gentle; there was in it only a dull, low sound of pain.

"Never mind, Martha. I thought it might be better if you would help me. Perhaps it would only have been worse, and you are quite right not to risk it with me. Let things be as they have always been between us two."

He went without further leave-taking. On the threshold he stopped an instant and looked back, but the girl did not raise her head, and he went quickly out.

"Well?" said the Manager, eagerly, as he came forward to meet his son. "Well?" he repeated more anxiously, for Ulric's face was not happy as that of an affianced lover.

"It was of no good, father," said Ulric in a low voice. "Martha will not have me."

"Will not have you?" cried the old man, as though the most astounding news in the world were being announced to him.

"No, and don't tease her with a lot of questions and talk about it. She knows well enough why she has refused me, and I know too, so there is no use in a third person meddling with it. Now let me go, father, I must get away."

He hurried past, evidently wishing to escape all further discussion. The Manager grasped his pipe with both hands; he was almost inclined to dash it to the ground, by way of giving vent to his vexation.

"Who can understand these women and their fancies? I could have staked my head upon it that the girl was fond of him, and now she sends him away with a No! and he ... I should not have thought he would have taken it so much to heart. He looked quite scared, and he is tearing along the road as if he were mad. But he will never explain it to me as long as he lives, I know him well enough to be sure of that, and Martha won't either."

The Manager went on pacing up and down the little garden, until gradually his wrath sobered down to a more resigned state of feeling. What could be done in the matter after all? They could not be tied together by force if they did not wish to be so tied, and it was of no use racking one's brains to discover why they did not wish it. With a heavy sigh the old man bade farewell to his favourite scheme, now hopelessly shipwrecked. These things cannot be forced!

He was still standing at the garden-gate, busy with his troubled thoughts, when he saw the younger Herr Berkow coming down the road which led past his cottage to the back of the park. Arthur seemed better acquainted than his wife with the mode of ingress. He drew a key from his pocket, destined, no doubt, to fit the lock which had so recently been broken open.

The Manager bowed deeply and respectfully to the young heir as he went by. With his usual scant sympathy, Arthur, hardly glancing aside at him, gave a lofty negligent little nod by way of recognition, and was passing on. A quiver of pain came into the old man's face, as he stood there still holding his cap in his hand and looking after the other with a mournful gaze which seemed to say, "So that's what you have grown into!"

Either Arthur saw the look or it occurred to him all at once that the old friend and playfellow of his childish years was there before him; he stopped suddenly.

"Oh, it is you, Hartmann! How do you do?"

He stretched out his hand in his lazy, indifferent way, and seemed rather surprised that it was not immediately grasped, but for years such a favour had not been granted, and the Manager hesitated before accepting it; when he did so at last, it was shily and with precaution, as though fearing to hurt the delicate white hand by the touch of his rough hard palm.

"Thank you, I am pretty well so far, Herr Arthur----I beg pardon, Herr Berkow, I mean."

"Keep to the Arthur," said the young man, quietly. "You are more used to it, and I would rather hear it from you than the other name. So you are all right, Hartmann?"

"Well yes, thank God, Herr Arthur. I have as much as I want. There is a bit of trouble and care in every house, and I am a little worried just now about my children, but it can't be helped."

"About your children? I thought you had only one son."

"Quite right, my Ulric. But I have a niece in my house, too, Martha Ewers."

"And she gives you trouble?"

"God forbid!" said the Manager, warmly. "The girl is as good as can be, but I did think the two might have made a pair, she and Ulric"----

"And Ulric will not?" interrupted Arthur, with a strangely rapid glance from the usually weary-looking eyes.

The old man shook his head.

"I don't know. Perhaps he did not really wish it, or perhaps he set about it badly; any way, it is over between them. And that was just my last hope, that he would get a good wife who would put some sensible notions into his head."

It was odd that the miner's simple uninteresting family affairs did not appear to "bore" the young man. He had not once yawned, as he was in the habit of doing, when not obliged to place some restraint on himself. His face even expressed a degree of interest as he asked:

"Are the notions he carries in his head at present the reverse of sensible then?"

The Manager looked up rather consciously at the speaker, and then down at the ground.

"Well, Herr Arthur, I need hardly tell you that. You must have heard enough about Ulric!"

"Yes, I remember. My father spoke to me about it. Your son is not in the good books of the gentlemen up there, Hartmann; very far from it."

The old man heaved a sigh.

"No, and I can't mend the matter. He will not listen to me, he never has listened to me. He always would think for himself and have his own way in everything. I let the boy learn a great deal more than the others, more, perhaps, than was good for him. I thought he would get on faster for it, and he is Deputy already, and will very likely be made Overman some day, but all the trouble has come from the learning though. He bothers himself about all sorts of stuff, and thinks he knows better about everything; he sits up all night over his books, and is just all in all with his mates. How he manages to take the lead everywhere, I don't know; but even when he was quite a little lad, he had them all under his thumb, and now it is worse than ever. What he says, they believe blindfold; where he stands, they will all stand together with him; and if he were to lead them into hell itself, they would go, always supposing he marched first. But this is not at all as it should be, particularly here on our works."

"Why here, particularly?" asked Arthur, drawing figures with the key on the wooden gate, and apparently immersed in thought.

"Because the people here are too badly off," burst forth the Manager. "Don't be angry, Herr Arthur, if I tell you so to your face. It is just the truth. I can't complain myself, I have always had more than my deserts, because your late mother was very fond of my wife--but the others! They toil and trouble day after day, and yet they can scarcely get bare necessaries for their wives and children. God knows they earn their bread hardly, but we must all of us work, and most of them would do it willingly enough, if they could only get their rights, as on the other works. But here they are pressed and harried for every farthing of their miserable wages, and the mines below are in such a state, that each man says his prayers before going down, because he keeps thinking that the whole concern will fall down some day and crush him. But there is never any money for repairs, and when a poor fellow gets into difficulties and distress, no money can ever be found to help him with either, and all the time they have to look on while thousands upon thousands are sent up to the city, in order that"----

The old man stopped suddenly, and clapped his hand over his indiscreet mouth in mortal fear. He had gone on speaking in such a zealous haste, that he had completely forgotten who it was that stood before him. The hot flush which rose to the young man's face at his last words, brought him back to a consciousness of what he was saying.

"Well?" asked Arthur, as he paused. "Go on. Hartmann, you see I am listening."

"God bless me!" stammered the old man, in sad confusion. "I did not mean that, I had quite forgotten"----

"Who spent the thousands? You need not make any apologies, Hartmann, but speak out like a man what you were going to say to me. Or perhaps you think I shall carry tales to my father?"

"No," said the Manager, heartily. "That you certainly won't do. You are not like your father, such an imprudent word as that to him would have lost me my place. Well, I was only going to say that all this makes bad blood with the hands. Herr Arthur"--he stepped up nearer, with a look of half-timid, half-trusting appeal, "if you would but take some interest in these things! You are Herr Berkow's son, and you will inherit all one of these days. No one has so much concern in it as you."

"I?" said Arthur, with a bitterness which happily escaped his unpractised hearer. "I understand nothing of your customs or of what is necessary here on the works. It is, and always has been, all quite strange to me."

The old man shook his head sorrowfully.

"Lord Almighty! what is there so much to understand? You need not study all about machinery and the shafts for that. You only need to look at the people and listen to them, as you are listening to me now. But nobody will do that. If a man complains, he is sent away, and then they say it is for insubordination; when a poor miner is dismissed on that score he finds it hard to get another place. Herr Arthur, I tell you, it is a crying shame, and that is what Ulric can't endure to see; it eats his heart out, and, though I am always talking and preaching against his notions, in point of fact he is right. Things can't go on in this way, only the means he would use to bring about a change are godless and sinful. They would bring him into trouble, and the others with him. Herr Arthur,"--the salt tears stood in the Manager's eyes as, without any hesitation now, he seized the young man's hand, still resting on the gate,--"for God's sake, I implore you, don't let matters go on like this. It can be good for no one, not even for Herr Berkow. There are troubles and disputes now on all the works around, but when once they break out with us, the Lord have mercy on us, for there will be awful work!"

During the whole of this speech Arthur had stood silent, gazing straight before him. Now he turned his eyes to the speaker and looked fixedly and gravely at him.

"I will talk to my father about it," he said slowly; "you may rely upon that, Hartmann."

The Manager let fall the hand he had grasped, and stepped back. Having poured out his whole heart, he had expected some better result than this poor promise.

Arthur drew himself up and prepared to go.

"One thing more, Hartmann. Your son saved my life not long ago, and he has felt hurt, probably, at receiving no word of thanks. I do not attach a great value to life in itself, and it may be, therefore, that I did not estimate aright the service rendered. But I should have made good my negligence, if"----the young heir frowned and his voice took a sharper inflexion, "if your Ulric had not been the man he is. I have no desire to find myself and my acknowledgments repulsed, as happened to my messenger a short time back; but in spite of this, I would not be thought ungrateful. Tell him I thank him, and as to the rest, I will confer with my father on the subject. Good-bye."

He took the road leading to the park. The Manager looked after him despondingly, and sighed heavily as he murmured: "God grant it may do some good--but I hardly think it."

CHAPTER XI

Up at the great house the carriage had been drawn out, and the coachman was busy putting to the horses.

"This is something quite new," said he to the footman who had brought him the order to make ready. "The master and mistress are going to drive out together. A red cross should be set against the day in the calendar."

The man laughed. "Yes, they won't find much pleasure in it; but you see they can't help themselves. The return visits have to be made in the town to all the great folk who were here at the dinner, and it would not do exactly for them to drive in separately, or, no doubt, that is what they would have done."

"A queer couple," said the coachman shaking his head. "And they call that being married! The Lord preserve a man from such wedded bliss as that!"

A quarter of an hour later the carriage containing Arthur Berkow and his wife was rolling along the road which led to the town.

The weather had been tolerable enough during the morning, but had now changed for the worse. The sky was lowering and overcast; the wind, which had risen almost to a hurricane, drove the grey clouds before it, and every now and then a heavy shower fell from them on to the already over-saturated earth. It was, in truth, a rough and stormy spring, of a sort thoroughly to disgust those accustomed to a town-life with a sojourn in the country.

Although the month of May had come, the bare leafless trees in the park showed hardly any symptoms of sprouting forth. The piercing wind and cold rains had destroyed all the flowers, to the distraction of the head-gardener who had been at so much pains to train them to perfection in the beds and on the terraces, and every bud was mercilessly nipped and blighted so soon as it showed itself. The impracticable roads and drenched forests made all excursions, possible only in a close carriage, as unpleasant as they were objectless.

Day after day nothing but storms and heavy rain; a grey cloudy sky, mountains veiled in mist, through which, ever and anon, a pale ray of sunshine would struggle faintly; and with all this a joyless, desolate home, where the mists gradually sank deeper and deeper, so that there, at least, no sunshine could penetrate, where every blossom, possibly ready to unfold, was frozen by the icy breath of bitterness and hatred.

In this home two people endured, as a kind of martyrdom from which each strove to escape as much as possible, that undisturbed seclusion which is looked on by most newly-married couples as the height of bliss. Surely this was enough to account for the bride's pale face and for that expression of pain about her mouth which no amount of self-control could obliterate; to account also for the melancholy look with which she gazed out at the landscape.

She had given her strength credit for more than it could bear. The sacrifice had been promptly made in the flush of courage and of filial love, but the days and hours succeeding the sacrifice, the passive endurance of her chosen lot, called now, for the first time, all her moral courage, all her power of will, into action, and however much Eugénie might possess of both, it was yet plainly to be seen that this after-time was very bitter to her.

Her husband, leaning back in the opposite corner as far off as possible, so that the folds of her dress hardly touched his cloak, did not seem to carry the burden of his happiness much more lightly. His face had, it is true, always been as pale, his eyes as expressive of fatigue, his bearing as languid as now, but there were lines in his countenance which had not been there before--dark, bitter lines, stamped on it by the events of the last few weeks, and which no amount of the coolest indifference would ever again efface.

He too looked out silently through the window, and made no more attempt than Eugénie to renew the conversation. They had met for the first time that day when about to set out on this journey, and some formal little speeches had been exchanged about the weather, the drive and the object for which it was being made; then they had relapsed into an icy silence which was to last, apparently, until they reached the town.

The expedition, conducted in this fashion, was not very agreeable; though in the comfortable close carriage nothing was felt of the inclement weather without, yet even the softest cushions could not prevent their feeling some inconvenience from the bad state of the roads, and the heavy barouche could only advance slowly, though drawn by fine and powerful horses.

They had accomplished nearly half the distance when a sudden jerk, more violent then any preceding, nearly threw the carriage over on its side. The coachman swore and stopped the horses. He and the footman both dismounted from the box, and then a lively discussion went on between them out in the road.

"What is the matter?" asked Eugénie, leaning forward uneasily.

Arthur, for his part, did not seem much to care what was the matter. He would no doubt have quietly waited until some announcement on the subject had been made to him, but he felt himself called on now to let down the window and to repeat his wife's question.

"Don't be alarmed, sir," said the coachman, stepping up to the door with the reins in his hand. "We have had a very lucky escape, we were within a hair of upsetting. Something must have snapped in the hind-wheel. Frank has gone to see what it is."

The report, which Frank brought back after due examination, was not precisely of a consoling nature. The wheel was so much injured that it was clearly impossible to move the carriage on even a hundred paces in that state. Both the men looked at their master helplessly.

"I am afraid, under these circumstances, we must give up the intended visits," said Arthur coolly, turning to his wife. "By the time Frank has gone back to the house and brought us back another carriage it will be too late to drive as far as the town."

"I am afraid so too. There is nothing to be done then but to get out and turn back."

"Get out?" said Arthur in amazement "Do you think of going back on foot?"

"Do you think of sitting in this carriage until Frank has returned with another?"

Arthur appeared to have entertained the idea; he would probably have preferred to wait two hours, stretched in his comfortable corner where he was sheltered from wind and weather, than to undertake a pedestrian tour through the cold wet woods. Eugénie noticed this, and her lips curled disdainfully.

"As for me, I prefer going back on foot to waiting in that wearisome useless manner. Frank will go with me, he must return any way. You will no doubt remain in the carriage. I would not take upon myself the responsibility of giving you cold for the world."

That which the misadventure had not had power to do, was effected by the overt irony of these words. Arthur was roused out of his corner. He got up, pushed open the door, and next minute was standing on the step, offering his hand to help her alight. Eugénie hesitated.

"I beg of you, Arthur" ...

"I beg of you not to make a scene before the servants and to show them that you prefer the footman's escort to mine. Allow me."

She gave an imperceptible little shrug; there was no choice for her, however, but to accept the proffered hand; the coachman and Frank were, in truth, standing close by. She got out, and Arthur turned to the two men.

"I will see your mistress home. You must contrive to get the empty carriage to some farm where it can stay for the present, and follow us as quickly as possible with the horses."

The men took off their hats and prepared to carry out the instructions they had received. Under the circumstances it was really the only thing to be done. With a slight gesture Eugénie declined her husband's offered arm.

"I think we can hardly walk here as on a promenade," said she, evading it. "We must each look to ourselves and make our own way as best we can."

She attempted this indeed, but only to sink at the very first step into the soft slippery mud; taking refuge on the other side of the road, she found herself suddenly in water an inch deep which splashed under her feet. She stood still in it helpless. The road had not looked so bad to her from the carriage.

"Here, at any rate, we shall never get on," said Arthur, who had tried a like experiment with the like result. "We must go back through the woods."

"Without knowing our way? we should lose ourselves."

"Hardly that. I remember when I was a child there used to be a path which led right through the wood, over the heights and down into the valley. We must try and find it."

Eugénie still lingered, but the evidently impracticable state of the main road, half flooded and full of ruts, left her no alternative. She followed her husband who had already turned off to the left, and a few minutes later they were in the midst of the dusky green and thickly planted pine trees.

Now at least it was possible to advance over the roots and moss-covered ground, nay, it would even have been easy to feet trained to such exercise. To a lady and gentleman accustomed to the smooth floor of a drawing-room, having carriages and riding horses at their disposal for every excursion, and whose pedestrian feats were limited to a turn round the park when the weather proved unusually fine, this path offered difficulties enough--and then the foggy tempestuous weather to boot! It had left off raining certainly, but everything about them was dripping wet, and the clouds threatened a fresh shower at any moment. Several miles from home, in the midst of the woods, straying like a pair of adventurers trusting to chance, without conveyance or servants, without the smallest protection from wind or rain, Herr Arthur Berkow and his high-born wife were in a situation so extraordinary as to seem almost desperate.

But the lady had already accepted the inevitable with characteristic resolution. The first ten steps had shown her how impossible it would be to save her light silk dress and white bernous, so she abandoned them to the mercy of the wet moss and dripping trees, and walked bravely on. Her attire was ill-suited to such wanderings on foot, and utterly incapable of affording her any protection from the inclemency of the weather. She wrapped herself more closely in the thin cashmere, and shivered in spite of herself as the cold wind met her.

Her husband noticed this and stopped. Although they had started in a close carriage, he had, in his effeminate way, thrown a cloak round him which covered him completely. He took it off in silence, and would have put it round his wife's shoulders, but she moved aside with prompt decision.

"Thank you, I do not want it."

"But you are chilly."

"Not at all. I am not so sensitive to the weather as you are."

Without saying another word Arthur took the cloak back, but instead of folding it about him again, he threw it negligently on one arm and walked on at her side, clad only in his light dress suit. Eugénie struggled against a feeling of rising anger. She hardly knew herself why this conduct vexed her so much, but she would far rather have seen him wrap himself carefully in the despised cloak and so take care of his precious health, than witness this reckless exposure of himself to wind and weather. It was for her, and her alone, to show a quiet, well-considered acquiescence in the decrees of Fate.

It was incomprehensible to her that her husband should for once lay claim to the same right, that he, who had been alarmed at the very idea of this journey home on foot, should appear now hardly to feel its inconveniences, while she was already more than half repenting of her resolve. A gust of wind tore his hat off and blew it down a steep bank where it could not possibly be reached. Arthur looked calmly after the fugitive and tossed his long brown hair back with an almost defiant movement. His feet sank deep into the wet moss at every step, and yet his gait had never seemed to Eugénie so firm, so elastic, as now. As they advanced into the forest, his languid air gradually vanished, his eyes brightened as they glanced sharply round in quest of the wished-for path. The dark damp woods seemed to have a re-animating power over him, in such deep draughts did he drink in the bracing pine-scented air, so briskly did he lead his wife along under the whispering trees. All at once he stopped and cried triumphantly,

"There, that is the way!"

Before them there was indeed a narrow footpath which ran straight through the forest, and, at some distance farther on, seemed to decline gently. Eugénie looked at it in surprise. She had not believed that her husband would prove a sure guide, and had quite made up her mind to losing their way completely.

"You seem very familiar with the country," said she, as she entered the path at his side.

He smiled, but the smile was less for her than for the place he found himself in; he looked round, scanning it on all sides with interest.

"I have not forgotten my old friends the woods yet, though it is long, very long, since we have seen each other."

Eugénie raised her head in astonishment. She had never heard such a tone in his voice; there was deep strongly-repressed feeling in it.

"Are you so fond of the woods?" she asked, involuntarily keeping up a conversation which would probably else have lapsed into the usual silence. "Why have you passed a whole month then without once setting foot in them?"

Arthur did not answer. He was gazing dreamily down at the green depths shrouded in mist.

"Why?" said he at last, sadly. "I don't know. Perhaps because I was too lazy. One loses everything in that city of yours, even one's taste for solitude in the woods."

"In that city of mine? I thought you were brought up there as well as I."

"Certainly, but with this difference, that my life ended when my so-called bringing up began. All that was really worth living for I left behind me when I entered those walls, for the joyous sunny years of my early boyhood were the only ones worth having."

He spoke in a tone half bitter, half resentful. But in Eugénie's mind the old angry feeling blazed up hotly again. How dared he speak as if he had ever had anything to give up? What did he know of sacrifice, of renunciation? For her, indeed, childhood and happiness might truly be said to have come to an end together. As her father's confidant, early initiated into all the family affairs, she had made acquaintance on her first entrance into life with that graduated scale of care, humiliation, and despair, with that bitter school of sorrow, which had steeled her character, but had also robbed her of all the joys of youth. How different had been her husband's position, how different all his past life! And yet he spoke as if he had known unhappiness!

Arthur seemed to read these thoughts in her face, as he turned to hold back a drooping branch which would have brushed against her.

"You think I, of all people, have no right to complain? It may be so. At any rate I have always been told that my existence is a most enviable one. But I assure you a life like mine is sometimes desperately void and wretched. When fortune heaps all her gifts before a man, he just treads them under foot, because he does not know what use to make of them. The life is so empty and miserable that one would gladly escape in the end from this gilded felicity they vaunt so loudly, and rush out of it anywhere--anywhere, even into the midst of storm and tempest!"

Eugénie's dark eyes were fixed in speechless astonishment on his face. He flushed suddenly, remembering perhaps that he had been guilty of an unpardonable mistake; he had betrayed some feeling in his wife's presence. The young man frowned and cast a reproachful angry glance at the forest which had thus led him astray. Next minute he resumed his old indifferent manner.

"Just now we have more storm and tempest than we care about," said he negligently, going on in front so as completely to turn his back on her. "It is blowing a gale up there on the hills. We shall have to wait until the worst is over; we cannot go down at present."

And truly the storm met them with such force, as they issued from the wood, that they had some trouble to keep their footing. It was plainly out of the question to go on now, for at this spot the road grew steep and led straight down into the valley; they would have been in danger of being caught up by the wind and hurled bodily into the depths below. There was therefore nothing for it but to wait here under the shelter of the trees until the hurricane should subside.

They stood under a mighty pine-tree which reared itself high aloft on the very verge of the forest. The storm roared and rustled in its great green arms, as it stretched them protectingly over its younger and weaker fellows, and swayed them groaning up and down every now and then in spite of their strength, but the giant, whitish-grey trunk, offered shelter and support to Eugénie, who stood leaning against it. Two persons might have found room there in case of need, but they would have been placed in the closest proximity to each other, and it was this consideration, no doubt, which induced Arthur to remain standing some paces off. He was but very imperfectly sheltered, and the raindrops, accumulated on the branches from the last shower, poured down plentifully upon him as the wind moved them to and fro; his hair was blown about and the drops chased each other over his uncovered brow, still he made no attempt to change his place.

"Would you ... would you not rather come here?" asked Eugénie, hesitating and squeezing herself to one side, so as to make room for him on the only dry spot.

"Thank you. I do not wish to inconvenience you."

"Put the cloak on then, at least." This time it sounded almost like an entreaty. "You will be quite wet through."

"Certainly not. I am not so sensitive to the weather as you imagine."

She bit her lips. It is not pleasant to be fought with one's own weapons, but far more than this it angered her to see him expose himself thus to wind and weather, just for the sole purpose of teaching her a lesson. True, this sort of defiance seemed to her supremely absurd; she did not really suffer by his persistency, and she did not very much care if he caught cold or fell ill through it or not. Still it irritated her that he should stand there calmly and keep his place in spite of the storm, with an effort, perhaps, but still keep it, while, but half an hour before, he had been lying, sleepy and shivering, in the cushions of the comfortable carriage and appearing painfully affected by every breath of air which found its way through the windows. Were storm and tempest really needed that he might prove to her he was not quite the weakling she had hitherto considered him to be?

Arthur hardly looked just now as if he had the intention of proving anything to her. He stood with folded arms, gazing at the chain of wooded hills, a commanding view of which was to be had from this eminence. As his eyes turned slowly from one summit to another, Eugénie suddenly made the startling discovery that they were very handsome. It was a great surprise to her; up to this time she had only known that the half-closed lids veiled two sleepy, tired-looking orbs which she had not troubled herself to examine more narrowly. When, by any chance, he raised them, he did it slowly, in a lazy fashion, as if it cost him an effort which he felt would be ill repaid, and yet this look of his was well worthy of notice. To judge by the expression of his face, one would have expected the usually drooping lashes to cover eyes of a cold pale blue, but instead of this they proved to be brown, clear and deep, though lacking animation, and it seemed as if they might yet light up with energy and passion, as if in their depths a whole world lay perdu, long forgotten and sunk out of sight, yet awaiting only the magic word which should break the spell and call it up afresh to life and action.

Once more there flashed into the young wife's mind the thought which had crossed it when, at their entrance into the woods, he had turned from her so suddenly, the suspicion of all the havoc made, of the great wrong done, by the education his father had given him, a wrong too great to be justified or ever to be redressed.

They stood together alone up there upon the hill. The forest lay before them with its veil of mist, closely wreathed in the grey shadows which clung to the sombre firs, waved from their crests in long gauzy stripes, floated ghost-like over the earth. And over the hills yonder the same misty veil hovered and fluttered, now torn asunder, now rushing together in one compact mass, clothing alike the hill-tops and steaming valleys. One continual surging and swelling, ebbing and flowing; mountains and woods seeming, at one time, to open forth their innermost depths, then again to close, withdrawing themselves from every mortal eye.

All around the storm howled and raged, tearing through the great secular pines as through a cornfield. The mighty trunks groaned as they swayed up and down, and bent their lofty crests murmuring before the wind, whilst overhead chased in disordered flight the great, seething formless masses of grey cloud. Such a storm as can only burst forth in the heart of the mountains--yet in all its uproar, it brought a message of spring. She came riding on its rustling wings, not sunnily smiling as on the plains below, but in rough wild humour. It was her breath which swelled the hurricane, her cry which resounded through all the clamour.

In these great disturbances of Nature may be traced a promise of the glowing sunshine and scent of flowers, so soon to be spread through the earth, a prevision of all those creative forces at work, struggling to bring their thousand germs forth to the light of day. And they heard her cry and answered her, those murmuring forests, those precipitous brooks and vaporous valleys. In all this commotion and fury and foam, there was yet Nature's shout of gladness as she threw off the last chains of winter, her hail of rejoicing as she greeted the coming deliverer. The spring is at hand!

There is something mysterious in such an hour. The legends of those mountain parts allot to it a peculiar romantic charm. They tell how the spirit of the hills travels through his kingdom at such times, and uses his power for a blessing or a curse to the lives of all tarrying within his dominions. "To meet then is to cleave together, to part then is to part for all eternity." For those two standing on the height together, there was indeed no question of such meeting. They were bound by the closest tie which can unite two human beings, and yet they were as far apart, as strange one to the other, as though worlds lay between them.

The silence had lasted some time. Eugénie broke it first.

"Arthur."

He started as from a dream and turned to her.

"Yes?"

"It is so cold up here--Will you not .... lend me your cloak now?"

Again the bright flush rose to the young man's face, as he looked at her in speechless astonishment. He knew she was so proud, she would rather have been frozen by the icy wind than condescend to beg for the once despised covering; yet she did so now in the hesitating tone, and with the downcast eyes, of one confessing a fault.

In a minute he was at her side, and holding out the cloak to her. She allowed him to put it round her shoulders in silence, but when he was about to return to his former post, he met a glance of dumb yet earnest reproach. Arthur still hesitated for one second, but had she not almost asked for forgiveness? He, too, allowed himself to be disarmed, and remained standing by her.

A great rampart of fog had risen out of the valley and closed in round them, fastening them to the spot. Mountains and woods disappeared in the grey vapour. Only the mighty pines towered high above it, and looked gravely down on the two human beings who had come to them for protection and a refuge. Overhead the dark branches rustled and whispered noisily as with a thousand mysterious voices, and ever and anon struck in the fuller-toned chords of the forest. It became painfully oppressive up here in the midst of this fog, beneath all this eerie fluttering and stir.

Eugénie started up all at once, as if she must extricate herself from some danger, from some toils which held her enchained.

"The fog gets thicker and thicker," said she anxiously; "and the weather more dreadful than ever. Do you think there would be any danger for us on the road?"

Arthur looked at the swelling masses of vapour, and stroked the drops from his damp hair.

"I am not well enough acquainted with our mountains to know how far their storms may be dangerous. If it were the case, would you be afraid?"

"I am not fearful, but one always hesitates when it is a question of life."

"Always? I should have thought our life, the life we have led for the last month, was not of a nature to make any one afraid of risking it. You especially have cause to feel this."

She looked down.

"So far as I know, I have annoyed you by no complaints."

"Oh, no. Nothing like a complaint has escaped your lips. If you could only force some colour into your cheeks as easily! You would do it, I know, if you could, but there even your power of will fails. Do you think it can afford me any great pleasure to see that my wife is drooping away at my side, and that just because a hard fate has driven her there?"

This time the hot glow mounted to Eugénie's face; it was not called up by the reproach contained in his words, but by the strange expression he had used towards her for the first time.

"My wife" he had said. Yes, she had certainly been married to him, but it had never yet occurred to her that he could have the right to call her "his wife."

"Why do you touch upon this subject again?" asked she, turning away. "I hoped after that one necessary explanation it would be done with for ever."

"Because you seem to be in error and to fancy that I shall hold you all your life long in chains which, truly, are as oppressive to me as they ever were to you."

His tone was cold in the extreme, but Eugénie looked quickly up at him. She could read nothing in his countenance, however. Why were those eyes instantly veiled whenever she attempted to search their meaning? Was it that they would not submit to be questioned, or that they feared to betray themselves?

"You allude to--to a separation?"

"Do you imagine I could look upon the union between us as lasting after the expression of--of esteem, which I was forced to hear from your mouth on that first evening?"

Eugénie was silent.

Over their heads the pine-branches rustled and waved hither and thither once more. The voice of the forest, exhorting, remonstrating, was wafted down to this wedded pair about to utter the word which should separate them, but neither he nor she would understand the meaning.

"We are neither of us free enough to lay all considerations on one side," continued Arthur, in the same tone. "Your father and mine are both too well known, each in his own sphere, our marriage attracted too much attention for us to be able to dissolve it immediately, without affording inexhaustible matter for gossip to the whole town, and making ourselves ridiculous as the hero and heroine of a hundred stories. People do not separate after four-and-twenty hours, or even after a week, without some appreciable cause; for appearances' sake they bear with one another for a year or so, in order to declare, with some show of likelihood, that there is incompatibility of temper. I had hoped we could have borne to live so long together, but it seems that our strength is not equal to the task. If we go on in this way, we shall both of us succumb."

The arm which Eugénie had wound round the trunk of the great tree trembled slightly, but her voice was steady as she answered.

"I do not succumb so easily when I have once taken a task upon me; and, as for you, I really did not think you were in the least affected by our painful position."

In his brown eyes there flashed once more that rapid lightning-like gleam which vanished as quickly, leaving no trace behind it. His look was quiet and expressionless as before, when he replied after a short pause.

"You really think so? Well, it does not signify whether I am affected by it or not. I should not have touched upon the subject, if I had not seen the necessity of reassuring you by a promise that our marriage should be dissolved as soon as circumstances permit. Perhaps now I shall not see you look so white as you have done for the last few days, and perhaps you will believe now what you have, so far, looked upon as a lie, namely, that I had no knowledge of the machinations by which your hand was obtained for me, but imagined that it was given voluntarily and of your own free will."

"I believe you, Arthur," said she in a low voice. "I do believe you now."

Arthur received this first mark of his wife's confidence with a smile of exceeding bitterness. It came to him at the very moment he was giving her up.

"The fog begins to clear," said he, changing the subject, "and the storm seems to abate too for a few minutes. We must take advantage of it to get down. In the valley below we shall be protected, and shall soon reach the farm, where, I hope, they will be able to lend us a carriage. Will you follow me?"

The way was steep and slippery, but Arthur seemed wishful to-day of giving his whole nature the lie. He walked down the hill with a firm sure tread, while Eugénie, with her thin boots and long dress, impeded still further by the cloak, could hardly advance. He saw that he must come to her assistance, but on such a road he could not simply offer her his arm. He must, of necessity put it well round her if his help were to be of any avail, and that ... that would hardly do!

The husband hesitated to render his wife a service which he would have done to any stranger; and that which a stranger, under the circumstances, would have at once accepted, the wife felt averse to receiving from her husband.

After some moments of indecision he did finally place his arm round her waist. She quivered a little at his touch, but neither of them spoke while making the descent, which lasted about ten minutes. At every step they took downwards Eugénie's face grew whiter. It appeared to be intolerable to her that his arm should thus support her, that she should be forced to lean on his shoulder, so near him that she could feel his breath on her face. Yet he did what he could to spare her. He never glanced at her once. All his attention seemed directed to the road, which, certainly, was of a nature to make care and prudence needful to prevent their both sliding down it unawares. But, quiet as he seemed, there was that same treacherous little twitch about the young man's lips, and, when at last they reached the valley below, he released his wife from his arms with a long, deep-drawn breath, which showed he had been anything but calm during their strange little journey.

Already the farm-buildings were visible glinting through the trees, and they hastened down the path which led to them, as though feeling that on no account must they remain longer alone together. Overhead the storm raged afresh, and high up on the hill the fog thickened again round the stout old pine which had spread its branches protectingly over these two, and given them shelter in the hour of which the old legends say:

"To meet then is to cleave together, to part then is to part for all eternity."

CHAPTER XII

Herr Berkow had arrived in the afternoon of the day on which Arthur and his wife had made their excursion through the forest, and had received them on their return home. This time he did not appear to be in such excellent spirits as on the occasion of his previous visit, when he had revelled in the first triumph procured for him in his own house by his grand new connection.

He was, it is true, now as ever, full of politeness to his daughter-in-law and of indulgence towards his son, but his manner, even on the evening of his arrival, showed that he was ruffled, uneasy, abstracted, and this was still more evident next morning when Arthur went to his room and asked for an interview.

"Another time, Arthur," said he, evading it, "another time. Do not tease me about trifles now that my head is full of most important affairs. The city business and money matters have caused me an immense amount of worry. Everything is at a standstill, or bringing loss instead of gain, but you understand nothing about it, and very likely don't care. I will soon bring things into shape again myself, but pray spare me all talk about your private concerns just now."

"It is not a private concern of my own this time, sir, the subject has its importance for you too. I am sorry to take up your time now that you are overwhelmed with business, but I cannot help it."

"Well--after dinner then," returned Berkow impatiently. "You can very well wait till then. I have not a moment now; all the officials are waiting for me over in the committee-room, and I have sent word to the chief-engineer that I will go down the shaft with him as soon as the meeting is over."

"Go down with him?" asked the young man, growing attentive. "Do you mean to inspect the mines personally?"

"No, I am going to see after the alterations in the lifting-apparatus which have been begun in my absence. What should I do down in the mines?"

"I thought you were going to ascertain personally whether things are in as bad a state down below as they pretend."

Berkow turned round suddenly as he was going out, and looked at his son in surprise. "What do you know about the state of things in the mines? Who has put such notions into your head? I suppose the Director, finding I turned a deaf ear to his last demands for cash, has since applied to my son. Well, he has got to the right man there!"

He laughed out loud, not noticing the displeasure in Arthur's face; the latter replied with some sharpness:

"But it must be looked into, to find out how far these improvements are necessary, and as you are going down with the engineers, you might take advantage of the opportunity to make a more thorough examination of the shafts and galleries."

"That I certainly shall not," returned Berkow curtly. "Do you think I want to risk my life? Things are dangerous in their present condition, there is no doubt about it."

"And yet you send down hundreds of men every day?"

The tone of this question was very peculiar, so peculiar that his father frowned with annoyance.

"Do you mean to lecture me, Arthur? I fancy a sermon from you would sound rather odd. You seem to have taken refuge in philanthropy from the monotony of your stay in the country. I would let that alone if I were you. It is an expensive pursuit, particularly in our circumstances. Besides, I shall take good care no accidents happen; I should incur a loss by it which would be exceedingly ill-timed just now. The necessary repairs shall be made and things kept in order; but as for extensive improvements, I have in the first place no money for them, and in the second, I cannot allow the works to be stopped even for a day. To have enabled me to do that, your requirements should have been rather more moderate than they were for some time before your marriage. But I really don't understand why you a troubling yourself all at once about things which you generally ignore altogether. You had better busy yourself with the arrangements for your salon and for the soirées you will be giving in the city this winter, and leave to me the care and responsibility of matters which you understand nothing about."

"Nothing," assented the young man with rising bitterness. "You have taken care of that."

"I do believe you mean to reproach me!" exclaimed Berkow. "Have you not enjoyed every pleasure in life? Have I ever recoiled before a sacrifice which could procure you enjoyment? Shall I not leave you a wealthy man, I who began life without a penny in my pocket? Have I not, by this marriage of yours with the Baroness Windeg, got you introduced in the ranks of the nobility to which you will one day belong? I should like to see the father who has done so much for his son as I have!"

During the whole of this speech, Arthur had stood silent, looking out of the window.

"You are quite right, sir, but I see you have neither time nor patience to listen now to what I had intended saying to you. I will wait until after dinner."

So saying he went out. Berkow looked after him and shook his head. This son of his was growing incomprehensible to him; but he had, indeed, no time to spare. He locked his desk hastily, took up his hat, and went over to the committee-room with a look on his face which presaged but little sunshine for those who there awaited him.

Meanwhile the miners had assembled about the shaft, ready to begin the second shift of the day. They were waiting for the overman, who had not appeared as yet. In and about the shed at the shaft's mouth were grouped together men of every age and skilled in every branch of industry which active mining operations call into play. The various Deputies of the various divisions were there also, but the most prominent figure of all was Ulric Hartmann, who stood in the midst of them, with one foot on the steps, his arms crossed, silent at present, and yet distinguishable as the leading man.

No real discussion could have been held then, both time and place were unfitted for it, but even at these short casual meetings the talk turned on the one subject which now occupied all the men on the works.

"You may depend upon it, Ulric, they will not follow us on the other works," said the young miner Lawrence, who was standing next to Hartmann. "They think it is too soon; they are not ready; in short, they have no mind to begin, and would rather wait and see how things turn out."

Ulric tossed his head defiantly. "What do I care? We will go forward alone then, we have no time to spare."

A movement of surprise was to be seen amongst the miners. "Alone?" asked some. "Without our mates?" added others, and the majority repeated anxiously "Now? Already?"

"Now, I say," declared Ulric imperiously, as he threw a challenging look around him. "If any man among you is of a different way of thinking let him say so."

A not inconsiderable number of those present seemed to be of a different way of thinking, but no one ventured on a decided opposition; only Lawrence said gravely:

"But you thought yourself it would be better if all the works in the neighbourhood struck at the same time?"

"Can I help it if they dally and shilly-shally until our patience is worn out?" asked the young Deputy vehemently. "If they will go on waiting, we can't, and that they know right well. But they want to send us on first under fire, that they may see how the thing goes with us. Right good fellowship that! Well, we will manage without them."

"And you really think that he"--Lawrence glanced in the direction of the château--"that he will give in?"

"He must," said Ulric decidedly, "he must or else ruin himself. Several of his speculations have just failed, he has had to meet his son's debts, and the new house in town will be a matter of some thousands. If there is a stoppage on the works for a couple of months or so just now when the great contracts have been entered into, it is all up with their fine doings. Two years ago he might have weathered it, but not now. We shall get all we want if we threaten to strike."

"God grant we may!" said an elderly man with a pale sunken face and anxious look. "It would be terrible if we took all that care and trouble upon us for nothing, if we and our wives and children were to go on starving for weeks together, and, after all, find things just as they were. Had not we better wait until our mates ...?"

"Yes, if we were to wait for the others?" was heard from several voices.

"Talk, talk, and nothing but talk!" broke out Ulric fiercely. "I tell you now is the time, and we must set about it. Will you go with me, or will you not? Answer."

"Don't flare out like that," said Lawrence pacificating. "You know well enough we shall all go with you, if it comes to that. Let them do as they will on the other works, we are united among ourselves; not a man of us will desert you."

"I would not recommend any one to remain behind, if once things become serious," said Ulric, glowering darkly at the corner whence the opposition had proceeded. "We can't have any cowardice. Every man must be answerable for his fellow, and woe to him who is found wanting."

The young leader seemed to have adopted the right way of stifling any possible germs of resistance; his comrades were awed by his despotic treatment of them. The few dissentient voices, those exclusively of middle-aged men, were silenced, and the rest of the miners, especially the younger ones, flocked round Hartmann with loud demonstrations of approval. He continued more quietly:

"Besides, this is not the time to discuss it all, this evening we will"-
---

"The overman!" broke in several voices, while the looks of all turned to the door.

"Fall apart!" commanded Ulric; obedient to the order, the men dispersed at once, each miner taking up his safety-lamp which he had previously placed on one side.

The overman, coming in upon them suddenly and rather unexpectedly, probably saw the group separate quickly at his approach, and perhaps heard the word of command, for he looked keenly round the circle.

"You seem to have your men in capital discipline, Hartmann," said he coldly.

"Pretty fair, sir," returned the other in the same tone.

The overman must have known as well as the other officials what was going on among the hands, but he preferred to see and hear nothing. He went on in a matter-of-fact way:

"Herr Berkow is going with the engineers to inspect the pumps and the lifting apparatus. You are to wait with Lawrence in the shaft, Hartmann, until the gentlemen come up. Deputy Wilm can lead your men with his own, and you can follow later on."

Ulric received his instructions in silence and remained behind with Lawrence, while the others, conducted by the overman, began the descent. When the last of his comrades had disappeared, the young miner turned in his wrath.

"They are all cowards together," he muttered angrily. "One can't get them to move for their fears and their indecision. They know as well as I do that we must make use of the present time, and yet they won't go forwards, because the others are not at their back. A very good thing that it is Berkow we have got to deal with and no other. If he were the right sort of man, and knew when to show his teeth and when to give them good words, they would never go through with the business."

"Do you think he will not know?" asked Lawrence, rather distrustfully.

"No, he is a coward like all tyrants. He will talk loudly and harass us so long as he has the upper hand, but when his skin or his money-bag is in danger, he will sing small. He has made himself so thoroughly hateful, and he persists so in driving them on to the last extremity, that soon not a man among them will hold back, and then it will be all right. We shall have him in our hands then."

"And the young master? Do you think he won't interfere when the troubles break out?"

An expression of unconcealed contempt played about Ulric's mouth, as he answered disdainfully,

"He counts for nothing. He will run away back to the city at the first alarm and put himself in safety. If we had only him to deal with, we should settle the business very quickly. He would say yes to everything, if you threatened not to let him have his sleep out. The father will give us rather more trouble."

"He is going to inspect the pumps," said Lawrence, reflectively. "Perhaps he will go into the mine as well?"

Ulric laughed out bitterly.

"What are you dreaming of? Men like us must risk their lives daily. That is what we are fit for, but our lord and master will remain where it is safe in the shaft. I wish I had him alone once with me, face to face. He should learn what it is to tremble, as we so often have to do down below."

The young man's look and tone were full of such savage hatred that his more moderate companion thought it better to be silent, and so, for the time being at least, let the conversation drop.

A long pause ensued. Hartmann went up to the window and looked out impatiently. All at once he felt the touch of a hand on his shoulder, and, turning, saw Lawrence standing at his side.

"I want to ask you something, Ulric," began the latter with some hesitation. "I think you will tell me if I ask it of you. How do matters stand between you and Martha?"

Some seconds passed before Ulric answered.

"Between me and Martha? What do you want to know for?"

The other looked down.

"You see, I have been courting the girl so long. She would never take me, because ... because there was some one else. Well, I can't blame her"--with a wistful glance of admiration at his friend--"and if it is really a fact that you are standing in my light, well, I must manage to drive the whole thing out of my head; so tell me, are you of one mind?"

"No, Karl," said Ulric, in a low voice. "We are not of one mind, and we are not likely to be. We know that now both of us. I shall not stand in your way any longer with the girl, and I think, if you will try your luck once more, she will take you."

A gleam of joy passed over Lawrence's face, and he drew himself up erect with a deep-drawn breath of relief.

"Do you really mean that? Well, if you say so, it must be true, and I will try once more this very evening."

Ulric frowned.

"This evening? Don't you remember that we have a meeting to-night, and that you have to attend it, instead of going courting! But you are no better than the others! Now when we are going into the fight your head is full of your love-making; now when a man should be thankful to be without wife and child you are thinking of nothing but of getting married. There is no bearing with you all!"

"Well, I may ask Martha any way," said Lawrence somewhat hurt. "And if she really does say yes, it will be some time yet before the wedding. You don't know how a man feels when there is some one he cares for that he can't have, how sick at heart he gets when he sees another man with her day after day, only needing to stretch out his hand to take that which he would give his life for, and yet not caring to take it. You"----

"Have done, Karl." Ulric interrupted him with lips working with agitation, and letting his clenched fist fall so heavily on the wood-work that it groaned again. "Go to Martha, marry her, do what you like, but don't talk to me any more of such things. I can't, I won't bear it."

The young miner looked at his friend in amazement. He could not comprehend so violent a repulse. There was no doubt that Ulric gave the girl up freely .... but he had no time to ponder over it, for at this moment Berkow's sharp voice was heard outside, saying in very ungracious tones to the officials who accompanied him:

"And now I must beg of you, gentlemen, to have done. The old ventilators have lasted all this time without an accident, and they will last longer. We need no expensive novelties which it pleases you to consider necessary, because they would not be paid for out of your pockets. Do you think I want a model philanthropic establishment here? I want the returns to be increased, and the funds required for that purpose will be granted. All the other items will be erased. If the miners have to run risks, I can't help that. They earn their bread by it. I can't throw away thousands to insure a few hewers and trammers against an accident which might have happened any day, but never has happened yet. The repairs in the shafts and mines will be limited to what is strictly necessary to keep things in good working order, and so there is an end of it."

He pushed open the door of the shed and seemed unpleasantly surprised at seeing the two men, whom he had certainly not expected to find there, and who must have overheard his last words. Their presence appeared to be even more unsatisfactory to the chief-engineer.

"Hartmann, what are you doing up here?" he asked in some embarrassment.

"The overman told us we were to go down the shaft with the gentlemen," answered Ulric, keeping his darkly gleaming eyes fixed on Berkow.

The chief-engineer shrugged his shoulders and turned to his principal, with a look which said plainly enough, "He might as well have chosen some one else," but he made no reply.

"All right," said Berkow, shortly. "Go on, we will follow you."

The two miners obeyed. When they were out of sight of the others, Lawrence stopped a moment.

"Ulric!"

"What?"

"Did you hear?"

"That he can't throw away thousands just to insure the lives of a few hewers and trammers? But the returns are to be increased by tens of thousands! Well, no one is safe here down below, and he means coming with us to-day. We shall see whose turn comes first. Off with you, Karl."

CHAPTER XIII

It seemed that the long-looked-for spring had indeed conquered her kingdom by the might of yesterday's storm, with such magic swiftness had the weather changed over night. Fog and cloud had vanished without leaving trace behind, and with them were gone also both wind and cold. The mountains lay clear and distinct, bathed in bright sunshine, the air around them was warm and balmy, and so at last one might dare to hope that the continual rain and tempests of the last few weeks were over at last, over for the long sunny spring and summer time.

Eugénie had stepped out on to her balcony, and was looking at the landscape from which the veil had at length been lifted. Her eyes were fixed dreamily on the mountains out yonder. Perhaps she was thinking of yesterday's mists up on the heights, perhaps the rustling and swaying to and fro of the great pine branches still sounded in her ears, but all these recollections were suddenly put to flight. The note of a post-horn was heard close by, and immediately afterwards a chaise drew up before the terrace below. With a cry of joyful surprise she flew back from the balcony.

"My father!"

Yes, it certainly was Baron Windeg who stepped so quickly from the carriage and up into the hall, where he found his daughter already waiting to welcome him. It was the first time they had met since her marriage, and, in spite of the presence of two servants who had rushed to the door to receive so distinguished a guest, the father took his child in his arms, eagerly, as he had done on the evening of her wedding-day, when she had come in her travelling dress to take leave of him. At length she drew herself gently free and led him with her to her favourite room, the little blue boudoir.

"What a surprise, papa!" said Eugénie, radiant with joyful agitation. "I had no idea of this visit."

The Baron, with his arm still round her, sat down by her side on the sofa.

"And I did not propose to visit you, dear, but I had to make a journey to this part of the country, and I neither could nor would resist going a few miles out of my way that I might see you again."

"A journey?" Eugénie looked up enquiringly at her father and met his eyes, which were searching her face, as though trying to read there the story of the weeks during which she had been separated from him. As her look fell accidentally on the hat he was still holding, she shrank back, pale and startled.

"For Heaven's sake, papa! tell me the meaning of that crape. My brothers" ...

"They are well and send their love," said the Baron soothingly. "Do not be alarmed, Eugénie, you have no cause to fear for any who are dear to you. The mourning which has fallen on our house does not, I regret to say, deeply affect our hearts. But you shall hear all about that later on, now you must tell me" ...

"No, no," interrupted his daughter uneasily. "I must know first for whom you wear this crape. Why are you in mourning?"

"Windeg placed his crape-bound hat on one side and drew his child more closely to him; there was something convulsive, something painful, in the manner of his tenderness towards her.

"I am on my way to pay the last marks of respect to our cousin Rabenau. His property lies in this province."

Eugénie started up. "Count Rabenau? the owner of the entailed estates?"

"Is dead," continued the Baron, speaking with difficulty. "In the fulness of life and strength, a few weeks before his intended marriage. No one could have foreseen that."

Eugénie had grown deadly white. It was evident that the news awakened in her some terrible emotion which yet was not grief. She said no word, but her father seemed to understand her agitation.

"You know that we have been strangers to each other for a long time," he went on sadly. "Rabenau's rough, fierce ways made it impossible for us to be on good terms, and I shall never forget the bitter repulse I met with from him six months ago. He could have saved us if he would, it would have been but a light thing to him. He refused harshly and peremptorily, and now he is dead, leaving no issue. I succeed to the entailed property, now that it is too late, that I have sacrificed my child!"

There was such misery in his tone that Eugénie made a great effort to control herself, and succeeded after the lapse of a minute or two.

"O papa, you must not think of me now! I--I am quite relieved to know that you will be so richly compensated for all the past humiliations. I was only a little startled, taken by surprise at the sudden news. We never could have counted on the succession."

"Never!" said the Baron gloomily. "Rabenau was young and strong, he was about to be married. Who could have guessed that a three days' illness would have carried him off? But, if he was fated to die, why, oh! why could this event not have happened sooner? A month ago, half, nay, a quarter of the wealth now flowing in upon me would have saved us. I could have flung back his money to the rogue who brought my misfortunes on me, with the hundredfold rate of usury which he claimed, and my only daughter would not have been the price of his vile bargain. I accepted your sacrifice, Eugénie, God knows not for my own sake, but for that of the name we bear, and to secure my sons' future. Now, when I think that all that bitter sacrifice was in vain, that a short chance delay of a few weeks would have spared it us both, I cannot endure this mockery of Fate."

He pressed her hand tightly in his. But, by this time, Eugénie had won back all her pride and complete composure. If this "too late" were terrible in its effect upon her, she did not allow it to be seen.

"You must not speak so, papa," she replied firmly. "It would be unjust to your other children. Count Rabenau was such, that we can only formally mourn his death, and it sets you free from much trouble and embarrassment. My marriage only averted the most threatening danger. There remained burdens enough upon us, which weighed heavily and might one day have brought you again into degrading dependence on that man. All fear of this is now over for ever, you can pay him back the whole of what you have received, we shall owe him nothing more!"

"But he will owe us," interrupted Windeg bitterly, "and he will take good care never to pay his debt; it is the thought of that which turns my joy to gall. A short time back I should have greeted this deliverance with delight, and with the keenest sense of relief, now it drives me to despair on your account."

Eugénie turned away and bent over some flowers which bloomed in a vase at her side.

"I am not so unhappy as you and my brothers perhaps fancy," said she, in a low voice.

"Not? Do you think your letters could deceive me? I knew beforehand that you would do all to spare us, but if I could have had a doubt, your pale face would have told the story plainly enough. You are unhappy, Eugénie, you must be unhappy with this man who"----

"Papa, you are speaking of my husband!" The young wife spoke with so much warmth, and rose so hastily from her seat, that her father stepped back and looked at her, astonished at her tone and at the crimson flush which overspread her countenance.

"Forgive me," said he, recovering himself, "I cannot accustom myself to the thought that my daughter belongs to an Arthur Berkow, and that I am at the present moment in his house. They oblige me to enter it if I wish to see my own child! But you are right, I must spare you in speaking of the man you have married, though I can see plainly how much you have suffered, and still have to suffer through him."

The deep glow was fading slowly from Eugénie's face, but there was still a lingering flush on it, as she answered hurriedly,

"You are mistaken, I have no complaint to make of Arthur. He has held himself aloof from the first with a forbearance for which I can only thank him."

The Baron's eyes kindled.

"I would not advise either him or his father to forget the regard which is due to you. They, of all people, least deserved the honour you have brought to their house, where there was no great honour before. And one satisfaction I can give you, Eugénie: you will not long have to bear a name to which attaches so much meanness, so much roguery to us and to others, roguery none the less shameful that the law cannot touch it. I have taken care that, at least, there shall be an end of that."

His daughter looked at him in surprise.

"What do you mean, papa? An end of what?"

"I have taken the necessary steps to obtain for your"----the Baron seemed to have some difficulty in pronouncing the word, "your husband an elevation to the peerage. Only for him, not for his father, I will render him no service, and I will not have him, even formally, admitted into our ranks. It is not unusual that such a change of position should be accompanied by a change of name, and so it shall be in this case. You can choose yourselves among the names of your estates that which may seem to you the most suitable for the noble race you are about to found. Your wishes will be taken into consideration."

"The noble race we are about to found!" repeated Eugénie almost under her breath. "You are mistaken, papa, and if you only wish for this elevation of rank on my account ... but you are right! It will be best in any case. The thought has been dreadful to me that I had to accept back, as a free gift from Arthur's generosity, that which he had bought and paid for. Now, we can offer him something for it. The patent of nobility will be ample compensation for all that he gives up."

In the bitterness of this outburst there was an undertone of suppressed pain. To Windeg one was as incomprehensible as the other; his daughter's speech was an enigma to him, and he would have asked her for an explanation, if a servant had not just then appeared and announced Herr Berkow, who wished to wait upon the Baron.

Arthur entered and approached his father-in-law with some polite speech about the latter's unexpected visit. The young man had resumed his old blasé manner. He welcomed his guest as a mere matter of etiquette, and his guest, in return, just submitted to the welcome as to a necessity. This time no strangers were by, so even the form of shaking hands was omitted. They contented themselves with bowing coolly, then the elder man took up his position again at his daughter's side, and the younger remained standing, evidently intending to shorten, as much as might be, this enforced visit to his wife's boudoir.

Windeg would not have been the consummate man of the world he was, if, notwithstanding the exciting nature of his talk with Eugénie, he had failed to fall back at once into a conventional tone. The usual inquiries were then made, and information given as to different members of the family. Count Rabenau's decease was mentioned as the cause of the journey, and formal condolences were offered by Arthur, who certainly had no idea of the change which this death would bring about in the circumstances of his new relations. At length the Baron introduced a new subject.

"But," said he politely, "I bring some news from the city which must have a real interest for you, Herr Berkow. I take it for granted that your father's wishes respecting an elevation of rank have been no secret from you, and I am in a position to assure you that they are likely to be fulfilled. On one point, certainly, I find the obstacles to be insurmountable. There are certain--certain prejudices against Herr Berkow personally, which can hardly be set aside, but, on the other hand, there is every disposition to distinguish him, as one of the leaders of the industrial movement in this country, by conferring a title on his son. In short, I hope soon to offer you my congratulations thereupon."

Arthur had listened without any change of countenance. Now he raised his eyes, and Eugénie's gaze was immediately riveted on them, with an interest inexplicable even to herself.

For the moment, however, there was but little to be read in his face.

"May I ask, Baron, whether the wishes of my father were alone consulted in this matter, or whether the question has been raised out of regard to your daughter?"

Windeg felt slightly embarrassed; he had reckoned so surely on some expression of thanks, and now instead there came this singular inquiry.

"Our wishes on the subject became naturally identical, when once the alliance between us was accomplished," he returned rather stiffly. "Besides, I did not conceal from Herr Berkow my doubts as to any personal benefit accruing to himself. I received an assurance from him that he would, if necessary, lay aside his own claims in favour of his only son and heir, his sole anxiety being to secure for him a brilliant career in the future."

"Then I regret that my father has not made me acquainted with the progress of this affair. I only knew of it as a vague project," said Arthur coolly, "and I regret still more that you should have used your influence to procure for me an honour, which I, unfortunately, must decline."

The Baron started up and stared at his son-in-law.

"Excuse me, Herr Berkow, did I hear aright? I understood you to speak of declining"----

"Of declining a peerage, were it offered to me. Yes."

Windeg was utterly disconcerted, a thing which rarely happened to him. "Well then, I must beg of you to give me your reasons for this, to use a mild term, very singular refusal. I am extremely anxious to hear them."

Arthur looked across at his wife. She had started as he spoke, and the deep flush had again mounted hotly to her cheeks. Their eyes met, and they gazed for a second at each other, but the young man found in his wife's face no inducement to yield. He answered with a decided ring of defiance in his voice.

"My refusal is less singular than the proposal, as it is made to me. Had a title been conferred on my father, on account of the services he has indisputably rendered to the industry of the country, I, as his heir, should have joined in accepting it. Such a recognition is honourable as any other. It has not been thought fit to grant it to him, and I, of course, am no judge as to the prejudices which may stand in the way. But, for my part, I have not the very smallest claim to such a distinction, and therefore I think it better not to set afloat a report in the city that a connection by marriage with the Windeg family will necessarily imply a peerage."

He let fall the last words very quietly, but Eugénie pressed her lips angrily together. She knew he meant them for her alone. Was he bent on freeing himself from everything that could justify her contempt? Her wish to feel such contempt was stronger than ever.

"I seem indeed to have been in error as to the motives which led you to desire our connection," said the Baron slowly, "but I must confess I was not prepared to find that you held such views. They must be of somewhat recent date, for, before your marriage, you appeared to entertain quite different ideas."

"Before my marriage!" A smile of infinite bitterness played about Arthur's lips. "I was somewhat ignorant then as to the way in which I myself and my position in society were looked upon in the upper circles. This has since been clearly pointed out to me in a rather unsparing fashion, and you can therefore hardly feel surprise that I should renounce all idea of forcing my way into them as an unwished-for intruder."

Eugénie's fingers closed tightly round the rose which she had drawn out of the vase and was still holding in her hand. The tender flower shared the fate her fan had lately met with in Arthur's grasp; it fell crushed to the ground. Arthur did not notice it, he had now almost turned his back on her and stood facing her father, who stared as though in doubt as to whether it really were his son-in-law he saw before him.

"I cannot, of course, divine who may have made such very exaggerated disclosures to you," he replied gravely, "but I do beg of you in this matter to have some consideration for Eugénie. The rôle she will, in all probability, have to play in the city this winter makes it impossible for her--excuse me, Herr Berkow--impossible, I say, for her to bear a middle-class name. That was never intended either by your father or by me."

Arthur looked again at his wife long and sternly. She still took no part in the conversation, interfering by no single word, though she generally knew right well how to make her views known and her will felt.

"Before the winter, the situation may have shaped itself differently than at present appears. Leave that to Eugénie and to me. For the time being, I regret that I must maintain my decision. As this high position is offered to me alone, I certainly have the right alone to accept or to decline, and I must decline, for--pardon me. Baron--I do not wish to owe it to my wife's aristocratic name."

Windeg rose offended.

"Then there is no course left open to me but to recall as speedily as possible the steps which have already been taken in this business, so that I may not be compromised further than I am at present. Eugénie, you are quite silent. What do you say to the views you have heard your husband express?"

The young wife was spared all answer, for at this moment the door was, not noiselessly opened by the servant as was usual, but hastily flung back, and, unannounced, with pallid face and an utter disregard of those forms to which he was wont to pay so much attention, in rushed Herr Wilberg.

"Is Herr Berkow here? Excuse me, my lady, I must speak to Herr Berkow at once."

"What has happened?" said Arthur, going up to the young man, whose disturbed countenance betrayed ill tidings.

"An accident!" said Wilberg breathless. "Down below in the shaft. Your father is hurt, grievously hurt. The Director sent me"----

He got no further in his report, for Arthur had hurried past him to the door. The young official was about to follow him, but outside in the corridor he was stopped by the Baron.

"Have you told the son the whole truth?" asked he gravely. "You need hide nothing from me. Is Herr Berkow dead?"

"Yes," gasped Wilberg. "He was ascending with Deputy Hartmann--the ropes gave way--Hartmann saved himself by springing on to the last stage but one--Herr Berkow was carried down into the depths. No one knows how the accident happened, but it cannot be concealed. Prepare her ladyship for the news, I must go."

He hastened after Arthur, while Windeg turned back into the room, where his daughter met him in a state of great excitement.

"What have you heard, papa? The face of that messenger of woe spoke of something more than a mere injury. What has happened?"

"The worst," said the Baron deeply moved. "But a few minutes ago, Eugénie, we were uttering bitter accusations against the man, now all our hatred and the enmity between us are over. Death has smoothed them away."

CHAPTER XIV

The first solemn weeks succeeding the accident had passed by, but that sense of oppression, which rests upon every house of mourning, had not yet been dispelled; it made itself even more keenly felt now that all the busy arrangements, the visits and condolences, were over. There had been no lack of outward marks of sympathy. Berkow's position, his numerous acquaintances and large connections made his death an event of importance. The cortége which followed him to the grave, including, of course, all the officials and workmen on the estate had been of endless length. Cards and letters strewed the heir's writing-table, and the whole neighbourhood came to pay visits to his wife. Every attention was shown to the young people; it was felt that, so far as they were concerned, there were no "prejudices," as Baron Windeg had diplomatically expressed it, to be overcome.

The loss cut no one to the heart, perhaps not even the dead man's only son, for whom he had done so much. Where all esteem is wanting, it is not easy to love. But it would have been hard to decide whether Arthur were deeply moved by his father's death or not. The composure he showed in the presence of others led to the belief that he had not been seriously affected by it, and yet, ever since the catastrophe, he had been almost solemn in his gravity, and had become inaccessible to all with whom he was not necessarily brought into relations. Eugénie's calm could surprise no one who knew anything of the circumstances. Her hatred, like her father's, had died out, certainly, at Berkow's death; any other sentiment towards him had been out of the question with her, and, unfortunately, her views in this respect were shared by many who had but too good cause for such a state of feeling.

The officials had been too often wounded by the arrogant and unconciliating behaviour of the man who, having made his own way up in the world, looked upon their knowledge and abilities as so many wares to be at his absolute disposal, in consideration of the salary paid;

they could have no deep regrets for the loss of a principal who cared little either for character, personal qualities, or individual talent, but was exclusively bent on extracting the greatest possible amount of service from each in his separate capacity.

Among the workmen a still worse temper was noticeable; they showed an utter absence of all feeling, they were moved neither by sympathy nor compassion. Whatever reproaches Berkow had earned, he had incontestably proved himself to be an industrial genius of the very first order. By his own efforts he had raised himself from poverty and lowliness to the height of prosperity--had called into being operations on so grand a scale as to vie with any in the land--had won for himself a position which he might have used as a blessing to thousands. He did not so use it, had not been willing to do the good he might, and, therefore, through all his belongings, throughout his vast establishment, a deep breath of relief was drawn when his sudden death became known. "Thank God!" was the thought unexpressed, but felt by all, and in this manner judgment was passed on his memory.

Whether the inheritance of such a life and all that it had sown year by year were, in reality, as desirable as appearances suggested, shall not here be decided. However that might be, its first effect on the young heir was to lay on his shoulders such a heavy burden of care and business as, according to the general opinion, he was of all men least fitted to bear. He had, it is true, officials for each separate department, representatives and authorised agents, but the very fact that his father had thoroughly understood how to keep them all in subjection to himself and under his sovereign control, made the present need greater, the absence of the guiding eye and hand of the master himself more keenly felt. The son had now to take the reins in hand, and, before ever he could do so, the significant shrugs of all his dependants showed their unanimous judgment, or rather condemnation, of him. They were all of one mind as to this: he was to be counted on for nothing, or next to nothing.

The entire staff of officials was assembled in the committee-room, awaiting the arrival of the new proprietor who had convoked the meeting for this hour. Any one who saw these gentlemen's irresolute disturbed countenances, some of which bore traces of real anxiety, would have been convinced that more important matters were on hand than the mere formal introduction of the heir, now that the first days of mourning were over.

"That was a blow," the Director was saying to Herr Schäffer, who had come out from the city, "the very worst that could have happened to us! We knew long ago what they were concerting and planning among themselves, and the same thing is going on now on all the neighbouring works. We could see it coming, and we should have taken some precautionary measures, but now, just at this juncture! It places us altogether at their mercy."

"Hartmann has chosen his time well," put in the chief-engineer bitterly. "He knows what he is about in going ahead like this, without waiting for the other works. The master gone, all the affairs in confusion and at a standstill, the heir incapable of any energetic action--now is the very time to push his claims! I always told you this Hartmann would be a thorn in our flesh. The people are not ill-disposed; we cannot blame them for wanting to secure for themselves safety in the mines and the necessaries of life. They have held out under oppressive circumstances as no others have, and they would have made reasonable demands which might have been granted. That which they want to dictate to us now under their present leader passes all belief. It is a regular revolt against all existing institutions."

"What will the young gentleman do.'" asked Wilberg, rather timidly. Among these helpless, anxious men, he was most helpless, most anxious of all.

"What, under the circumstances, he can't help doing," returned Herr Schäffer, gravely. "Agree to whatever they ask."

"Excuse me, he cannot do that," cried the chief-engineer. "There would be an end of all discipline, and before the year is out he would be a ruined man. At any rate, I should not remain on any works where that course was adopted."

Schäffer shrugged his shoulders.

"And yet there is hardly any alternative left him. I have told you already that things are by no means so brilliant with us as they appear to be. We have had losses of late, very heavy losses. On every side there have been deficits to cover, sacrifices to make, and, with all this, so many engagements to meet.... In short, we have nothing to reckon on but the actual returns from the works. If they remain idle for a few months, and we cannot carry out the contracts we have undertaken for the year, then--it is all up with us."

"Something of this must have got wind among the hands," said the chief-engineer, thoughtfully, "or they would not have dared to show so bold a front. But they know full well that what has once been conceded can never be recalled. Hartmann will strain every nerve to gain his end, and if, owing to the stress of circumstances, he should really succeed!... What said Herr Arthur when you acquainted him with the state of his affairs?"

It was noticeable that none of the officials even spoke of him as Herr Berkow or as their principal. They seemed not to be able to associate such terms with their late master's son. They called him Herr Arthur or "the young gentleman," as they had been in the habit of doing. At the last question all eyes were turned on Schäffer.

"Nothing," said Schäffer. "'I am obliged to you, Schäffer.' That was all. But he kept the papers, which I had taken with me for his edification, and shut himself up with them. I have not spoken to him since."

"I spoke to him yesterday evening when I had to submit to him our people's demands," said the Director. "At the first mention of the bad news, he turned deadly pale, but he listened in silence without answering a syllable, and when I gave him a few words of counsel and encouragement, feeling sure that it would end in a consultation, he sent me away. 'He wished first to consider the matter alone.' Imagine, if you please, Herr Arthur considering! This morning I received instructions to summon you all to a conference."

The old sarcastic lines showed round Herr Schäffer's mouth.

"I am afraid I can tell you the result of our conference beforehand. 'Consent to everything, gentlemen, give way unconditionally, do what you like, only make sure that the works are kept going for the present.' And then he will make the announcement that he is going back to the city with her ladyship, and intends to leave matters here to Providence and to Herr Hartmann."

"But blow after blow is falling upon him just now!" broke in Wilberg, taking the part of the absent with chivalrous warmth. "A stronger man than he might well succumb."

"Yes, weakness always finds sympathy from you," said the chief-engineer, derisively. "But, during the last few weeks, you seem to have had a very decided leaning in the opposite direction. Herr Hartmann was in the enjoyment of your special friendship. Do you still rave about him?"

"Good Heavens, no!" cried Wilberg, with almost a look of consternation. "I have felt a horror of the man ever since--ever since Herr Berkow's sudden death."

"So have I," said the chief-engineer shortly, "and so, I suppose, have we all. It is revolting to have to treat precisely with him, but when there are no proofs, one does well to be silent."

"Do you seriously believe then in the possibility of a crime?" asked Schäffer lowering his voice.

The Director shrugged his shoulders.

"At the inquest, they only proved the fact of the ropes having given way. They may have given way of themselves; whether it really was so or not, can only be known to Hartmann. As I said before, the inquest brought nothing to light, and there certainly would have been no just grounds for suspicion had any other man been his companion. This fellow is capable of anything."

"But, remember, his own life was in the greatest peril. He saved himself by a spring, which was a daring feat not one in ten could have attempted, and which, assuredly, not one in ten would have made successfully. He must have expected to go down with the other and be dashed to pieces."

The chief-engineer shook his head.

"You little know Ulric Hartmann, if you think he would hesitate to risk his life in any undertaking he was bent on carrying through. You stood by that day when he rushed before those horses. It was his humour then to come to the rescue. When the fancy takes him to destroy, he will care little about bringing destruction on himself. That is just the dangerous point about this man. He is utterly without consideration either for himself or for others. He would sacrifice himself in case of need, if"----

He broke off suddenly, for at this moment the young proprietor came in.

Arthur was greatly changed. The deep mourning he wore made his naturally pale face appear still more pallid, and his eyes looked as if he had known no sleep for many a night. He returned the officials' greeting quietly, as he stepped in among them.

"I have sent for you, gentlemen, that I might confer with you on the subject of those business concerns which have passed into my hands through my father's death. There is much in them to set in order and much to change, more, possibly, than we at first supposed. Up to the present time, I have, as you are aware, held myself completely aloof from all these matters, and I shall not be able to feel my way at once, though, during the last few days, I have attempted to do so. I must, therefore, rely entirely upon your goodwill and readiness to assist me, and, as I shall, doubtless, make many claims on you for both, I offer you beforehand my sincere thanks."

The gentlemen bowed; marks of astonishment were already visible on most of their faces, and the chief-engineer cast a glance at the Director, which seemed to say, "So far, he is rational enough."

"All these things," continued Arthur, "must give place for the moment to the misfortune, the danger with which we are threatened by the demands our miners have made upon us, and by the suspension of work which might follow on our non-agreement to them. Of course, there can be no question as to our decision."

This time it was Herr Schäffer's turn to shoot a glance over to the chief-engineer; it spoke as plainly as its predecessor: "Did not I tell you so? he makes unconditional surrender. Now he is going to announce his departure."

But the young proprietor seemed in no haste to do so; he went on:

"In the first place, we must find out who drills the people, and who leads them?"

A pause of a few seconds followed. None of the officials cared to pronounce a name they had so lately associated with the recent accident. At last the chief-engineer said:

"Hartmann leads them, and so there can be no doubt that they are in able hands, and that the movement has been well organised."

Arthur looked thoughtfully before him.

"I fear so too, and there will be a battle, for, as to a complete concession on our part, of course, there can be no question of it."

"Of course, there can be no question of it!" repeated the chief-engineer triumphantly, thereby giving the signal for a very animated debate, in which he most resolutely defended the views he had previously expressed. Herr Schäffer, who represented the opposition, was not less eager in his endeavours, by all sorts of hints and covert allusions which were understood by his young principal but too clearly, to prove to the latter that there was no help but to yield.

On the other hand, the Director preserved a sort of neutrality, advising delay and some negotiations. The remaining officials let the heads of the different departments have the discussion to themselves, risking only an occasional remark, or modestly expressed opinion.

Arthur listened to it all in silence, and apparently with much attention, neither leaning to one side nor the other, but when Schäffer brought one of his longest speeches to a close with the explicit words "we must!" he raised his head suddenly with an air of resolution which hushed all the voices round him.

"We must not, Herr Schäffer. There is something more to be considered in this than the question of money; my position here as master would be ruined for ever if I were thus to surrender at discretion. Though I am but little acquainted with these things, I can plainly see that such demands as are now made overstep all bounds. You allow that, gentlemen? Abuses may have crept in, the miners may have grounds for complaint" ....

"That they have, Herr Berkow," interrupted the chief-engineer stoutly. "They are in the right when they ask for a thorough examination of the mines, and for the necessary repairs and improvements; they are right in requiring that their wages shall be raised, and there is something to be said also in favour of relief to be granted in the division of labour. Beyond this all is arrogant presumption, and due solely to their leader Hartmann. He is the soul of the whole business."

"Then we will hear him first. I have already sent him word that his presence, and that of the other delegates, might be necessary here. They are in attendance. Herr Wilberg, will you call them in?"

Herr Wilberg obeyed, his open mouth and almost stupid expression of countenance betokening extreme amazement. Herr Schäffer raised his eyebrows and stared at the Director. The latter took a pinch of snuff and stared at the others, and then they all turned their gaze collectively on the new proprietor, who thus suddenly made arrangements and gave out orders in a tone which fairly bewildered them. The chief-engineer was, perhaps, the one exception. He turned his back on his colleagues, and took up his stand at Arthur's side, knowing well by this time where his allegiance was due.

Meanwhile Wilberg had returned, followed by Ulric Hartmann, Lawrence and another miner. As though it were a matter of course, these two remained some steps behind and let the young Deputy advance alone.

"Good day!"[1] said he, and "Good day!" repeated his two comrades; but the tone of the greeting seemed to contradict its meaning. Ulric's bearing had always been imperious and defiant, but it had never assumed so challenging and absolutely insulting an air as now that, for the first time, he came before the master and assembled officials, no longer as a subordinate to receive orders and instructions, but as a delegate who had not to submit his terms, no, but to dictate them!

His attitude betrayed, it is true, no low-minded arrogance, but rather that disdainful sense of superiority, which the consciousness of his own strength and others' weakness bears in upon a man. He let his moody blue eyes travel slowly round the circle until they fixed themselves, at last, upon the principal, and his lips curled contemptuously as he awaited in silence the opening speech.

Arthur had not seated himself during the previous discussion. He stood now, grave and collected, and faced the man, who, as every one declared, was principally to blame for the blow which threatened him. Of that far deeper blame connected with his father's last moments, he, the son, was happily quite unsuspicious. He began the negotiation, therefore, with perfect composure.

"Deputy Hartmann, you submitted to me yesterday, through the Director of this establishment, the claims put forward by all the miners employed on my works, and in case of these not being conceded, you threatened a general cessation of work."

"Just so, Herr Berkow," was the short decided answer.

Arthur leaned with his hand on the table, but his tone was cool and business-like; it betrayed no emotion whatever.

"Before we go any further, I wish to know what you really have in view in this proceeding. These are no reasonable demands, they amount to a declaration of war, for you must say to yourselves that I neither can nor will make any such concessions."

"Whether you can make them or not, I don't know, Herr Berkow," said Ulric coldly, "but I believe that you will have to make them, for we are determined to let the works lie idle until you have agreed to our terms. You won't find men to replace us in the whole province."

The argument was forcible, and little could be objected to it, but the tone in which it was put forth was scornful in the extreme.

Arthur's brows contracted angrily.

"It is far from being my intention to refuse you everything," he explained steadily. "Among your demands are several the justice of which I acknowledge, and those I am ready to meet. An examination of the shafts and mines shall be made and the necessary alterations at once completed. The wages will, in part at least, be raised. To accomplish this, I shall have to make heavy sacrifices, more, perhaps, than in a business point of view I am justified in making, but it shall be done. On the other hand, the remaining clauses must be withdrawn. They tend solely to take all power from me and my agents, and to relax that discipline which, in such a concern as this, is a question of paramount importance."

Ulric's contemptuous expression had disappeared and given place to a look of surprise and distrust. He turned his eyes first on the officials and then on their leader, evidently suspecting that the latter was reciting a lesson previously learnt by heart.

"I am sorry, Herr Berkow, but the clauses must stand!" he returned defiantly.

"I can well believe that to you they form the main point at issue," said Arthur, "nevertheless, I repeat it, they must be withdrawn. In my concessions I will go to the extreme limit of what seems practicable. There I shall stop, and shall attempt nothing further. That which I am ready to grant should and would content every man who is seeking honest remunerative labour. Those who are not satisfied with it are seeking something quite different, and with such there can be no hope of coming to an understanding. I give you my word of honour that all necessary precautions shall be taken for the safety of the men who work in the mines, and that there shall be an increase of wages. I shall only require from you some confidence in my word. Before, however, we begin to discuss the matter, the second part of your claims must be given up. They can never be made good, for no consideration on earth would induce me to subscribe to them."

He had maintained throughout the same quiet business-like tone, but the whole tenor of his speech differed so widely from the young heir's habitual style and manner that it could not fail to have some effect on Ulric. He could hardly believe his own ears, but the more unexpected resistance was to him, coming from a quarter where he had surely reckoned on some timid compromise which should serve as a bridge to absolute surrender, so much the more did such resistance anger him, and his fiery spirit broke at once through the unaccustomed restraint.

"You had better not put the matter from you in that way, Herr Berkow," said he, in a threatening voice. "There are two thousand of us, and the works are as good as in our hands. The time is past when you could make slaves of us and crush us at your liking. Now we demand our rights, and if we can't get them by fair means, we shall take them by force."

A movement, half of anger, half of uneasiness, passed through the circle of bystanders. They felt that a scene was at hand, and dreaded lest, through Hartmann's savage temper, it might end with some deeds of violence.

Arthur had grown crimson. He stepped forward a few paces and stood close to Ulric, facing him.

"First of all, Hartmann, have the goodness to alter your tone, and remember you are addressing your employer. If you wish to be received here as a delegate, if you lay claims, as such, to some sort of equality, you must behave with the propriety which is customary on such occasions, and not fling in our faces threats of violence and revolt. You exact discipline from your people, and I exact it from you. Lord it outside over your comrades as much as you choose, but so long as I stand here before you, it is I who am master of these works--and I intend to remain so. Keep that fact in mind."

A thunderbolt falling into the committee-room could not have had a more startling effect than these words, spoken with great energy and in commanding accents. The officials receded in their first surprise, and then moved round their leader as if to protect him, but he quietly waved them back.

The two miners, standing in the background, stared at him half stupefied by their astonishment; but, of all present, Ulric was most seriously affected by this sudden display of vigour. He had grown deadly pale and stood bending forwards, with trembling lips, with eyes wide open, as though he could not, would not, understand that which he saw and heard. A great blaze of anger flashed into his face, and he was about to rush at his enemy like an enraged lion, when he met a look so clear, so calm and steadfast, that it quelled him as it would have quelled the kingly beast he resembled.

Arthur still stood motionless, he had but opened his eyes wide and full, and with his eyes alone had ordered back within bounds that furious spirit in the very act of breaking forth. Only a few seconds did they gaze at one another; then the fortune of the day was decided. Gradually Ulric unclenched his right hand; gradually the wild look of menace vanished from his countenance and his eyes sought the ground. He had recognised in his young employer an equal, if not a superior mind, and he bowed before it.

Arthur stepped back. His voice sounded cold and quiet again as he continued: "And now let your comrades know what I can grant and what I cannot. You may add that I shall not retract a single word of all that I have said. So we have done for the present.

"We have," Ulric's voice was low and hoarse, half stifled by repressed passion. "I must inform you then, in the name of the miners employed on these works, that all hands will go on strike tomorrow morning."

"Very well, I was prepared for it. And now, I warn you, Hartmann, once for all, to take no extreme measures. They say you have unlimited power over your comrades. Look to it then that quiet and order are maintained, and do not hope to intimidate by noisy disturbances. I and my friends here will do all and everything to avoid a conflict. If it is forced upon us, we shall take up a defensive position, and, if it comes to the worst, I shall use my rights as master of the place. Spare both me and yourselves that."

Ulric turned to go. In the hate and fury of his parting glance there mingled a something other, deeper, undivined by any; a something which tightened round his wild passionate heart with a cramp-like hold. He had so taught himself to despise this 'weakling,' and so triumphed in the thought that he must be despised ... elsewhere also. But if the man showed himself elsewhere as here, then there must be an end of all contempt, and the great brown eyes, which had compelled obedience from him, might there compel some other feeling than hatred and repugnance. The pallor, which had overspread the miner's face on receiving that reprimand, became almost livid as he turned away.

"We shall see who holds out longest. Good day."

He went, accompanied by his two comrades, whose faces showed that the scene they had just witnessed had worked differently on them than on their leader. They cast back a look half shy, half respectful at their master, and their manner, on leaving the room, was hesitating and uncertain.

Arthur looked after them with a scrutinising gaze, and then turned to the officials.

"There are two already who follow him in a half-hearted way. I hope the majority of them will come to their senses, if we give them time. For the present, gentlemen, we must yield to necessity and close the works. I quite appreciate the danger of our position here, in a secluded place with two thousand excited men having a leader like Hartmann at their head, but I am determined to stand my ground, and not to give way an inch until all is decided. It must, of course, depend entirely on your own choice whether you follow me or not. As almost all of you were opposed to my decision, I, naturally, cannot force the consequences of it upon you, and I am quite ready to give leave of absence to any one who thinks a temporary removal from the works desirable."

This proposal was answered by a unanimous and indignant negative. All the officials pressed round their principal with almost passionate eagerness, assuring him that not one of them would budge from his place. Even the timid Herr Wilberg seemed suddenly to have acquired the courage of a lion, so earnestly did he give in his adhesion. Arthur drew a long breath of relief.

"I thank you, gentlemen. We will discuss things further this afternoon, and agree as to the measures to be taken. I must leave you now. Herr Schäffer, in an hour I shall be glad to see you over in my study. Once more, gentlemen, I thank you all."

Only when he had gone, and the door had fairly closed behind him, did all the different feelings of astonishment, approval and apprehension find vent, which up to this time had been restrained by his presence.

"I am trembling in every limb," said Wilberg, forgetting his superiors' close vicinity and letting himself fall on to a seat. The excitement of the moment seemed to have done away with all considerations of etiquette. "Good Heavens, that was a scene! I thought that savage, Hartmann, would rush upon him! but his look! his way of speaking! Who could have expected it from him?"

"He was too sharp, a great deal too sharp," said Schäffer disapprovingly; but, even in his disapproval and in the thoughtful shake of his head, there was quite another expression to that which he had lately manifested in speaking of Arthur. "He talked as though he had still command over millions, and as though it were not a question of life and death with him to keep the works going. With all the father's arrogance, he would have given way here unconditionally, for, as far as the business is concerned, it would have been salvation to him, and he was not troubled by many considerations as to his dignity and his position. The son seems to be made of different stuff, but that kind of speech, though a year ago it might have answered very well, is out of place now. He should have been more prudent, rather more vague in his expressions, so as to have left open a way of retreat in case of"----

"The deuce take your prudence and your hesitation!" interrupted the chief-engineer hotly. "Excuse me for any rudeness, Herr Schäffer, but it is quite evident that you have been accustomed to office life, and have never had great masses of workmen under your command. He just hit the right nail on the head. He awed them, and, in a case like this, that is everything. They would have taken a kindly exhortation as a proof of weakness, and a cold and distant address for pride. You must put it to them in their own language, 'make your choice between this and that,' and our principal knows right well how to do it. You could see that by Hartmann."

"I only fear that, with it all, he under-estimates the struggle before us," said the Director gravely: "If our people were alone, they would declare themselves satisfied with the concessions made to them, but, with a leader like Hartmann, it will be different. He will admit of no sort of arrangement, and they all follow him blindfold. But our principal is right. He has gone as far as he possibly can. To overstep these limits would be to deliver himself, his position, and all of us, up into their hands."

They began to speak now of "our principal," as if it were a thing of course. In one hour Arthur had won the title for himself; it seemed now the only proper designation for him. He must indeed have shown himself well fitted to rule.

The three delegates had left the house, and walked away in the direction of the works. Ulric spoke no word, but Lawrence said in a low voice:

"You were saying a little while ago that if some one knew when to show his teeth, and when to give them good words, then .... Well, Ulric, I think there is some one up there that does know."

Ulric did not answer. He cast a look up at the windows, and a thunder-cloud gathered on his brow.

"So all that lay hidden behind those sleepy eyes of his, which looked fit for nothing in the world but napping," he murmured between his tightly set teeth. "'So long as I stand here, I am master of these works!' I really believe the man has the making of it in him."

They here met a group of miners, special partisans of Ulric, who had not made the descent into the mine with the others, and who now pressed round the three ambassadors with much noisy questioning.

"Ulric will tell you all about it," said Lawrence, drily. "I think we have gone to the wrong man. He does not mean to give way."

"Not?"

All the miners looked disappointed. They had evidently reckoned on another answer. Some angry exclamations and menaces against the young proprietor were heard, and his name was several times mentioned in terms of undisguised contempt.

"Hold your tongues, lads!" called out Ulric imperiously. "You don't know the man we have just seen. I thought we should have had easy work, now that the father is out of the way. We have all been mistaken in the son. He has got something no one would have looked for in such a milksop; he has got a will of his own. I tell you, he will give us some trouble yet."

CHAPTER XV

It was quite early morning. Mountains and woods were sparkling in the dewy freshness of the young spring day, and the air was full of balmy odours, as Eugénie Berkow rode alone and unattended along the forest path. She was an excellent horsewoman and passionately fond of riding, yet here in the country she had indulged in it much less frequently than had been her wont.

At first the weather had not permitted of any long excursions, later on she had lacked all inclination for it; but the chief reason, no doubt, was that her beautiful mare had been a present from her husband in the days of his courtship, and that her dislike to the donor was habitually transferred to everything that came directly from him. On her wedding day it had cost her a struggle to put on the costly diamonds which had been his bridal gift, and, since that day, they had never been taken from their cases.

In the midst of the luxury and splendour which had surrounded her since her marriage, she had moved as one constrained and ill at ease. Even the beautiful creature, which had cost a fabulous sum, and had excited the admiration of the whole city when Eugénie appeared on it for the first time, riding by her betrothed's side, was neglected by its mistress in a remarkable manner, and altogether given over to the care of the domestics.

These latter were, therefore, not a little surprised when her ladyship that morning ordered Afra to be saddled, and intimated to the servant who was preparing to accompany her that she wished to ride alone. Though her commands caused no little wonder, they were, of course, obeyed, and she set out on her journey without any attendant.

Arthur, naturally, knew nothing of it. She saw him now more rarely than ever, for he frequently excused himself from dining with her, and their lives were so entirely separate, that it was a most unusual thing for one to know what the other intended doing on such and such a day.

Eugénie trotted quickly through the forest, without meeting a human being. It was, indeed, most solitary up here in the woods, but the freshness and beauty of the morning, the very solitude itself, had a reviving effect upon the young wife, who for several days had not been beyond the park-gates.

The works lay idle; an unnatural calm brooded over the whole settlement, contrasting with its usual restless activity, for now the centre of action was transferred to the master's study, which the latter but rarely left.

The officials came and went, conferences were held, books and papers were examined; Schäffer was continually on the road between the capital and the estates; letters and despatches flew backwards and forwards; but a shade of sombre gravity hung over all this zeal and busy movement, as though some misfortune were looming in the distance, which they were striving to avert or, at all events, preparing to meet.

Eugénie knew, of course, that a disagreement existed with the work-people; Arthur had told her so himself, and had added that the matter was of no importance and would very soon be settled. He had spoken very quietly and coolly, and had only begged her, if she went out to drive, to avoid the miners' villages as much as possible, a somewhat irritable spirit being abroad just now. The officials must have received hints not to alarm her ladyship, for when Eugénie endeavoured to learn from them something more definite, she was always met by a polite evasive answer, or by some comforting assurance.

They told her there was really nothing to be uneasy about, the difficulty was not of a serious nature, and an arrangement might be looked for any day. Yet Eugénie had a distinct perception of the danger which was thus denied, and a perception as keen of the change which had come over her husband since the elder Berkow's death, though his behaviour to her was just the one point which remained unaltered.

The young wife was of too fearless and too proud a nature not to feel as a sort of offence the being thus shut out, and so obviously spared all unpleasant knowledge. True, she had no right to exact a frank and open statement, no right to share the anxieties and, perhaps, perils, which might assail her husband. That privilege, to which other women could assert a claim, lay immeasurably removed from her.

When once the decisive word of separation has been spoken, when people are only bearing with one another for a few months "for appearances' sake," and in order to give the world as little matter for gossip as possible, there can hardly be any interests in common. She understood this, and, had she not understood it, Arthur's conduct would have made her sensible of the fact. For, as he every day roused himself more and more from his former indolence, and applied himself to the most strenuous exertion, so in proportion did he become colder and more distant in his manner to her. She was grateful to him, really, that by thus treating her already as a perfect stranger, he should seek to render the step they proposed taking easier and less painful to her.

Eugénie did not conceal from herself that Berkow's death had cleared away a great obstacle to the fulfilment of her wishes. He would hardly have consented to the dissolution of a marriage for which he, in his ambition, had so long striven, and which he had bought so dearly. His son viewed the matter in another light. To him the marriage was as indifferent as the wife, whom he, in his former easy passivity, had suffered to be forced upon him.

He had voluntarily offered her the separation before she had made any attempt to obtain his consent to it, and the step, which almost invariably costs so many a struggle, such tears and bitterness of feeling, which, not unfrequently, rouses from their depths all the passions of the human heart, would, in this case, be taken quietly and temperately, with perfect mutual accord, and in so thoroughly cold, polite and heartless a manner, it was really worthy of all admiration.

All at once Afra reared high in the air. She was not accustomed to the touch of the whip, much less to so very smart a cut as she had just received. Her mistress's impatience tried her greatly this morning, and if Eugénie had not been perfectly at home in the saddle, the fiery excitable animal would have given her trouble enough. As it was, she bridled in her horse with some little effort, but her delicate eyebrows were knitted and her lips firmly set, as if in anger. Whether this anger were aroused by Afra's opposition, or by the failure of opposition in another quarter, must remain undecided.

Meanwhile she had reached the farm, distant a mile or two from the works, and lying farther up the valley. Now she must begin to climb, not indeed by the steep footpath by which she and Arthur had made their descent, and which would have been impracticable on horseback, but by a carriage-road leading not far from thence up, by long but easy windings, to the not very elevated summit. Her horse, unused to mountain-climbing, chafed at the exertion required, and on reaching the top of the hill, she was obliged to halt to give it time to recover itself.

The veil of mist, which had hovered over the country when last she was there, had vanished now, and the clear sunshine flowed down brightly warm upon the earth, as though there had never been a time when the rain and the wind had here striven for the mastery, and when the whole landscape around had been shrouded in one grey shapeless mantle of fog.

The valleys lay once more blue and vaporous in the cool morning shade, and the mountains stood out in bolder relief by the contrast, their countless crests rising one above the other, seeming to press each other into the background; nothing but one great sea of forest, stretching right away to the range of blue peaks in the horizon. The dark pines had dressed themselves in a tender light green. Blossoms of a thousand hues and forms bloomed, not only in the fruitful soil within the woods, but in the rocky ground without, in every nook and cranny where a reed could find room for itself or a tiny plant take root, and the air was full of their sweet fragrance.

Then the brooks ran foaming down into the valleys below, the springs rippled gently, and overhead was spread a cloudless azure canopy of sky. All around was so golden clear, so grand and free, it seemed as though the newly awakened life of Nature must have power to heal every wound, to break every fetter, as though here nothing could draw breath that was not allied to freedom and to happiness.

And yet Eugénie's look was strangely thoughtful. There was a tension of pain in her face, as if for her there lay some secret torture in all this surrounding beauty. She should have breathed freely now, remembering the promised liberty which would be hers before the earth had been greeted by another spring.

Why could she feel no relief? Why, at this thought, did a sensation nearly akin to pain dart through her soul? Was the memory of that troubled hour still so potent within her, of that hour when, for the first time, the word of separation had been spoken and accepted? She longed so ardently for this separation, to be free to go back to her own people; she suffered so cruelly from her chains, she felt as if she could hardly bear them any longer; since their conversation up here it had become impossible for her to bear them.

Up to then she had been firm and steadfast in her self-sacrifice for her father's sake, in her resignation to the lot forced upon her and in her hatred to those who had so forced it, but, from that hour, all her feelings seemed to have undergone a change. From that hour dated the secret contest within her, the struggle against something which lay obscure and unexpressed down in the farthest depths of her soul, and which, she was determined, should never gain dominion over her.

Yet it was this indefinite something that had driven her out this morning and dragged her almost against her will up to this spot; it alone was to blame for the fact that Baron Windeg's daughter had so far lost sight of all etiquette as to leave behind the groom who always attended her on her expeditions.

She neither could nor would have any observant eyes upon her to-day, and it was well that she had none, for, as she halted there alone upon the heights, there came over her, in the midst of all this bright spring sunshine, a sort of vague longing for the mysterious charm of that hour when clouds and fog encircled her, when the pine crests rustled above them and the storm raged in the ravines and valleys below, when those great brown eyes, unveiling themselves for the first time, awakened within her a dim intuitive consciousness that of the man before her much, nay almost anything, might perhaps have been made, if only--before his own father's hand had drawn him down into that vortex where so many a life is wrecked--if only he could have loved and been loved in return.

And, with the remembrance of this, there welled up within her a feeling which Eugénie Windeg had never known, which it was reserved for Arthur Berkow's wife to experience, a sorrow far quieter, but also far deeper, than any she had yet endured. She laid her hand over her eyes, as a torrent of hot tears burst irrepressibly from them.

"My lady!"

Eugénie started, and, at the same moment, Afra, taking fright at the sound of a strange voice, sprang violently to one side. In an instant a powerful hand had seized her bridle, forcing the animal to be still. Ulric Hartmann stood close by its side.

"I did not know the horse was so easily scared, but I caught hold of the bridle at once," said he apologetically, casting a look half anxious, half admiring, at the young rider who had kept her seat so steadily in spite of the surprise.

Eugénie brushed her hand quickly across her face, trying to wipe away all trace of tears, but it was too late, her fit of weeping must already have been observed, and the thought of this drove a deep crimson to her cheeks and lent a tone of vexation to her voice, as she said quickly and rather imperiously:

"Let go the reins. Afra is not accustomed to be held by strangers, and it frightens her to feel their touch. You are bringing danger on me and yourself too by standing so near."

Ulric obeyed and stepped back. Eugénie passed her hand caressingly over the animal's neck, and Afra, who had never ceased snorting and fretting while she felt a strange hold on her rein, a hold too powerful, as she at once knew, to be resisted, soon quieted down under the influence of her mistress's petting.

In the meantime Hartmann's gaze had never swerved from the young horsewoman, and, in truth, few of her sex, when mounted, could show to such advantage as she. The dark habit, the little hat and veil set lightly on the rich plaits of her fair hair, and crowning becomingly the beautiful face with its heightened colour, her easy and assured bearing, quite unruffled by Afra's restlessness, all served her admirably and brought the just proportions of her slender figure into fullest evidence. As she sat her handsome horse there in the bright full sunlight, she looked a perfect picture of graceful strength.

"You were up here, Hartmann?" asked she, in the faint hope that he might only just have reached the heights at the moment he had first addressed her, and so not have seen her tears. "I did not notice you before."

"I was standing up there," he pointed to an opening in the forest which had certainly not attracted her attention. "I saw you riding up and stayed waiting for you."

Eugénie, about to ride past him into the wood, stopped at these words in surprise.

"Waiting for me?" she repeated. "And why?" Ulric evaded a reply.

"You are alone, my lady, quite alone? you have not even a servant with you as usual?"

"No, you can see I am by myself." Ulric stepped up quickly, but more cautiously this time, to the horse's side again.

"Then you must turn back at once. I will go with you, at all events until we come in sight of the works."

"But why all this?" asked Eugénie, more and more amazed at the proposal and at the young miner's darkly knitted brows. "Is there any danger here in the woods, or what else is there to be afraid of?"

Ulric cast a scrutinising look at the road below, which could be seen in most of its windings from the spot where they stood.

"We have been up to the forges in the hills, I and some of my mates," he said at last slowly. "I took the shorter cut because I wanted to get back sooner, the others followed the high road. You might come upon them, my lady, and I would rather be with you--any way."

"I am not timid," Eugénie declared firmly, "and I should suppose they will hardly go so far as to insult me. I know there is a disagreement with the miners on the works, but they tell me it is of no importance and will soon be settled."

"Then they lie to you!" broke in Ulric roughly. "It is no trifling matter, and it is not likely to be settled. Herr Berkow has declared war upon us, or we upon him, it comes to the same thing; any way, we are at war, and there will never be an end to it until one side or the other is fairly worsted. I tell you so, my lady, and I ought to know."

A slight pallor overspread the young wife's face as she heard this confirmation of the fears which had so long haunted her; but his arrogant tone and rough manner of disclosing facts offended her, and she replied with some haughtiness:

"Well, if that is the case, I cannot possibly accept the company, still less the protection, of a man who so openly avows himself to be my husband's enemy. I shall go on alone."

She would have given her horse the rein, but Ulric started forward at the movement, and, with a hasty imperious gesture, placed himself before her, barring the road.

"Stay, my lady, you must take me with you."

"I must?" Eugénie raised her head proudly. "What if I will not?"

"Then .... I implore you to yield."

Again there was the same abrupt transition from ruthless menace to almost supplicating entreaty which had disarmed her once already.

It melted her anger now as she looked down on the young miner, dark and wrathful, but yet gazing up at her in unmistakable anxiety.

"I cannot accept your offer, Hartmann," said she gravely. "If your comrades are stirred up to such a pitch of irritation that I cannot meet them without being exposed to insult, I fear it has been your doing alone, and a man who bears us so deadly a hatred" ...

"Us!" interrupted Ulric impetuously. "I bear you no hatred, my lady, and I'll take care you are not insulted. Not a man among them dares say a word against you when I am by, and if he dared to do it once, he would not a second time. Let me go with you!"

Eugénie hesitated a few seconds, but her fearless nature and the thought of his former hostile tone turned the scale against him.

"I will turn back and avoid the high road," said she quickly. "You must stay here, Hartmann. Consideration for Herr Berkow requires it."

At the sound of this name his long pent-up anger burst forth. His eyes flashed, and a gleam of savage hatred darted like lightning from them.

"Consideration for Herr Berkow!" he broke out, "for Herr Berkow, who shows you such tender care, allowing you to ride out alone, when he knows we have been up at the forges and must be about the woods now. But the truth is, he never has given himself any concern about you. It is all the same to him whether you are unhappy or not, and yet the whole responsibility of it lies at his door."

"Hartmann, how dare you speak so!" exclaimed Eugénie, glowing with anger and indignation, but she strove in vain to stop him. He went on with ever-growing excitement.

"No doubt, it is a great crime to have caught you crying, when you thought there was not a soul about to notice it; but I am pretty sure that you have shed tears enough, my lady, since you came here, only no one has been by to see, as I was just now. I know who is to blame for it, and I will make him" ...

He stopped suddenly, for Eugénie had drawn herself up erect in her saddle, and was looking at him with that air of crushing haughtiness she could assume at times to keep others at a distance. The tone of her voice was sharp and freezing; worse still, she spoke as a mistress addressing an inferior, ordering him now imperiously.

"Be silent, Hartmann. Say one word, one single word, more against my husband, and I shall forget that you saved his life and mine, and answer your outbreak as it deserves."

She turned her horse's head quickly, and would have ridden past him; but Ulric's giant form stood before her in the path, and he would not yield a step. At that tone of command, which he then heard for the first time from her lips, he had grown deadly pale, and the hate burning in his eyes seemed now to include her also.

"Out of my way!" commanded Eugénie still more imperatively than before. "I will pass."

But she was dealing with a man who cared little for orders given him, and who was stung to fury at receiving one from her mouth. Instead of obeying, he took one step forward, which brought him close up to her side, and again, this time with a grasp of iron, seized the bridle, paying no heed to the rearing horse or to its rider's danger.

"You should not speak so to me," he said in a deep low voice. "Don't urge on your horse," he continued desperately, as she was about to touch Afra with her whip, in the hope of breaking free from him and getting away. "You cannot ride me down; but, by Heaven, I will drag the beast to the ground, as I did that day with the other two."

The threat contained in his words was terrible enough, but there was a still worse menace in his look. For the first time Eugénie saw turned against herself that savage temper so feared by all, and she suddenly awoke to a full sense of the danger of her position. Instantly, however, with quick presence of mind, she caught at the only means which could save her.

"Hartmann," said she reproachfully, but her voice had grown gentle and almost soft, "not long ago, you offered me your protection, and now you use threats towards me yourself. Yes indeed, I can see what there might be to fear from your comrades, if you can behave so to me. I should not have ridden out to the forest if I could have had the least suspicion of it."

The reproach and, still more, the voice, brought Ulric to his senses again. His wild fury subsided, when he no longer heard that imperative tone which had exasperated him.

"Up to this time I have never feared you," continued Eugénie softly, "in spite of all the bad things they say of you. Do you wish to make me fear you now? We are close to the edge, and it is very steep below. If you go on irritating the mare in this way, if you attempt to carry out your threat, there will be an accident. Will the man who once threw himself under my horses' hoofs, that he might rescue a perfect stranger, actually bring danger upon me now? Let me go, Hartmann."

A quiver shot through Ulric. He looked down at the steep slope and saw how very near it they were. Slowly he let go his hold on the bridle, very slowly, as though yielding to some irresistible force, he stepped to one side and let her pass.

Eugénie looked back involuntarily. He was standing there silent and still, his fiery eyes fixed on the ground; without a syllable of response or of leave-taking he let her go on her way unhindered.

CHAPTER XVI

Eugénie drew a deep breath of relief, as Afra's swift pace soon carried her from that dangerous neighbourhood. Fearless as she was by nature, she had trembled. Our heroine would have been no woman, if, after such a scene, she had not known that which she had long suspected, namely, that the man's behaviour to herself, so enigmatical and full of contradictions, concealed some other and far more dangerous feeling than hate.

Once again he had yielded to her influence, but he had been on the very point of bursting his bonds. She had a proof now that, when once the barriers were broken down, he was no whit inferior in blind and raging fury to that "untamed element of Nature" to which she had likened him.

She had reached the valley, and, bearing in mind the warning she had received, was about to turn out of the main road, when she heard the sound of a horse's hoofs, and, looking round, saw that its rider was galloping towards her at a speed which soon brought him to her side.

"At last!" cried Arthur, out of breath and reining in his horse. "What imprudence to ride out alone to-day of all days! But, to be sure, you had no notion of the risk you ran."

Eugénie looked at him in surprise, as, panting and glowing from his hasty ride, he walked his horse by her side. He was not dressed for riding, he wore neither spurs nor gloves. He must have mounted just as he was, in his house-dress, and set out in her pursuit.

"I only heard of your fancy half-an-hour ago," he continued, mastering his excitement. "Frank and Anthony are looking for you in different directions, I was the only one to find the right track. They told me at the farm you had ridden by here a little while ago."

Eugénie did not inquire as to the reason of all this uneasiness; she knew it well enough, but the uneasiness itself surprised her a little. He might simply have sent the servants out after her. No doubt, the idea that his wife might be insulted by the miners would be very distasteful to the proprietor of the works, and it was probably in his character as master of the place that he had rushed after her himself.

"I have been up there," said she, pointing to the goal of her expedition.

"Up on the heights? Where we took refuge from the storm that day? You have been up there?"

Eugénie grew crimson. Once again she saw in his eyes that strange gleam of light which had been absent from them for weeks, and then, why did he question her so eagerly, so breathlessly? Had he not long ago forgotten that hour, the remembrance of which still troubled her so often?

"I came upon the place accidentally," said she hurriedly, as though trying to acquit herself of blame. Her plea succeeded, and was at once followed by the desired result.

The light vanished from his eyes, and his voice was cold and steady again as he returned:

"Accidentally? Ah, yes, I might have known that such a mountain excursion as that would not form part of your plans. Afra always shows so much dislike to climbing. But you might also accidentally have taken the road to M----, and that was what I feared."

"And what was there to be afraid of there?" asked Eugénie, looking keenly at him, while together they left the broad high-road and entered a path which led through the woods.

Arthur tried to evade her look.

"Something unpleasant might have occurred there on this particular day. Our miners have been up to the forges in the hills to try and stir up resistance there also. Hartmann's fulminating speeches have made them all red hot. I hear there were already disturbances up there yesterday, and a band of men, returning in an excited state from the scene of such disorders, may, unfortunately, be ready for anything. They must be on their way back now."

"I should have avoided the high road in any case," said Eugénie quietly. "I had been warned already."

"Warned! By whom?"

"By Hartmann himself. I met him not a quarter of an hour ago up in the forest."

This time it was Arthur's horse which reared violently. Its rider had startled it by a sudden twitch at the reins.

"Hartmann? And he dared to go near you--to address you, after all that has happened during the last few days?"

"He only did it to warn me, to offer me his escort and protection. I declined both. I thought it was due to you and your position."

"You thought it due to me," repeated Arthur in a cutting tone. "I am immensely indebted to you for such consideration, and you did well to take it into account; for, if you had allowed yourself to be escorted by him--much as I try to avoid giving any pretext for an open conflict--I should have had to make him feel that the author and chief instigator of the whole revolt must keep himself at a distance from my wife."

Eugénie was silent. She knew him now well enough to be aware that, in spite of his apparent coldness, he was greatly irritated; she understood the close setting of the lips and the slight tremor of the hand. Just so had he stood opposite her on the first evening of their arrival, only now she knew better what lay concealed behind that calm demeanour.

They rode on in silence through the sunny woods, the horses' hoofs falling noiselessly on the yielding moss. Here, as up yonder, the scent and breath of spring were everywhere; here as there, was the clear deep-blue sky, vaulting in the pine trees overhead, and here too the secret sorrow at her heart, but keener now and far more poignant than it had been up on the heights above.

The horses walked side by side in the narrow path; as they went, the heavy folds of Eugénie's habit brushed against the bushes, and her veil went fluttering back over Arthur's shoulder. Brought into such close neighbourhood as this, she could not fail to observe that her companion was looking terribly pale, now that the exertion of his hasty ride was over. True, he had never had the fresh, healthy colour of youth, but this was quite a different pallor from that of the young dandy who spent his evenings in heated salons and his nights in play, and then, wearied out and satiated, would lie all day long on the sofa, with the curtains closely drawn, because his weakened eyes could not endure the sunlight.

His present paleness came, no doubt, from the same source as the dark lines of care upon his brow, and the grave, almost sombre, expression of his face which formerly bore an expression of lazy indifference only. To most men such a change would have been unfavourable, but to Arthur Berkow it proved an infinite gain.

Eugénie now saw plainly for the first time that her husband had claims to be considered handsome. In earlier days she had not been willing to see this. His languid air and evident want of interest in all around him had outweighed for her those advantages which were now, all at once, brought out into bold relief by the new and unaccustomed stamp of energy imprinted on his countenance and entire bearing; an energy which possibly may have been long latent within him, but which, like so many other qualities had been repressed, and well-nigh crushed, by too early and too satiating an experience of life and its enjoyments. Ah, yes! the world lying perdu beneath was indeed rising from its depths at last, roused by the sound of the approaching storm which alone ...!

Eugénie felt something like bitterness at the thought that she herself had had no share in this awakening, that hers was not the magic charm which had loosed the spell. He had broken through it of his own strength, and needed no help from a stranger's hand.

"I am sorry I had to spoil your ride," said Arthur, breaking the silence at last, but addressing her in his usual tone of distant politeness. "It is a glorious day."

"I am afraid you stand more in need of a ride in the open air than I." The young wife's voice betrayed a perhaps unconscious anxiety. "You are looking pale, Arthur."

"I am not used to work," said he with a kind of bitter pleasantry. "That comes from being so effeminate. I cannot do what the people I employ have to do every day of their lives."

"It seems to me, rather, that you are doing too much, you are pushing it to the very extreme," returned Eugénie, quickly. "All day long you hardly leave your study, and, at night, I see the light burning there until morning."

A sudden flush passed over the young man's face.

"And how long is it since you have favoured the windows of my room with so much attention?" asked he with quiet sarcasm. "I did not suppose you knew of their existence."

She reddened a little now in her turn, but soon overcame her confusion, and answered with firmness:

"Since I have known that the danger you are so determined to make light of is drawing nearer day by day. Why did you deceive me as to the importance of this dispute and its possible consequences?"

"I did not wish to alarm you."

She made an impatient gesture.

"I am no timid child to be so carefully spared, and if there is anything threatening us"----

"Us!" interrupted Arthur. "Excuse me, the danger threatens me alone. I have never intended to treat you as a child; but I thought it my duty not to importune the Baroness Windeg with matters which must be quite indifferent to her, and which, before long, will be as completely removed from her as the name she now bears."

The tone of his reply was frigid in the extreme. It was her own tone, one she had often enough adopted towards him, when she found it necessary to remind him of her descent or of the compulsion to which she had yielded in marrying; and now it was used as a lesson to herself! Something like anger shot up into her dark eyes as she fixed them on her husband.

"So you decline giving me any information about your affairs for the future?"

"No, not if you wish for it."

Eugénie struggled a moment with herself; at last she said,

"You have refused your people's demands?"

"All that it was possible for me to grant, and all that the people themselves required, I have granted; but Hartmann's terms are so extreme, they will not bear discussion. They would, of necessity, lead to the complete destruction of all discipline, to a state of positive anarchy, and they are in themselves a downright insult. He would hardly have ventured to propose them, if he had not known all that is at stake for me in this struggle."

"And what is there at stake?" asked Eugénie, listening with breathless attention. "Your fortune?"

"More even, my existence as a mine-owner."

"And you will not give way?"

"No."

She looked up at her husband, at the man who, barely three months before, could not endure a "scene" with her, because it affected his "nerves," and who now quietly faced a struggle on which his whole future depended. Was he really the same being? That "No" of his had an iron clang about it; she felt that the most violent threats would extract from him no other answer.

"I fear Hartmann will go all lengths," she returned. "He hates you."

Arthur smiled contemptuously.

"I know it, and the feeling is certainly mutual."

Eugénie thought of the eyes which had flashed so wildly when she pronounced her husband's name up there on the heights, and a sudden terror took possession of her.

"You must not under-estimate that man's hatred. He is terrible in his passions as in his energy."

Arthur looked her steadily in the face, frowning as he did so.

"Are you so well acquainted with him? You certainly always have had an admiration for this hero in a blouse. A cheap sort of energy, his, defiantly setting itself to work to bring about the impossible, and preferring to drag hundreds down into misfortune rather than listen to a word of reason. But even Hartmann may find a rampart against which his obstinate will may spend its strength in vain. From me, at least, he will obtain nothing, though I should have to fight on until I am completely ruined."

He reined in his horse all at once, and Eugénie instantly did the same. The path through the woods was here intersected by a bend in the high road, and there, drawn up just before them, they saw the very men they had wished to avoid. A troop of miners had come to a halt at that spot and appeared to be waiting for some one.

Arthur knitted his brows.

"It seems we are not to be spared a meeting."

"Shall we turn back?" asked Eugénie in a low voice.

"It is too late, they have seen us already. We cannot avoid them now; to turn back would savour of flight. It is a pity we are on horseback, that will irritate them still more, but we must show no weakness; we must go on."

"And yet you feared this encounter?"

Arthur looked at her astonished.

"I? It was only you who were not to meet them. It cannot be helped now; but, at all events, you are no longer alone. Keep Afra well in hand, and stay close by me. Perhaps there will be no conflict, after all."

These words were exchanged quickly and almost in a whisper as they paused for one minute. Then they rode slowly forward and out into the high road, where their approach had evidently been remarked.

Arthur was right. The circumstances of the meeting could hardly be worse. The men were in a turbulent mood, embittered and excited by the scenes which had taken place up at the forges. They were already beginning to suffer from the consequences of their resistance, and now they came face to face with the master who had refused to yield to their demands. They saw him well mounted, riding by the side of his high-born wife, and returning, as they supposed, from some excursion of pleasure.

It was a dangerous sight for men already battling with want. A significant growl of discontent was heard, some muttered threats and insulting words were spoken; but, as the two emerged from the forest on to the main road, there was silence, the troop, as if by a preconcerted movement, forming itself into a compact mass ready to bar the passage.

Arthur's lips showed that slight nervous quiver which, with him, was the only outward mark of emotion, but his hand was perfectly steady as he grasped Afra's bridle, so as, come what might, to keep her close at his side.

"Good day."

The greeting was unanswered. Not a man of the whole troop responded to it; on all sides hostile glances were showered upon the new-comers, and the men standing nearest to them pressed round more closely.

"Will you not let us through?" asked Arthur gravely. "The horses will grow restive if you press round them so. Give way."

In spite of the danger of their situation, a danger she thoroughly understood, Eugénie looked up at her husband in wonder. It was the first time she had ever heard this tone from his lips, very quiet, no doubt, but nevertheless conveying all the authority of a master over his subordinates.

This behaviour on Arthur's part was certainly full of danger at such a moment, but it would have been attended with complete success, if the troop had remained without a leader; the men would have obeyed him. But now all eyes were turned in one direction, as though awaiting from thence alone the signal for compliance or resistance.

Some little distance off stood Ulric Hartmann, who had just come down from the heights, and whom they had probably expected to meet here. He stood motionless, his arms folded, and his eyes fixed on Berkow and his wife with an expression which boded them little good.

Arthur's looks had followed those of the men about him. He faced round now.

"Hartmann, are you in charge to-day? It is for you to see, then, that a way is made for us. We are waiting."

If, in these words, there had been the slightest trace of command or of entreaty, no matter which, it would have been as a spark falling into a powder-magazine, and Ulric seemed really to be only waiting for some such spark; but by thus recognising his authority and coolly calling on him to keep order, as if it were a well-understood part of his duty, Arthur took him by surprise, without, however, disarming him. He drew near slowly.

"Oh, so you want to ride on, Herr Berkow?"

"Certainly, you see we wish to pass through to the other side."

A look of withering contempt crossed Ulric's features.

"And you call on me to help you? You are master of your works and of your men. Why do you not order them to make way? Or"--here his voice took a hollow, threatening sound, "or, perhaps, you think that here I am master, and that I need only say one word to prove it to you--to prove it to you both!"

Eugénie had grown very pale, and pressed her horse still closer to Arthur's. She knew that the menace in those glittering eyes was not for her, but it was not for herself she trembled. She had no courage now to try and use that power before which Ulric had so lately bent; besides, she felt the spell would not work while he beheld her at her husband's side.

"In case of assault, a hundred can always have the mastery over one," said Arthur coldly, "but I suppose you hardly mean that, Hartmann. You would feel no uneasiness yourself, would you, if you came, alone and unexpectedly, into the midst of my officials? I consider myself as safe here as in my own house."

Ulric made no answer. He looked up with a scowl at the man before him, who was facing him with such perfect composure and steadily scanning his face with those clear brown eyes, just as on the day when the strife had first broken out.

On that occasion, however, he had stood in his own committee-room, surrounded and protected by his agents; now he was alone in the midst of an excited crowd, only awaiting the signal to proceed to insults, possibly to deeds of violence, and yet not a muscle of his face quivered; his bearing was as proud and assured, his look as fearless, as though he felt and knew himself to be master even here.

This quiet confidence of his did not fail to have its effect upon the crowd, trained in the habit of obedience. The only question for the men now was to know whom they should follow. They turned another inquiring glance on Ulric, who stood by in silence. He looked up once more, then aside at Eugénie's white face. Suddenly he stepped back.

"Make way, let the horses through! To the left, face about!"

The order was executed with a celerity which showed it was not unwelcome. In less than a minute a broad path was opened, and Berkow and his wife rode through unhindered. They turned from the high-road into the forest again, and soon disappeared among the trees.

"I say, Ulric," Lawrence went up to his friend with a sort of good-natured remonstrance, "you flew at me just now because I preached peace up at the forges. What have you been doing here, yourself?"

The other was still gazing over at the trees. Now that the young proprietor's personal influence was no longer felt, he seemed to repent him of his fit of generosity.

"'A hundred to one,'" he murmured bitterly, "and 'I am safe among you.' Yes! they are never wanting in fine speeches when there is anything that frightens them, and such as we are always ready to catch at the old bait."

"He did not look as if he were frightened," said Lawrence decidedly. "He is certainly not at all like his father. Ulric, we ought" ...

"What ought we to do?" interrupted Ulric hastily. "To give way, don't you mean? So that you may have peace and quiet again, and that he may go on worse than his father ever did, when he sees he can succeed in everything. If I let him go to-day, I did it because he was not alone, because his wife was with him, and because" ...

He broke off suddenly. The proud self-contained man would rather have bitten out his tongue than have confessed to his comrade what influence had really compelled him to forbear.

Meanwhile, Arthur and Eugénie had ridden on in silence. Perhaps the common danger they had just passed through had linked them more closely together, for their horses went on side by side, and Arthur still held Afra's rein, though the widening path would now have afforded them room enough, though there was nothing more to fear, and all further care of so consummate a horsewoman was plainly superfluous.

"Do you understand the danger of to-day's excursion now?"

"Yes, and also the danger of your situation."

"I must bear it. You see yourself what blind obedience Hartmann can command. One word from him, and they let us ride on; not a man ventured to murmur, yet they were only waiting a sign from him to turn against us."

"But he did not give the sign," said Eugénie emphatically.

Arthur turned the same strange, searching gaze upon her.

"No, not to-day. He knows best what held him back, but it may happen to-morrow, or the next day, or whenever we meet. I am quite prepared for it."

Leaving the wood now, they set their horses into a trot and arrived a quarter of an hour later at the terrace before the château. Arthur swung himself from his saddle--with what elasticity compared with his former languid movements! He offered his hand to help his wife dismount. Her face was still deadly pale, and she trembled a little as he placed his arm round her, trembled still more as it held her firmly a second longer than was usual on such occasions.

"Were you frightened?" he asked softly, as he took her arm to lead her into the house.

Eugénie gave no answer. Yes, she had been a prey to mortal terror all through that scene, but she would rather he should think her a coward than let him guess it was for his sake she had felt alarm. A suspicion of this seemed, however, to dawn upon him.

"Were you frightened, Eugénie?" he asked again in soft, low tones, pressing her arm more and more firmly to his breast. She raised her eyes to his, and, once more, saw that bright illumining, more radiant now and more significant than she had ever seen it yet. He bent down to her, as if to lose no syllable of her reply.

"Arthur, I----"

"Baron Windeg and his eldest son arrived half-an-hour ago," announced a servant, hastening forward, and the words were hardly spoken when the young Baron, who had probably been watching for them from the window, rushed down the stairs with all the ardour of his eighteen years, eager to greet his sister whom he had not seen since her marriage.

"Ah, Con, is it you?"

She felt something like a pang at this arrival of father and brother, an arrival for which she had before so earnestly longed.

Arthur had let her hand fall as the name of Windeg was mentioned. She saw the glacial expression which stole over his features, and heard the freezing tone of his voice as he greeted his young brother-in-law with distant politeness.

"Will you not come up with me?" she asked, seeing that he remained standing at the foot of the staircase.

"Excuse me if I ask you to receive your father alone. I had ... forgotten something which has just been recalled to my memory. I will wait on the Baron as soon as I possibly can."

He stepped back while Eugénie and her brother went up the stairs by themselves. The latter seemed rather surprised, but a glance at his sister's pale face made him suppress the question which was on his lips. He knew pretty well, he thought, how matters stood here. Perhaps during their ride that parvenu had taken occasion to inflict some fresh mortification on his wife. The young fellow cast a threatening look below, and turned to his sister with impetuous tenderness.

"Eugénie, I am so happy to see you again, and you"----

She forced herself to smile.

"And I too am happy, infinitely happy!"

She looked down into the vestibule again. It was empty. Arthur must already have left it.

She drew herself up with a movement of wounded pride.

"Let us go to my father. He is waiting for us."

CHAPTER XVII

Among the dwellers on the Berkow estates there was probably only one person who viewed the strife, which had so violently broken out between master and men, in any but its most alarming aspect. This person was Herr Wilberg. In that official's foolish young head there lurked so much vague exaggerated romance that he could not help thinking it all highly interesting. His fancy was taken by this situation so fraught with peril, by the knowledge that the low ferment of discontent reigning all around might at any moment explode and bring about a catastrophe.

The admiration he had felt for Hartmann had been promptly transferred to the new proprietor, when the latter had placed himself at the head of affairs, grasping the helm with a vigour which no one expected from so weak and effeminate a hand. But in Arthur's strenuous efforts to make himself thoroughly at home in the new field of labour and to stem the torrent of dangers and losses pouring in upon him on all sides, the superior officials alone were called on to aid by their sympathy and support. The younger members of the establishment enjoyed an involuntary leisure in consequence of the general lull, and Herr Wilberg employed his idle hours in plunging deep into his so-called passion for his liege lady, and by doing his very best to feel as unhappy in it as possible.

To tell the truth, this last was somewhat difficult, for he was, in reality, quite in his element and extremely proud of this hopeless attachment. His idea was that love, to be poetical, must of necessity be unfortunate, and a happy affection would have been really embarrassing to him. This adoration from afar suited him perfectly, and he found ample opportunity of indulging in it, for he now seldom or ever saw the object of his idolatry.

Since the day on which he had accompanied Eugénie through the park, he had only spoken to her once. Accidentally meeting him one day, she had tried to learn from him something more definite about the strike then just breaking out. Strict orders had, however, been issued by Herr Berkow to the effect that his wife was in no way to be alarmed, and Wilberg obeyed them so far as to avoid all reference to the actually existing state of affairs; on the other hand, he could not resist giving a faithful description of the scene which had taken place in the committee-room between her husband and Hartmann.

Coming from his lips, the whole history naturally took a dramatic colour, and Arthur, in his suddenly awakened energy, rose to such a pitch of heroism, it was really incomprehensible how such a story could have entirely failed in its effect.

Eugénie had listened, it is true, with evident and eager attention, but she was pale and unusually still while listening; and, when he came to the end, the narrator waited in vain for a word of remark from her lips. She thanked and then dismissed him with cool politeness, and the young man left her, feeling rather surprised and a good deal hurt at such a want of sympathy on her part.

So she too had no perception of the poetical, or perhaps the situation had appeared less imposing to her, from the fact that her husband had been the hero of the hour. Another would very likely have triumphed in this thought, but Wilberg's romantic fancies generally distinguished themselves by the complete reversal of all natural sentiments.

He felt injured that his recital had produced no greater effect. When in Eugénie's company, he was apt to feel something of that glacier-like atmosphere which, according to the chief-engineer, constantly surrounded her. She was so high, so distant, so unapproachable, and never more so than when she condescended to some act of kindness.

In presence of such condescension, no choice was left a man but either to bow down in absolute adoration, or for ever to bear about with him the sense of utter insignificance and nothingness. As the latter alternative could not possibly suit Herr Wilberg, he was fain to choose the former.

Buried in such thoughts as these, he had strolled on in the direction of the Manager's house; it being his habit to look neither to the right nor to the left, he came, as he stepped on to the bridge, into violent collision with a lady who was crossing from the other side. Startled at the sudden shock, she gave a little cry and sprang for safety to one side. Wilberg looked up now, and stammered an excuse.

"I beg your pardon, Fräulein Mélanie, I did not see you. I was so taken up with my thoughts, I paid no heed to where I was going."

Fräulein Mélanie was the daughter of the chief-engineer, at whose house the young clerk occasionally visited; but his ideas had confessedly taken so high a flight that he had bestowed but small notice on the girl of sixteen who, with the exception of a graceful figure, a sweet young face, and a pair of roguish eyes, had nothing in the least romantic to recommend her.

She was far from his poetical standard, and the young lady, for her part, had up to this time troubled herself very little about the fair-haired Herr Wilberg; she had even thought him rather tiresome. But now he evidently considered it his duty to make reparation for his involuntary rudeness by addressing to her some polite speeches.

"You are coming back from a walk, Fräulein Mélanie? Have you been far?"

"Oh no, not far. Papa has forbidden me to take long walks, and he does not much like my coming out alone. Tell me, Herr Wilberg, is all this about our miners really so dangerous?"

"Dangerous? How do you mean?" said Wilberg diplomatically.

"Well, I don't know, but papa is so grave sometimes, it makes me feel quite nervous and frightened. He has talked too of sending mamma and me into town on a visit."

The young man's face assumed an expression of deep melancholy.

"The times are full of grave earnest," he said, "of terrible earnest! I cannot blame your father for wishing to place his wife and child in safety. We must stand and fight to the last man!"

"To the last man?" cried the girl, horrified. "Good Heavens, my poor papa!"

"Well, I only meant that in a figurative sense," said Wilberg soothingly. "There is no question of personal danger; and even if it should come to that, your father's years and his duties as head of a family would exclude him from all perilous service. In that case, we young ones should step into the breach."

"Would you?" asked Mélanie, looking at him rather distrustfully.

"Certainly, Fräulein Mélanie, I should be the very first."

With a view to giving greater emphasis to this declaration, Herr

Wilberg was about to lay his hand solemnly on his breast, when all at once, he jumped back and hurried as fast as possible over to the other side, Mélanie following him with equal speed. Close behind them stood Hartmann's gigantic form. He had come over the bridge unnoticed, and smiled now a contemptuous little smile as he saw the evident emotion of the young people.

"You need not be afraid, Herr Wilberg," said he quietly. "I am not going to hurt you."

The young clerk seemed to feel the absurdity of his sudden retreat, and to perceive also that, as the companion and protector of a young lady, he was bound to adopt a different line of conduct. He summoned up all his courage and, placing himself before the no less intimidated Mélanie, answered with some show of firmness,

"I hardly suppose, Hartmann, that you mean to attack us in the open street."

"That is what you gentlemen seem to expect," said Ulric derisively. "You run away, all of you directly I show myself, just as if I were a highwayman. Herr Berkow does not, he is the only one," the miner went on speaking with a growl now as he uttered the hated name. "He holds his ground, no matter if I have the whole gang at my back."

"Herr Berkow and her ladyship are just the only two who do not suspect" ... began Wilberg imprudently.

"Who do not suspect what?" asked Ulric, turning a dark look on him.

Whether the young official were exasperated by the derision with which he and his colleagues had been treated, or whether he considered it necessary to play the hero for Mélanie's benefit, is uncertain; suffice it to say that he yielded to one of those fits of passion which not seldom carry timid natures into extremes.

"We do not run away from you, Hartmann, because you are stirring up the people to rebellion and making it impossible to come to an understanding with them. It is not on that account we get out of your way, but because,"--here he lowered his voice so that the girl could not overhear his words--"because the ropes broke that day when you went below with Herr Berkow--if you must know the reason why every one avoids you."

They were very thoughtless, very rash words, particularly to be spoken by a man like Wilberg, but he little dreamed of the effect they would produce. Ulric started, uttered a half-suppressed cry of rage which was full of menace, then grew ashy pale, and letting fall his clenched fist, caught convulsively at the iron railings of the bridge. He stood there with heaving breast and teeth tightly ground together, gazing down at the two before him in speechless fury.

This proved too hard a trial for the young folks' courage. Neither knew which ran away first, dragging the other with him or her; but they both made off with all possible speed, and only slackened their pace when they had put several houses between them and the object of their fear, and convinced themselves that they were not followed.

"For Heaven's sake, what did it mean, Herr Wilberg?" asked Mélanie anxiously. "What did you say to that dreadful creature Hartmann, that made him start like that? How rash of you to provoke him!"

The young man smiled, though his lips were still colourless. It was the first time in his life he had ever been accused of rashness, and he was conscious that the reproach was merited. Now only did he clearly see the full measure of the risk he had run.

"Offended pride!" he gasped. "The duty of protecting you, Fräulein! You see he dared not attack us after all."

"No, we got away in time," returned Mélanie naïvely, "and it was a good thing we did, for our lives would have been in danger if we had stayed."

"It was only on your account I ran," said Wilberg, feeling a little hurt. "I should have held my ground if I had been alone, even at the risk of my life."

"That would have been very sad though," remarked the girl. "You who write such beautiful poetry!"

Wilberg blushed with agreeable surprise.

"Do you know my poems? I did not think in your house ... Your father has rather a prejudice against my lyrical tendency."

"Papa was talking to the Director about it a little while ago," said Mélanie, and then suddenly came to a full stop. She could not tell the poet that her father had read aloud to his colleagues those verses, which to her sixteen-year-old imagination had seemed so touching, adding many a biting jest and malicious comment as he read, and finally throwing down the paper with the words:

"And the fellow can spend his time now on such rubbish as that!"

At the moment she had thought it rather cruel and unjust to the young man. He no longer seemed tiresome to her, now that she knew he had been crossed in love, as clearly as appeared from his verses. That explained and excused all the peculiarities of his behaviour. She hastened to assure him that, for her part, she thought his verses lovely, and in shy but fervent sympathy, tried to console him somewhat for his supposed misfortune.

Herr Wilberg suffered himself to be comforted. He found it indescribably refreshing to meet at last with a being who could understand him, and still more refreshing to feel himself compassionated by the said being. It was quite a misfortune that they had by this time reached the chief-engineer's house, and that the master of it, in his august person, stood at the window, watching them with surprised and rather critical looks. Wilberg had no wish to expose himself to his superior's jokes, which, he knew, would be inevitable, should it occur to Mélanie to relate their meeting with Hartmann and their common flight. He took leave of the young lady therefore, and Fräulein Mélanie ran up the steps, racking her brains to try and find out who the object of this interesting and unfortunate attachment could be.

Old Manager Hartmann sat at home in his cottage, leaning his head on his hand; not far from him, at the window, stood Lawrence and Martha. As Ulric suddenly opened the door, the three broke off their conversation so abruptly, that the new-comer might easily have guessed they had been talking of him. He did not notice it, however, but closed the door, flung his hat on the table and threw himself without a word of greeting into the great arm-chair by the fireside.

"Good day," said the Manager, turning slowly round to him. "Don't you think it worth your while now to say a civil word when you come in? I should have thought you might have kept that up, at least."

"Don't worry me, father," exclaimed his son impatiently, throwing back his head and pressing his hand to his forehead.

The Manager shrugged his shoulders and turned away. Martha left her place by the window and sat down by her uncle, taking up the work she had laid aside while talking with Lawrence. For some minutes there was an oppressive silence in the room, then the younger man went up to his friend.

"Deputy Wilms has been here to speak to you, Ulric. He will come back in an hour. He has been making the round of all the neighbouring works."

Ulric passed his hand over his brow, as though to chase away some tormenting dream.

"Well, and how goes it?" he asked, but in a listless mechanical way; he seemed hardly to know what the other was speaking of.

"They are going to join us. Our example appears to have given them courage, for the game is beginning everywhere now. The forges will strike first, and the other works will follow suit, unless all they ask is granted to them at once. That is out of the question, so in a week all the miners and works in the district will be empty."

"At last!" Ulric started up, as though electrified; all his dreamy listlessness and lack of interest had vanished. The man had regained his old elasticity. "At last!" he repeated, heaving a deep sigh of relief. "It was time; they have left us alone long enough!"

"Because we began alone in the first instance."

"May be so, but we could not wait. Things were not on the same footing here as on the other works. Each day's labour brought the Berkows a step forward and took us a step back. Has Wilms gone over to the villages? He ought to let the others know at once, it will raise their spirits."

"Not before they want it," said the Manager quietly. "Their courage seems to be on the wane. For the last fortnight not a stroke of the hammer has been heard. You are waiting and waiting, fancying that you will be asked to come back, or that, at least, some attempt at a bargain will be made up yonder, and yet they make no sign. The officials avoid you, and the master does not look as if he meant to give way an inch. I tell you, Ulric, it is high time you should find assistance somewhere."

"Nonsense, father," cried the young man. "We have hardly been off work a fortnight, and I told them beforehand, they might make up their minds to be idle a couple of months, if we meant to conquer, and conquer we must."

The old man shook his head.

"A couple of months! You and I and Lawrence, may hold out that long, but not those who have a wife and children to keep."

"They must," said Ulric coldly. "I did think, certainly, we should have managed it faster and with less trouble. I was mistaken in that. But, if they are determined up yonder to drive us to an extremity, we will let them have a thorough good taste of what it means."

"Or they us," put in Lawrence. "If the master really"----

Ulric gave an angry stamp with his foot.

"'The master,' always 'the master!' Can't you find another name for this Berkow? You used not to call him so, but ever since he has told you to your faces that he is, and will be, the first person here, you have not an opinion of your own about it. I tell you, if we go through with the thing, we shall be masters, he will only have the name then, and we shall have the power. He knows it very well; that is why he resists so strongly, and that is why we must persevere until he grants us all we ask. We must go on at any cost."

"Try it," said the Manager briefly. "See if you can turn the world topsy-turvy all by yourself. I have given up talking about it this long while."

Lawrence took his cap from the window-sill, and prepared to go.

"You must know best, if we are likely to succeed or not. You are our leader."

Ulric's face grew dark.

"Yes, I am, but I thought it would have been easier to keep you in hand. You make the work hard enough for me."

The young miner exclaimed indignantly,

"We! you can hardly complain of us. Every word you say is obeyed instantly."

"Obeyed!" And Ulric turned a dark and searching gaze upon his friend. "Yes, obedience is not wanting, and it is not that I am complaining of. But we are not as we used to be. Even you and I, Karl, are not as we used to be together. You are all of you so distant now, so cold and shy; it seems to me often as if you were all afraid of me, and--and that's all."

"No, no, Ulric!" Lawrence resented the reproach vehemently, it almost appeared as if the other had hit the right mark. "We have perfect trust in you, and you alone. No matter what you may have done, you did it for us, not for yourself. We know that, all of us, we none of us forget that."

"No matter what you may have done, you did it for us!" The words sounded harmless enough and may have contained no hidden meaning, but Ulric seemed to detect one in them, for he looked hard at the speaker. Lawrence avoided his gaze, keeping his eyes fixed on the ground.

"I must go," he said hastily. "I will send Wilms over to you. You will stay here, so that he will be sure to find you?"

Ulric made no answer. The flow of emotion of the last few minutes had subsided, and his face was pale again as at his entrance. He nodded affirmatively, and turned to the window.

The young miner took leave of the Manager and left the room, Martha rose and went out with him. During the whole of the foregoing conversation she had spoken no word, but had observed the two men attentively. She stayed rather long outside, but that could excite no wonder. Her uncle and cousin knew well enough that a newly-engaged pair have much to whisper to one another, and they seemed, indeed, to trouble themselves not at all about it.

The father and son remained alone together, and the silence now intervening was even more painful than that which had ensued on Ulric's entrance. He stood at the window now, leaning his forehead against the panes, and staring out without seeing anything before him.

The Manager still sat at the table resting his head on his hands; his sorrowful, care-worn face plainly showed the ravages which the last few weeks had made. The lines graven on it by old age were furrowed more deeply now, and his eye had grown dim. All the old animation and pugnacious vigour, with which he had been wont formerly to administer many a sermon to his son, had vanished; he sat there, quiet and depressed, making no attempt to renew the conversation.

At last the silence became intolerable to Ulric. He turned round hastily.

"And you say nothing to the news which Wilms has brought us? Is it really all the same to you whether we succeed, or whether we are beaten?"

The old man raised his head slowly.

"It is not all the same to me, but I can't take delight in your threats and your violence. Best wait and see who is most hurt by them, the gentlemen or ourselves. You do not care much about that, you have got your own way. It is for you to command now throughout the works. Every one appeals to you, every one bows down before you, obeys your slightest word. That was what you wanted from the first, what the whole business was set on foot for."

"Father!" cried the young man.

"Let be--let be," said the Manager, interrupting him. "You will not confess it to me, and perhaps not to yourself, but it is so. You took them all along with you, and me with the rest, for of what use to hold back alone? Take care where you lead us. The responsibility is yours."

"Did I begin the thing alone?" broke out Ulric vehemently. "Was it not decided unanimously that there must be a change, and have we not given our word to stand together until the change is made?"

"In case your demands were not granted--yes. But everything has been granted, or as good as everything, for what has been refused has really nothing to do with the demands of our people. You were the one to bring in all that, Ulric, and it is you alone who hold them to it. If it were not for you, they would have been at work long ago, and we should have peace and quiet on the works again."

Ulric threw back his head defiantly.

"Well, yes, I did start it, and I take no shame to myself that I can see farther, and provide for the future, better than the rest. If it will satisfy them that the old poverty should be made a little more bearable, and their miserable lives a little safer in the mines, it will not satisfy me, or any man of spirit among us. We ask for much, that is true, we ask for nearly everything, and if Berkow were the millionaire the world takes him for, he would never dream of giving himself into our hands. But he is that no longer, and his whole weal or woe depends upon whether these hands of ours are busy for him now or not. You don't know the state of things up there in the bureaus, and the reports which are read at the meetings, father, but I do, and I tell you, struggle against it as he may, he will have to yield when he is attacked on all sides at once."

"And I tell you he will not!" declared the Manager. "He will close the works first. I know Arthur well; he was like that as a child, quite different from you. You stormed at everything, and were always for using force, if your work, or your play-fellows, or even your garden hedge, did not please you. He never set about anything willingly, and sometimes it would be a long time before he made up his mind to it; but, when once he began, he would never leave off until he had mastered the thing, whatever it might be. He is roused now, and he means to show you the stuff he is made of. He holds the reins, and no one will be able to drag them out of his hands; there is something of your own obstinacy in him. Think of what I say, when some day he makes you feel it."

Ulric stood gloomy and silent. He did not contradict in his usual vehement way, but the fact that contradiction was impossible stirred up a feeling of wrathful resentment within him. Perhaps he had already felt something of his adversary's mettle.

"And however the thing may turn out," continued his father, "do you suppose that you can stay on here as Deputy, that they will suffer you to remain on the works, after what has happened?"

The young man laughed scornfully.

"No, certainly not, if it depends upon the gentlemen up yonder. They will never take me into favour again, that is very sure. But there will be no question of favour. We shall dictate our terms to them, and the first condition made by all the men unanimously will be that I am to remain."

"Are you so certain of that?

"Father, don't insult my mates," exclaimed Ulric. "They would never desert me."

"Not if the first condition up yonder is that you should go? The master will insist on that, depend upon it."

"Never; he will never obtain that from them. They know all of them that I have not done it for my own sake. I was not badly off, I have no need to starve, I can earn my bread anywhere. It was their misery I wanted to lessen. Don't talk to me, of it, father. They give me trouble enough often, but when things come to be serious, I shall pull through; there is not one of them who will desert me then. Wherever I lead they will follow, and where I stand they will stand by me, yes, that they will, to the very death!"

"They would have some time ago, they won't now." The old man had risen, and only as he turned to the broad daylight could it be fully seen how careworn his features were, and how bowed the figure which, but lately, had been so strong and vigorous.

"You said to Lawrence yourself that things are not as they used to be," he went on in a very low voice, "and you know well the day and hour when the change came about. I hardly need tell you so now, Ulric, but that day cost me the bit of peace and rest I had hoped for in my old age. It is all over with that now, for ever!"

"Father!" cried the young man again. The Manager stopped him with a hasty gesture. "Let it be as it is. I know nothing of what happened, I will know nothing of it, for, if I had to listen to the story in so many words, then all would be up with me indeed. The mere thought is enough; it alone has almost driven me out of my senses."

Ulric's eyes flashed angrily again, as when his friend had made that allusion a short time before.

"And if I were to tell you, father, that the ropes gave way, if I were to tell you that my hand had never been near them"----

"Tell me nothing rather," broke in the old man bitterly. "I should not believe you, and the others would not believe you either. You were always savage and prone to use violence. You would have felled your best friend to the ground in your wrath. Try it, go among your mates and say to them: 'It was nothing but an accident.' There is not one of them who will believe you!"

"Not one?" repeated Ulric, hoarsely. "And you doubt me too, father?"

The Manager fixed his dimmed eyes on his son.

"Can you look me in the face and declare that you were in no way to blame for the accident, in no way? that you"----he did not finish the question, for Ulric had not been able to bear his gaze. The eyes, which a minute before had flashed with anger, now sought the ground, a sharp quiver passed over him, he turned away and--was silent.

A great stillness fell upon the room. Nothing was heard but the old man's heavy breathing. His hand trembled, as he passed it across his brow, and his voice trembled still more, when at last he spoke in a low tone.

"Your hand was not near? Whether it were your hand precisely, or however it may have come about, they are all of opinion, thank God, that inquiries are useless, and that nothing can be proved, at all events in a court of justice. Settle it with yourself, Ulric, as to what befell down below, but don't bully your mates any more. You were quite right. They have been afraid of you since then, and nothing else. See how long you can manage them with fear alone."

So saying he went out. Ulric made a rapid movement as though about to rush after him, but stopped suddenly, striking his forehead with his clenched fist, while a sound like a suppressed groan escaped his breast.

Ten minutes may have passed before the door was again opened and Martha came in. Her uncle was gone, and Ulric lay back in the arm-chair, his head buried in his hands. That did not appear to surprise her much; she cast one glance at him, then went up to the table and began to put together her work. Ulric had raised himself as she approached. He stood up now slowly and went over to her. In general, he paid but little heed to the girl's doings, and would still less trouble to speak to her of what concerned herself. But now he did both these things.

Perhaps a moment had come when even his reserved unbending nature longed for a word, for a token of sympathy, at a time when all fled from him, all avoided him.

"So you and Lawrence have made it up?" he began. "I have not spoken to you about it yet, Martha, I have had so many other things in my head of late. Are you engaged?"

"Yes," was the short and not very encouraging answer.

"And when is the wedding to be?"

"There is time enough for that."

Ulric looked down at the girl, who with quick-coming breath and trembling fingers was busying herself with her work, without even raising her eyes to him. A sort of reproachful feeling rose up in his mind towards her.

"You have done right, Martha," he said, in a low voice. "Karl is a good fellow, and very fond of you, fonder, perhaps, than .... than others might have been. Yet you sent him away again without an answer after our last talk. When did you promise to marry him?"

"Yesterday three weeks."

"Yesterday three weeks! Why, that was the day after the accident. So it was then you promised?"

"Yes, it was then. I could not do it before. It was only on that day I felt as if I ever could be his wife."

"Martha!"

The man's voice swelled half in anger, half in pain. He would have laid his hand on her arm, but she started back involuntarily. He let his hand fall and moved away.

"You too?" he said hoarsely. "Well, yes, I might have known it."

"Oh, Ulric!" exclaimed the girl in wild despairing accents, "what have you done to yourself, to us all!"

He was still standing opposite her. His hand shook as it rested on the table, but his face had grown stern and hard again.

"Whatever harm I may have done myself, I shall take the consequences of it without troubling any one else. As for you all, why, there is not one of you that will even listen to me. But I tell you now, once and for good," here his voice grew hard and menacing, "I have had enough of your endless hinting and tormenting. I won't bear it any longer. Believe what you will and whom you will, it shall be just the same to me in future. What I have begun, I shall go through with, in spite of every one; and if there is really to be an end of all confidence, I shall, at least, know how to enforce obedience."

So saying he went out. Martha made no attempt to detain him, and she would certainly have tried in vain. He crashed to the door of the room behind him, making the little house shake in its foundations. Next minute he had left the cottage.

CHAPTER XVIII

The arrival of the guests up at the château had brought some animation to that divided household, but it had hardly drawn the young couple more closely together. Although the visitors' stay was limited to a few days, Arthur continually found pretexts and opportunities for withdrawing from their society, an attention for which his father and brother-in-law were both sincerely grateful.

The Baron was but now returning after a sojourn of several weeks on the Rabenau property, his own from this time forth. Notwithstanding the frightful catastrophe which had occurred on the occasion of his first visit, he had been forced to leave his daughter on the following morning, a nearer duty calling him to his cousin's grave. Even when the last offices were over, there remained much to be set in order, and the heir's presence had been indispensable.

He was now returning in company of his eldest son, whom he had sent for to join him, and, this time also, they made the short détour round by the Berkow estates, all the more readily that the young Baron Conrad had not seen his sister since her marriage.

More was intended by this visit than a mere family meeting, or so it appeared from a conversation which took place in Eugénie's boudoir on the day after their arrival, Arthur being absent as usual. His wife sat on the sofa listening to her father, who was standing before her, and just winding up a long peroration, while Conrad, leaning against a chair at a little distance from them, watched his sister with a look of eager expectation.

Eugénie sat resting her head on her hand so as to shade her face. When her father ceased speaking, she did not alter her position or look up, but replied in a low voice:

"No hints or allusions are needed for me to understand what you mean, papa. You are speaking of a separation."

"Yes, my dear," said the Baron, earnestly, "to a separation, no matter under what pretext, or at what cost. What is obtained by force must be kept by force, the Berkows should have remembered that. Now that I am once more master of my own actions, that I need be their debtor no longer, I will employ every means to free you from those chains which you took upon yourself solely on my account, and which, deny it as you may, are making you wretched in the extreme."

Eugénie did not answer. Her father took her hand and sat down by her.

"The thought is new to you and takes you by surprise? It flashed upon me directly I received the weighty news which brought about such an unexpected change in our circumstances. At that time it would have been difficult to realise it. The elder Berkow had left nothing undone to secure an alliance with our family. It was out of the question that he should consent to a dissolution of the marriage, for that would have shut him out from those circles to which he hoped to gain access through us; and with such a man as he, capable of anything in his utter unscrupulousness, we could not well proceed to open fight. His death put an end to all the difficulties at a blow, for his son's resistance can be got over. He has played a merely passive rôle throughout the business, and simply lent himself to be his father's tool. He will yield, I hope, to energetic action on our part."

"He will yield," affirmed Eugénie under her breath. "Have no fear on that score."

"So much the better!" replied Windeg. "We shall attain our end the more speedily."

He was, it seemed, desirous of pushing forward to that end without loss of time, and such was indeed the fact. To the poor nobleman, heavily laden with debt, there had been no choice left but to accept Eugénie's sacrifice, and so save his own and his sons' name and position; whatever it may have cost him, he bent to a hard necessity, and the very necessity of the case taught him how to bear it.

But, to the Lord of Rabenau, who had regained complete independence, and with it all his old sense of dignity, who could pay back with ease the sums he had received, this bond of restraint appeared a burning disgrace, and he looked upon his daughter's marriage as an act of injustice committed to her prejudice, and which he must repair at any cost. During his stay at Rabenau this thought had haunted him, and had gradually shaped itself into a plan which was now ripe for execution.

"It will certainly meet both your wishes and ours that this painful affair should be entered into and settled as quickly as possible," he continued. "I was going to propose that you should accompany us to the city under some pretext or other, and, when there, take the necessary steps to accomplish it. You need simply refuse to return to your husband, and insist upon a separation. We will take care that he does not make good his claims by force."

"Yes, by Jove, that we will, Eugénie!" broke in Conrad passionately. "If he should find he has made a bargain to his liking, and refuse to give it up, your brothers will compel him to yield at the point of the sword. He cannot threaten us now with shame and public humiliation as his father did. That was the only thing the Windegs feared, the only argument by which a daughter of their house could ever have been won from them."

His sister stopped him almost impatiently.

"There is no occasion for threats. Con, and none for your anxiety, papa. Both are equally uncalled for. That which you expect to have to fight for and win by force has long been a settled thing between Arthur and myself."

Windeg started up, and Conrad came a step nearer impetuously in his surprise.

Eugénie strove to give firmness to her voice, but she could not succeed; it quivered audibly as she went on:

"Before Herr Berkow's death we had come to an agreement about it, but we wished to avoid the éclat of too early and sudden a rupture, and so we imposed on ourselves the restraint of living for a time under the same roof."

"Before Berkow's death?" interrupted her brother. "Why, that was soon after you were married!"

"So you introduced the subject yourself?" said the Baron with equal animation. "Did you insist upon it?"

They neither of them seemed to understand the pain which was so plainly written on the young wife's face. She called up all her self-command and answered steadily.

"I never alluded to the matter. Arthur voluntarily offered me a separation."

The Baron and his son looked at one another, as though such a piece of intelligence overstepped their powers of comprehension.

"Indeed! I was not prepared for that," said the Baron, at last, slowly. "He himself! I should not have expected it!"

"No matter," cried Conrad with a sudden burst of tenderness, "no matter, so long as he gives you back to us, Eugénie. We have none of us been able to take any pleasure in the inheritance which has come to us, because we knew that you have been made unhappy for our sakes. My father will not be fairly at ease in the new life until you come back, no more will any of us. We have missed you so in everything."

He threw his arm round his sister, and she hid her face for a few seconds on his shoulder. It was as deadly white and cold in its beauty as it had been when she stood before the altar; yet now she was on the eve of returning to her father's house, from which she had that day been torn away.

The Baron looked at his daughter in some surprise, as she now raised her head and passed her handkerchief over her brow.

"Excuse me, papa, if I seem rather strange to-day. I am not quite well, not well enough, that is, to discuss this subject. You must let me go to my room, I"----

"You have had too much to bear of late," said her father tenderly. "I see it, my dear, even though you will not confess it. Go, and leave all to my care. I will spare you as much as possible."

"It is odd though, is it not, sir?" said the young Baron, as the door closed behind his sister. "Do you understand this Berkow? I don't."

Windeg paced up and down the room with a frown on his brow. He was not merely surprised, but wounded in his pride by this disclosure. To the aristocrat it had seemed quite explicable that a parvenu owning millions of money should employ all the means at his disposal, hesitating neither at intrigue nor sacrifice, to obtain a connection with himself, even though such endeavours were met with unbounded hatred and contempt. But that his plebeian son-in-law should have received the hand of a Baroness Windeg with perfect equanimity, as if there had been nothing extraordinary in such a marriage; that, as time went on, he should have shown himself as insensible to the honour done him as his father was the reverse;--these were things he never could forgive. And now this man, this Arthur Berkow, retired from the connection of his own free will, before any inducement to do so had been held out to him. This was too much for the haughty Windeg. He had been eager to struggle for, to re-conquer, his daughter's freedom, but that he should owe it to her husband's generosity or indifference was intolerable to him.

"I will speak to Berkow," he said presently, "and if he really does agree, which I doubt, in spite of what Eugénie has told us, we must set to work without delay."

"Without delay?" asked Conrad. "They have hardly been married three months, and I think they are right in wishing to avoid too early a rupture."

"No doubt they are, and I should give my complete approval, if I had not other reasons of my own for hurrying on the affair. Things are not as they should be here on the works. I have received a hint from a friendly source that these disturbances, which have broken out among the hands employed, may inflict a deadly injury upon the Berkow property, enormous as it is supposed to be. If a crash should come, his wife could hardly leave him at such a moment; for the sake of public opinion she must stay on. Though we have deeper and far more serious reasons for desiring a separation, his ruin would be looked upon as the real cause, and that must not be. Better we should be thought to stir in the matter prematurely than suffer our hands to be tied, as they would be, should a catastrophe occur. A vast undertaking like this does not fall to pieces in a few weeks. It would take a year at least, and in half that time a divorce may be obtained, if he puts no difficulties in the way. Eugénie must return to our house, must be free again, before the state of things here gets known in the city."

"I should have thought my sister would have taken up the idea more cheerfully and with greater zest," said Conrad meditatively. "To be sure, if they had settled the matter before between themselves, there was nothing in it new to her, but she seems as quiet and silent about it, as if it were no concern of hers, as if her liberty did not depend upon it."

The Baron shrugged his shoulders.

"She does not like the thought of the unavoidable talk it will excite, of all the unpleasant details of the law-suit which cannot be spared her. It is always a painful step for a woman to take, and yet it must be taken.

In this case we shall, at any rate, have the whole city on our side. It was unfortunately no secret why this marriage was arranged, and but little surprise can be felt that we should hasten to dissolve it."

"Here comes Berkow," whispered Conrad, as the door of the adjoining room was opened. "You wish to speak to him. Shall I leave you together?"

Windeg shook his head.

"You are the eldest son of our house, and at such discussions the presence of a third person often acts as a wholesome restraint. Stay here, Conrad."

While these words were being quickly exchanged in a low voice, Arthur had crossed the ante-room. He came in now, and the greetings on either side were polite and frigid as usual. The conversation began with the customary flowers of rhetoric. The guests regretted they should enjoy so little of their host's company, the latter put forth as an excuse the accumulation of business which deprived him of the pleasure, etc., mutual formalities believed in by neither party, but behind which each sheltered himself as affording, at least, some subject matter for talk.

"I hope Eugénie's constant company will make up to you for my enforced absence," continued Arthur, glancing through the salon as though in quest of his wife.

"Eugénie is slightly indisposed; she has just left us," returned the Baron, "and I should be glad to make use of this opportunity to express to you a wish of mine, the fulfilment of which depends mainly on yourself."

"If its fulfilment depends on me, you have but to command."

The young man took up a position opposite his father-in-law, while Conrad, who knew what was coming, withdrew, as though accidentally, into a window recess, and appeared to be steadfastly gazing out on the terrace below.

Windeg's bearing was full of stately calm and aristocratic dignity. He desired to be as impressive as possible, and so do away at once with any possible resistance on the part of his daughter's plebeian husband; for he looked upon Arthur's offer of a separation, at the most, as a hasty speech made in a moment of passion. He could not believe it to be serious.

"People seem to attach a greater degree of importance to this revolutionary movement on your estates than it probably has in reality," he began. "As I came by the town yesterday and paid a visit to the commandant of the garrison there, a very old friend of mine, the feeling among the hands over here was described to me as most dangerous, and an outbreak of disturbances was said to be extremely probable."

"They appear to take more interest in my works and in my people than I had supposed," said Arthur, coldly. "I have, at all events, not besought the Colonel for help in case of need."

The Baron understood the hint.

"As for me, of course, I can form no opinion on the subject," he replied quickly. "I only wished to draw your attention to the fact that there would be impropriety in exposing Eugénie to any such possible scenes of disorder. It is my desire to take my daughter with me to the city, just for a time, until the situation here has cleared a little."

A shade fell on the young man's face. Again he cast a quick glance over to the door which led to his wife's apartments, as though trying to divine whether the wish came from her. His reply was quite calm, however.

"Eugénie is mistress of her own actions. If she considers it necessary to leave she is perfectly at liberty to do so."

Windeg, highly pleased, bent his head affirmatively.

"She will accompany us then to-morrow morning. As to the length of her absence, there we approach a subject which is equally painful to us both, but I prefer to touch upon it by word of mouth, particularly as I know our wishes to be identical with regard to the main point at issue."

Arthur seemed about to start from his chair, but he controlled himself and kept his seat.

"Oh! so Eugénie has already been making communications to you?"

"Yes, does that surprise you? Her father would, of course, be the first person in whom she would confide."

Arthur's lips twitched nervously.

"I supposed that the matter would remain between ourselves until the time for action had arrived. I see I was wrong."

"Why postpone things when once a decision has been come to?" asked the Baron quietly. "The present time is most favourable for carrying it into execution. The existing state of affairs here affords the best, the most unexceptional pretext for my daughter's leaving. It need not be known at first that she is leaving definitively. In these summer months, when every one is away from the city, the preliminary steps can be taken with least notice. When an éclat cannot be avoided, it is preferable to give people at once an actual event to talk about. In that way gossip is soonest exhausted."

A long pause followed. Arthur looked again, this time with rather an enigmatical expression, at the door of his wife's apartments; then he turned slowly to her father.

"Did the wish that this affair should be hurried on come from Eugénie herself?"

The Baron thought proper to withhold the truth on this occasion. By so doing, he would attain his end more quickly, and Eugénie would certainly be grateful to him for it.

"I speak in my daughter's name," he declared gravely.

Arthur rose suddenly, and so hastily that his chair was thrown to the ground.

"I consent to everything, Baron, to everything! I thought I had explained to your daughter my reasons in favour of a delay. They were entirely dictated by consideration for herself, and did not concern me in any way. If, notwithstanding these, she still desires to hasten on the matter--be it so!"

The tone in which these words were spoken was so peculiar, that Conrad, who had all along been apparently intent on the terrace below, although, in reality, he had not lost a word of the discussion, turned round suddenly and looked at his brother-in-law in astonishment.

Windeg himself felt surprised. What reason was there for any show of temper? He simply wished that a tie, burdensome to both parties, should be loosed a little earlier than had been intended.

"You fully agree to a separation then?" he asked, a little uncertain.

"Fully."

The Baron breathed freely. So Eugénie had been right in declaring that her husband would consent at once. What remained to be settled would, he thought, hardly present a difficulty.

"I am very much indebted to you for meeting me thus," said he politely. "It will facilitate matters for both sides. There is one other thing which I must mention, though it has no bearing upon the subject in hand. Your father"--the present Lord of Rabenau flushed crimson at the remembrance--"your father was good enough to take up certain obligations of mine which I was not then in a position to discharge. I am able to do so now, and I should wish as speedily as possible"----

He paused, for Arthur had turned his eyes full upon him with a look which forbade him to go on.

"Had we not better let this subject rest? I really must beg that it may not be touched upon."

"It might be allowed to rest so long as our mutual relations subsisted," returned Windeg gravely, "but not when they cease to exist. You will not oblige me to remain your debtor?"

"There was no question here of a debt in the ordinary sense of the word. Those obligations, which my father agreed to meet were, in reality, held by himself alone. The documents relating to the transaction were destroyed, so far as I know, when"--here the young man's extreme irritation broke for an instant through his enforced calm--"when you paid the price for them."

The Baron rose offended.

"The marriage was concluded at that time, in pursuance, certainly, of Herr Berkow's wish; it is now about to be dissolved, more particularly at our desire. The circumstances are completely reversed."

"Is it absolutely necessary that we should keep up the business point of view and make a bargain of the divorce also?" interrupted Arthur with cutting sarcasm. "I hope that I and my wife may not be made the subject of traffic a second time. Once was quite sufficient."

The Baron altogether misunderstood these words, as he also misunderstood the agitation which prompted them. He answered with his haughtiest air.

"Remember, if you please, Herr Berkow, that the word traffic, which you are pleased to employ, can only have reference to one of the parties concerned. It cannot apply to us."

Arthur stepped back; his attitude was proud and dignified, such as the nobleman opposite him could but rarely assume.

"I know now how this marriage was brought about, and I know too how those obligations came to exist which forced you into giving your consent. You will therefore understand why it is I request that not another syllable may be said about this debt. I require of you, Baron, that you do not make a son blush for his father's memory."

Once before Windeg had been disconcerted by his son-in-law's behaviour, on the occasion when the latter had thought fit to decline the peerage offered him, but that had been done in a cool, half negligent manner, and quite in the former Arthur Berkow's style. The present scene and the way in which he now bore himself fairly petrified the Baron. Involuntarily he glanced at his son, who had come out of the recess, and on whose youthful countenance was depicted a boundless astonishment which he gave himself no trouble to conceal.

"I was not aware you viewed the matter in that light," said Windeg at last "It was not my intention to wound your feelings."

"I suppose not, so we will let the subject drop into the past. With regard to the divorce, I will give my solicitor instructions to meet yours in a friendly spirit, and to render him any assistance in his power. Should a personal application to myself be necessary at any time, pray consider me as quite at your disposal I will do all I can to bring the matter to an end as speedily and with as little unpleasantness as possible."

He bowed to both gentlemen and left the room. In an instant young Conrad was at his father's side.

"What can it all mean? What, in the name of goodness, has come over this Arthur Berkow during the last three months? I thought yesterday evening he was graver and had a more decided way with him than formerly, but I never should have imagined he would be capable of behaving with so much dignity."

The Baron had not yet recovered from his astonishment. His son's exclamation roused him. "He really appears not to have been aware of the part his father was acting towards us. That certainly alters the case," said he in some confusion. "If only he had not required me to remain in his debt!"

"He does perfectly right," said Conrad, firing up, "now that he knows by what a system of usury Berkow drove us to our ruin. Not a quarter of the prodigious sums, afterwards arrayed against us, was ever advanced or expended by him in buying up those bills, and not a penny can the son receive if he will not bring dishonour on himself too. One could see that he was filled with shame at the whole disgraceful story. But this interview of ours took a very strange turn. The painful, the humiliating rôle in it was, unquestionably, his, and yet he managed to make us feel almost ashamed of our offer."

Windeg seemed disposed to take this last observation rather ungraciously, perhaps because he could not gainsay it.

"If we were unjust to him before, I am ready now to do him full justice," said he, "and the more so that we really owe him some thanks for his conduct with regard to this divorce business. I did not expect it would be so easy, notwithstanding the indifference he has always shown about the marriage."

Conrad's face again assumed a meditative expression, which, certainly, was not proper to it.

"I don't know, sir; it strikes me that the thing is by no means so settled. Berkow was far from being as calm as he tried to appear, and it was the same with Eugénie. There was no indifference in that violent start of his when you declared that she insisted on an immediate separation, and in Eugénie's face, when she left us, there was still less. A very odd idea has occurred to me in consequence!"

The Baron smiled with great superiority.

"You are quite a child still in some things. Con, in spite of your epaulets and your twenty years. Do you imagine that the determination which, as it now appears, they have both long since come to, could have arisen without previous quarrels and unpleasantness? Eugénie has suffered much from these scenes; perhaps Berkow may have suffered also. What you so sagely remarked was the reverberation of storms gone by, nothing more. Thank God, there is plain sailing between us now, and the storms are over for good and all."

"Or perhaps they are only just beginning!" said Conrad to himself under his breath, as he left the room with his father.

CHAPTER XIX

Evening had come, and throughout the house there was a feeling of disquiet and much busy movement. Baron Windeg had had another and a longer interview with his daughter in the afternoon, and directly afterwards the lady's maid had received orders to pack up her mistress's wardrobe. Herr Berkow had previously informed the servants that his wife would leave in the morning with her father for a stay of several weeks in the capital, and had desired that the necessary preparations should be made.

Of course, this piece of news at once made the round of all the officials' dwellings, and there, as at home, excited more uneasiness than surprise. It was clear as day that the master was only sending away her ladyship because he was convinced there would soon be "a row" on the works. He wished to know that she was in safety, and had probably himself sent for her father to fetch her away. Windeg was right. The pretext was so plausible, it occurred to nobody to doubt it.

At first, the strangely cold relations between the young married pair had been much discussed and commented on; but that had gradually ceased. It was known that the marriage had not been one of inclination, but as no quarrels or violent scenes were ever heard of--and, had there been any such, they could hardly have escaped the servants' notice--as Berkow was always politeness itself in his behaviour to his wife, and Eugénie tranquillity itself in her manner towards him, it was concluded that they must have become accustomed to and satisfied with each other: the usual result of these marriages of convenience. Their peculiar way of life seemed to be only what was practised in the great world.

In the higher circles of the capital it was usual to live thus apart and on a politely cool footing, and it could therefore be a matter of no surprise that the Baroness Windeg and the son of Berkow the millionaire should adopt the same course. That this journey, which had been preceded by no quarrel, should contain in it the germs of a final separation, was suspected by no one, and it struck no one as strange that the family did not spend that evening in company as usual.

Dinner was served for the two guests in the dining-room; her ladyship, being unwell, ordered tea in her boudoir, and then, to her maid's astonishment, left it untouched. As to Herr Berkow, he did not dine at all, but retired to his study where he had "business" to attend to, giving strict orders that he should not be disturbed.

Without all was pitch darkness, and here within the lamp on the writing-table shed its light on a man who, for more than an hour, had been pacing restlessly to and fro. Behind those closed doors the mask of indifference he had worn so long, was thrown off at last, and an outlet given to the storm silently raging within him. This was no longer the blasé young heir, nor the resolute leader whose suddenly-aroused energy and presence of mind had impressed his subordinates with respect and inspired the officials with courage.

In this man's face were visible traces of a great passion, the extent of which had been unknown even to himself, until the moment when the object of it was about to be lost to him. That moment had now come, and, for a while, his passion claimed its right to be heard.

The pallor of his brow, his quivering lips and burning eyeballs told a tale of what that day's interview had cost him, though the Baron had asserted of it that he could not have supposed the matter would be so easily arranged.

It had come at last then, that much-dreaded day of separation! and it was well that another had stepped in and effected that which his will lacked strength to undertake. How often during the last fortnight had Arthur himself thought of using the pretext which the Baron now suggested to him, and so of shortening the torture of this life under a common roof; for that measured calm of exterior, belying at every moment, as it did, the inward glow at his heart, could no longer be sustained. It exceeded his powers of endurance! And yet he had taken no step.

It is an indisputable truth that what is unavoidable had best be done at once; but not every one who would, if necessary, courageously use the knife to a poisoned bodily wound, can pluck up resolution to tear a devouring passion from his breast. With it there comes irresistibly the dread of losing the much loved object.

They had been long separated, these two, but, at least, he could still behold that fair face with the dark, speaking eyes, and the proud and delicate features which had grown so grave of late, and then there came moments of bliss, fleeting as lightning, which made amends for whole days and weeks of bitterness; such as that time in the forest the day before yesterday, when, with evident anxiety, she had pressed her horse close to his, when she had trembled in his arms as he lifted her from her saddle.... It might be cowardly, but he could not voluntarily renounce all this before it was demanded of him. And now the demand was made!

The door was gently opened, and a servant appeared hesitating on the threshold.

"What is it?" exclaimed Arthur. "Did I not give orders"----

"I beg your pardon, sir," said the man timidly.

"I knew you did not wish to be disturbed, but as her ladyship herself"----

"Who?"

"Her ladyship is here herself, and wishes"----

The man had no time to finish. To his astonishment, his master tore the door from his hand and hurried past him into the ante-room. There he saw his wife, apparently waiting; in an instant he was at her side.

"You have yourself announced? What unnecessary etiquette!"

"You wished to see no one, I hear, and Frank told me the order applied to every one without exception."

"Arthur frowned, and turned to the servant, who said apologetically,

"I really did not know what to do. It is the first time my lady has come here."

He stammered these words in his confusion, meaning them as an excuse and nothing more, but Eugénie turned quickly away, and the reprimand on her husband's lips remained unspoken.

The man was right after all; he had received no instructions for such an exceptional case as that of his mistress paying a visit to his master's room. It was truly the first time she had been there. Hitherto, they had only met in her boudoir, at table, or in the drawing-rooms. The present visit might well create surprise among the servants.

Arthur signed to the man to go, and came back into the study with his wife. She hesitated a little on the threshold.

"I wished to speak to you," she said, in a low voice.

"I am quite at your service."

He closed the door and pushed forward an armchair, inviting her by a gesture to be seated. These few minutes had sufficed to give him back all that self-control which he had so constantly exercised during the past few weeks. He spoke and moved in a cool measured way, as though showing politeness to a strange lady in a strange salon.

"Will you not sit down?"

"Thank you, I shall not detain you long."

There was something shy and uncertain in her manner which contrasted oddly with her usual composure. Perhaps in these rooms she felt ill at ease, or perhaps she found it hard to open the conversation.

Arthur did not come to her assistance. He saw that she twice tried to find words and failed, but he stood at his table silent and constrained, and waited.

"My father has told me of his talk with you," she began, "and also of its result."

"So I expected, and--excuse me, Eugénie--it was just on that account I was surprised to see you here. I thought you were occupied with the preparations for your departure."

These words were probably intended to counteract any impression his agitation at seeing her might have produced, and they had the desired result. Some seconds clasped before she continued.

"You had already spoken of my journey to the servants in the afternoon?"

"Yes, I thought you would wish it, and it seemed best that the order for the necessary preparation should come from me. Had you thought of introducing the subject in any other way? If so, I regret that I was not earlier made acquainted with your views."

His tone was frigid, and Eugénie felt as though an icy breath had been wafted over to her. Involuntarily she retreated a step.

"I have no observation to make, only it surprised me that my departure, the date of which had once been fixed, should now be hastened on. You had, I thought, reasons which would have induced you to keep to our arrangement."

"I? On this point I yielded to a wish, to a request of yours. Baron Windeg gave me to understand, at least, that it was so."

Eugénie started. She drew a long breath of relief, and all shyness and uncertainty vanished, as though, with this one answer, her courage had wholly returned to her.

"I thought so! My father went too far, Arthur; he spoke in my name, when he was only setting forth his own wishes. I have come now to clear up this misunderstanding, and to tell you that I shall not go, at least not until I hear from your lips that you wish me to do so."

Eugénie watched him with breathless attention, as though striving to read in his eyes what was passing in his mind; but they were downcast still, and her words produced no visible effect. His features relaxed once as she spoke of a misunderstanding, or so she fancied, but the change in him was but momentary, and, after a pause of a few seconds, he replied coldly and composedly as ever: "You will not go? And why not?" She stepped up to him and said resolutely: "You told me yourself the other day that all your future is involved in the coming struggle. I know since our last meeting with Hartmann that it will be fought out to the uttermost, and that your position is even more critical than you will allow. At such a time I can and will not leave you, it would be cowardly, and" ...

"You are very generous," interrupted Arthur with ill-concealed bitterness. "But to perform an act of generosity, some one must be found willing to accept it, and I certainly am not willing to accept yours."

Eugénie's hand grasped the chair near her, she pressed her fingers tightly into its velvet cushions, as though in repressed anger.

"Not?"

"No. The plan was of your father's making, so be it. He is doubtless right in requiring that his daughter, who will shortly be his altogether again, should be placed in safety and protected from those rough scenes and excesses which, in all probability, may take place here. I am quite of his opinion, and I agree fully to to-morrow's separation."

She raised her head and said with spirit,

"And I only agreed to it when I thought it was your wish. I cannot yield in this matter to my father's will alone. I have taken upon myself the duties of your wife, in the sight of the world at least, and, so far,

I shall fulfil them. They command me not to desert you basely in the face of that which threatens you, but to remain at your side until the worst has been tided over, and the date originally fixed for our parting has come. Then I will go, and not before."

"Not if I expressly ask you to do so?"

"Arthur!"

He stood half turning from her, and crushing in his hand a paper he had mechanically taken up from his bureau. The self-control he had regained by so violent an effort was not proof against that look and tone.

"I have begged you once already not to play at generosity with me. I have no liking for such scenes. Duties! It may be the duty of a woman, who has willingly given her husband both hand and heart, to stay by him and share his misfortune, perhaps his ruin, as she has shared his prosperity. That is not our case. We have no duties to each other, for we never had any rights one upon the other. The only thing which I could offer you in our compulsory union was the possibility of dissolving it; it has been dissolved from the moment that we decided upon a separation. That is my answer to the offer you have made me."

Eugénie's dark eyes were still fixed on his face. The tell-tale lightning-like flash, which at times seemed to discover the unknown depths of his being, came not to-day, and yet to-day of all days did she long to conjure it up at any cost.

Whatever she may have seen or guessed by it--and something she must have divined, or her proud spirit would never have so far bent as to allow her to come hither with her proposal--he would not grant her the triumph of again beholding it or of convincing herself of its true meaning.

He remained perfect master of himself, and left her a prey to torturing doubt. Her woman's instinct had spoken unhesitatingly when Ulric Hartmann's look had glowed upon her yesterday up on the forest heights, and, with the knowledge of what lay behind, horror of it had seized her as well. Yet she had been quite calm then, through all the danger with which she was threatened by an insane passion.

Here, where there was nothing to fear, she shook from head to foot in a fever of emotion, and a thick veil seemed to fall on all around, just as the brown eyes opposite were veiled before her. The inward voice was silent now, and yet at this moment she would have given her life to have acquired a certainty.

"You should not make it so hard for me to stay." Her voice betrayed something of the perplexity within her; it wavered between pride and soft submission. "I had much to fight against and much to conquer before I came here. You know it, Arthur, and should spare me."

The words were almost supplicating, but Arthur had reached such a pitch of irritation, he could no longer understand this. The bitter rage, which had taken possession of him and now shook his whole frame, gave its own interpretation to her words, and he answered sharply.

"I do not doubt that the Baroness Windeg is making an immense sacrifice in resolving to bear a hated name yet three months longer, and to remain at the side of a man she so thoroughly despises, notwithstanding that immediate freedom is offered her. I had to hear once how repugnant both are to you, and can judge therefore of what the victory over yourself must have cost you."

"You are reproaching me with the conversation we had on the night of our arrival," said Eugénie in a low tone. "I ... I had forgotten it!"

His eyes blazed now, but not with the light she had sought and hoped for. He was too distant from her, too full of hostility, for that.

"Really? And you do not ask whether I have forgotten it. I was forced to listen then, but that was the limit of what I could bear. Do you think a man will allow himself to be trampled in the dust with impunity, as I was by you on that evening, and then rise from it without further ado when it pleases you to alter your opinion? I was not quite so miserably weak as you imagined; from that time forth I was not weak at all. That hour was decisive for me, but it was decisive for our future also. Whatever may befall me, I will bear it alone. During the last few weeks I have learnt so much, I shall be able to go through with that too, but"--he drew himself up with a glow of pride--"but the woman who on the day after our wedding repulsed me with such haughty contempt, without condescending to ask whether the husband to whom she had given her hand were really as culpable as she believed him, who received my assurance, my given word, that she was in error as the ready pretext of a liar, who, to my question as to whether it might not be worth while to try and redeem so lost a man, flung at me that contemptuous 'No'-- that woman shall not stay by me; I will not have her at my side while I am fighting for all my future in this world. I will stand alone!"

He turned away from her in his wrath. Eugénie stood overwhelmed and speechless. Great as had been the change in her husband of late, she had never before seen him roused to passion, and at this moment his violence almost frightened her. By the storm, now bursting over her head, she could measure all that had lain hidden behind the indifference which had so revolted her, all that had smouldered within him for months together, until at last it drove him out of that apathy which had become a second nature.

Ah yes, that cold disdainful No! She knew now better than any one how unjust she had been to him, and now that she saw how that word of hers had mortified him, she might have allowed the present hour to make amends for all the evil the other had wrought, if only those last unfortunate words had remained unspoken. They touched her pride, and, when once that was called into play, all clear judgment and reflection were at an end, even though she knew herself to be in the wrong.

"You will stand alone," she repeated. "Well, I will not impose my presence on you. I wished to convince myself that my father's plan was yours also. I see it is so, and therefore I shall leave."

She turned to go. At the door she stopped a moment. It seemed to her that, as she touched the handle, he made a rapid movement as though about to spring after her; but it must have been an illusion, for, when she looked round, he was still standing at the table, deadly pale indeed, but with that answer of hers, that harsh inexorable "No," clearly written on his face and entire bearing.

Eugénie summoned up all her courage for one farewell speech.

"We shall only see each other to-morrow in my father's presence, and never again perhaps after that, so ... Good-bye, Arthur."

"Good-bye," said he hoarsely.

The door closed behind her; she was gone. The last few moments they could spend alone together had fled; the last bridge between them had broken down. Neither had been willing to yield an inch; neither would speak the word which alone had power to help and save, the one word which would have made good everything, even had the breach between them been ten times as wide. Pride had won the day and sealed their fate.

Grey and gloomy the morning dawned over the hills. In the house all was stirring at an unaccustomed hour. It was necessary to start early, so that the travellers might reach the nearest railway junction in time for the train which should take them on to the capital the same evening. At present there was no one in the breakfast-room but Conrad von Windeg. The Baron was still in his apartment, Eugénie was not visible either, and the young officer appeared to be very impatiently waiting for something or some one. He had paced up and down, had stepped out on to the balcony, and finally flung himself into an arm-chair, but he jumped up quickly as Arthur Berkow came in.

"Oh, you are here already!" said the latter, greeting his youthful brother-in-law with the cool politeness usual between them.

Conrad hurried up to him.

"I wanted to say a few words to you; but, good Heavens! what is the matter with you? Are you ill?"

"I?" said Arthur quietly. "What can you be thinking of? I am perfectly well."

"Are you?" returned Conrad with a look at the pale drawn features which told of a sleepless night. "I should not have thought so!"

"I am not used to get up so early, it always makes one look only half awake. I am afraid you will have a bad journey. There is a terrible fog this morning."

He went up to the window to look out at the weather, and also to escape from his companion's unpleasant physiognomical observations. Conrad was not to be put off so. He stepped up to his brother-in-law's side.

"I wanted to be down first," began he, hesitating a little, "because I should like to say a few words to you while we are by ourselves, Arthur."

Berkow turned round, surprised as much by the mode of address as by the wish expressed. Conrad had never before called him by his Christian name. He had hitherto followed his father's example and employed the formal "Herr Berkow."

"Well?" said Arthur, surprised indeed, but friendly.

The young officer was evidently divided between doubt and confusion on the one hand, and some unexpressed feeling on the other.

After the pause of a minute or so, he raised his frank handsome face and looked at his brother-in-law earnestly.

"We have been unjust to you, Arthur, and I perhaps more than the rest. I was indignant at the marriage and at the compulsion we had been subjected to, and I honestly confess I have hated you with all my heart ever since the day you married my sister. I found out yesterday that we had been mistaken in our opinion of you, and so it is all up with my hatred. I am sorry, very sorry, and--and that is what I wanted to say. Will you shake hands, Arthur?"

He held out his hand heartily. Arthur grasped it.

"I thank you, Con," he said, simply.

"Well, thank God, that is over. I could not sleep for it all night!" exclaimed the young fellow, greatly relieved. "And, believe me, my father does you justice too. He won't own it to you, I daresay, but I know it is in his mind."

A fleeting smile crossed Arthur's face, but it did not clear his brow or bring a sparkle to his eyes. A heavy shadow lay on both as he answered quietly,

"I am glad of it. So we shall not part as enemies."

"Oh, about the journey," broke in Conrad, hastily. "My father is still up in his room, and Eugénie is all by herself in hers. Will you not go in and speak to her?"

"What for?" asked Arthur in surprise. "The Baron may come in at any moment, and Eugénie will hardly"----

"I will stand before the door and not let any one in. I will manage to keep my father here until you are ready."

Arthur's face flushed under the other's earnest gaze, but he shook his head gravely.

"No, Con, that is not necessary. I spoke to your sister yesterday evening, and we said all there was to say."

"About her leaving?"

"About her leaving."

The young officer looked disappointed, but he had no time to press his offer, for the Baron's step was just then heard outside, and immediately afterwards he came in.

Conrad retreated into the back ground with an air of vexation, murmuring to himself as he did so:

"But the thing is not on the square, for all that."

The inevitable meeting at breakfast was over, helped through by the Baron's formal politeness, and by the constant presence of the servants; and now the carriage drove up to the terrace below. The gentlemen took their overcoats, and the maid brought Eugénie's hat and shawl. Arthur offered his arm to his wife to lead her down, for the appearance of a perfectly good understanding between them must be kept up to the last.

Grey and gloomy the morning had dawned over the hills; grey and gloomy it descended now into the valleys below. Before the windows a sea of mist ebbed and flowed, and here within doors the cold frosty morning light streaming already into the great rooms gave to them a weird and desolate look. The splendour of their decorations seemed suddenly to have lost all lustre and colour, now that they were about to be left empty once more--very empty would they be, for their young mistress was leaving them without thought of return.

Conrad noticed that his sister had precisely the same look on her face as that which just before had startled him on Arthur's; but, beyond this, he could discover nothing unusual in their appearance or behaviour. They were both fully capable of playing the parts they had undertaken, although their features betrayed that the effort to do so had cost them a sleepless night. Perhaps this icy composure of theirs was not all assumed.

When a storm has spent itself, there follows that dead calm which so often helps us with relative ease over the most dreaded passages in life. It casts a veil over the soul, and this veil obscures from it all clear consciousness of the decisive moment. The struggle and combating subside into a dull prevailing sense of pain, through which, now and again, darts a fierce sudden pang, making the sufferer reflect as to the reason of his anguish.

Eugénie, leaning on her husband's arm, went down the stairs without really knowing why or whither they were going. As in a dream she saw the carpeted steps over which her dress rustled, the tall oleander trees standing in the hall, the faces of the servants bowing as she went by. It all passed before her in an indistinct shadowy way.

Then all at once something sharp and almost painful smote her forehead; it was the cold morning air, and she shuddered as she went out into it. Before her stood the carriage ready to bear her away; she saw this and nothing else, for terraces, flower-beds and fountains, all had vanished, and the pale morning twilight gleamed only on a thick curtain of vapour. Once again the eyes of husband and wife met, but they spoke no word to each other. The cloud lay heavy and thick between them too.

Then Eugénie felt that a hand, cold as ice, was laid in hers, heard some distant polite farewell speech, the words of which she did not comprehend; but it was Arthur's voice which spoke, and, at that sound, the sharp stinging pain darted once more through her dull dream. After that came the stamping of horses' hoofs and the roll of wheels, and away they went out into the faintly illumined mists which surged and swelled around them, as on that spring day when, up on the forest heights, the separation had been decided on, in the hour of which the old legends say: "What parts then, parts for all eternity."

CHAPTER XX

"We shall have it in earnest now, I tell you," said the chief-engineer to the Director, as they were walking together towards their respective homes. "Their august leader seems to be only waiting for us to furnish him with a pretext, in order to give the signal for attack. They regularly challenge us now, and insults are the order of the day. The whole district has been raised by them; the same thing is rife now on all the works around, only we had the honour of being first in the field. That brings grist to Hartmann's mill. He carries his head as high as ever again."

"Herr Berkow seems to be prepared for anything," said the Director. "He has placed his wife in safety as speedily as possible. That shows better than all else what he fears from his own people."

"Bah! our people!" broke in his colleague. "We should soon come to terms with them, if it were not for that one man. So long as he is in command, there is no peace or rest to be thought of. If Hartmann were away from the works but one week, I would answer for a settlement of the whole business."

"I have thought already"--the Director looked round cautiously, and lowered his voice--"I have thought already whether we could make use of the suspicion which is in every one's mind, and which, we may be sure, does the fellow no injustice. What do you say?"

"It will not do. We have suspicions enough, but where are the proofs? Nothing was found amiss with the pulleys or with the ropes. They broke, and that was all that could be discovered, though the matter was thoroughly sifted when the judicial inquiry was made. How it came about, and what happened down below, can only be known to Hartmann, and he is a match for any man. No one would make him commit himself. It would result in nothing; they would have to set him free again."

"But a criminal charge would deprive him of all power to harm for the time being. If an accusation were lodged against him, he would be imprisoned for a few weeks, and then"----

The chief-engineer frowned ominously.

"And the fury of our people, when they see hands laid upon their leader, will you take that upon yourself? I will not. They would storm the house down over our heads, if the manœuvre were seen through, as it assuredly would be."

"That might be a question. There is no longer the old love between him and them."

"But there is the old fear. He rules with it more despotically than ever; and, besides, you do our men a wrong in supposing they would desert their comrade, their leader, just on a mere suspicion. They may be shy of him, may fall off from him in time; but the moment we were to attempt to touch him, they would rally round and protect him at all hazards. No, no; it won't do. The very thing we want to avoid, a bloody conflict, would be inevitable then: and more than this, I am convinced Herr Berkow would not lend a hand to it."

"Does he still guess nothing of the suspicions which are afloat?"

"Nothing. No one has cared to allude to the matter before him, and I think it will be best to spare him further. He has enough to bear as it is."

"Yes, more than enough; and the evil tidings of the last few weeks, together with Schäffer's letters from the city, seem to have produced some effect upon him. I believe he is seriously thinking of giving way."

"Nonsense," said the chief-engineer. "Before announcing that ultimatum to the people, he had the alternative of risking his money or of submitting to Herr Hartmann's rod while it might please that worthy to chastise us; after the way he met them then, there could be no further question of giving in. Every trace of authority would be gone irretrievably, if he did not show a steady front now. He must go forward, and it is always an advantage in battle to feel that there is nothing for it but to advance boldly."

"But if his fortune is at stake?"

"But if his honour is at stake?"

The two then fell into one of those heated and fruitless debates which commonly ended in each retaining his own opinion. This was the case now when they parted shortly afterwards.

"Neutrality is a fine thing!" growled the chief-engineer after his colleague, as he turned into his house. "Just a little proper anxiety, a little proper caution, keep fair with both parties, because you never can tell which may get the upper hand at last I wish all the sneaks--Wilberg, what the deuce are you about there with my daughter?"

The two young people, at whom these words were levelled, sprang apart as though they had been detected in a crime. But in truth, Herr Wilberg had only ventured to kiss the young lady's hand in the most innocent manner possible. He was looking so tender, however, and Mélanie, for her part, was feeling so moved, that the advent of her father, already vexed and irritated by his talk with the Director, came upon them both like a thunderbolt.

"I must entreat your forgiveness," stammered the luckless clerk; while Fräulein Mélanie, conscious that, after all there was nothing so very wicked in allowing one's hand to be kissed, stood by unabashed.

"I beg you will give me an explanation of all this," said the chief-engineer angrily. "What are you doing down here in the hall? Why don't you go up into the drawing-room, which is the proper place for you?"

The explanation thus demanded could hardly be given in two words, though the young people had been guiltless enough in the matter of this meeting. Wilberg had gone up to his superior's house with a commission from Herr Berkow in his head, and deep melancholy at his heart. The latter was naturally called forth by the departure of his liege lady. He had heard that this departure was intended on the evening before it actually took place, and the knowledge of it had not roused him from his dreams on the fatal morning. The young clerk was no early riser, and would never have committed the imprudence of exposing himself at that hour to the cold foggy air, which might have brought on an attack of rheumatism.

It was not he who, at break of day, was standing under the pines there where the high road turned into the forest, patiently waiting for the one minute in which the carriage would roll by, for the one look at a face within, which, after all, was looked for in vain, for it lay, with closed eyes, buried in the cushions, and altogether hidden from view.

As he, who had so waited, passed under the young poet's windows on his way home to the Manager's house, Herr Wilberg was still in the enjoyment of undisturbed repose. That, however, did not prevent his feeling unutterably wretched on his awakening, and the whole week through he bore himself with an air of such profound melancholy, that Fräulein Mélanie, meeting him accidentally in the hall, could not help asking him compassionately what ailed him.

The unhappy lover was just in the humour to unburthen himself to this sympathising listener of his long-pent-up woe. He sighed several times; made a few vague allusions, and, of course, ended by pouring out his whole heart, to receive, equally, of course, a still warmer show of sympathy in return.

If the young lady had felt curious before, she was touched beyond all expression now. She thought the story beautifully romantic, and poor Wilberg worthy of her sincerest pity. It was, therefore, in no way disconcerting to her when, at the end of all these disclosures and comfortings, he seized her hand and imprinted on it a grateful kiss. There could not be the slightest danger that he would ever love another!

And now the master of the house broke in on this touching scene with all the prose of his paternal authority, and demanded to be told why these outpourings of the heart took place in the hall, and not upstairs in the drawing-room, where her mamma's presence would naturally have acted as a restraint upon them. Herr Wilberg, feeling that a great wrong was being done to him, shook himself together and managed to explain.

"I have a commission from Herr Berkow."

"Oh, that is different. Mélanie, go upstairs; you hear it is a business matter."

Mélanie obeyed, while her father remained standing at the foot of the stairs, not inviting his visitor up as usual. The latter was therefore obliged to discharge his errand on the spot.

"All right," said the chief-engineer calmly. "The plans in question are at Herr Berkow's disposal; I will take them up to him. And now, Herr Wilberg, a word with you. In spite of our mutual antipathy, I have always done you full justice." Herr Wilberg bowed. "I look upon you as a capable official." Herr Wilberg bowed again. "But I consider that you are a little crazy."

The young man, just in the act of bowing for the third time, started up suddenly erect and stared at his interlocutor in speechless amazement; the other went on imperturbably:

"With regard to your mania for scribbling, I mean. That is no business of mine, you would say? I should hope it is not. You have alternately sung the praises of Hartmann, of her ladyship, and of Herr Berkow. You are quite at liberty to do that, if it pleases you; but don't take it into your head to sing about my Mélanie. That I forbid. I won't have such nonsense put into the child's head. If your poetical feelings are in want of a fresh object, take me or the Director; we are quite at your service."

"I think I shall decline that," said Wilberg, highly affronted.

"As you like; but remember, my daughter is not to be trifled with. If ever a poem 'To Mélanie,' falls into my hands, I shall be down upon your iambics and your alexandrines, or whatever the nonsense is called. That was what I had to say to you. Good-bye."

With that this ruthless personage turned his back on the poet, whose finest susceptibilities he had so cruelly wounded, and walked upstairs. In the sitting-room his daughter met him.

"O papa, how could you be so hard and so unjust to that poor Herr Wilberg? He is so miserable."

The chief-engineer laughed out loud.

"Miserable! He? He is a miserable scribbler, that is what he is, always stringing abominable verses together; and the more one tries to make him understand it, the more madly he insists upon rushing into rhyme. As to that kiss"----

"Good gracious, papa! you are entirely mistaken," interrupted Mélanie, very decidedly. "It was only out of gratitude. He is in love with Lady Eugénie Berkow, and has been, quite hopelessly, of course, ever since she was married. It is natural he should feel wretched, and that her going away should drive him to despair."

"Oh, so it was his wretchedness and despair which made him kiss your hand. Odd, very. But how do you know all this, Mélanie? You seem very well informed about this fair-haired minstrel's love affairs."

The young lady raised her head with an unmistakable air of self-complacency.

"I am his confidant. He has poured out his whole heart to me. I tried to comfort him, but he will not be comforted; he is far too miserable for that."

"Here is a pretty story!" cried the chief-engineer, highly incensed. "So it has gone as far as that already, has it? Outpourings of the heart and attempts at consolation! I should not have thought that Wilberg was so clever. He, who speculates on the pity of you women, is pretty sure to--but we will put a stop to the thing at once. In future, you will be so good as not to listen to such confidential communications. They are most improper. As for the consolation business, I forbid it, once for all. I will take good care that he does not set his foot in the house again, so there's an end of it!"

Mélanie turned away, pouting. Her papa showed no great knowledge of mankind when he fancied that, with his dictatorial fiat, he had really put an end to the matter and laid the spectre, which had suddenly risen up before him in the guise of a verse-making, guitar-playing son-in-law. He ought to have known that, now for the first time, Fräulein Mélanie would seriously resolve upon offering any consolation in her power to the poor misunderstood Wilberg, whenever an opportunity of doing so should occur, and that Herr Wilberg would that very evening sit down to compose a poem "To Mélanie." Such matters are not settled by the mere words, "It is not to be, so there's an end of it."

CHAPTER XXI

The day was drawing to a close. The sun, as it went down, broke through the gathering clouds once more with a bright crimson glow which flooded woods and hills with a brief transitory splendour. Only for a few minutes; then the great red ball of fire sank slowly below the horizon, and with it disappeared all the brilliancy and colour which it had lent the earth for one fleeting moment.

Arthur Berkow had just opened the iron gate which gave egress from the park, and stepped outside. There he stood still, arrested by the sight before him, and gazed long and sadly at the departing sun. His countenance bore the expression of that perfect calm for which he had so striven, but it was not the confident calm of a man who, having victoriously thrown off one weakness, girds himself up for fresh endeavours.

He who stays behind on a sinking ship, and sees disappear in the distance the boat which is bearing all he prizes on earth away to safety and the far-off coast, while the ship itself drives helplessly nearer and nearer the rocks on which it must inevitably perish, such a one may hold out with unflinching courage, but he can be light-hearted no more. When the last hope has fled, there comes a great hush. He is able and ready then to meet the worst; and it was this stillness which lay on Arthur's features. He had dreamt his dream, and the days at hand were such as to require a full and complete awakening.

He crossed the meadow, and took the direction leading to the officials' dwelling-houses. The broad ditch, full of water, which ran along the upper end of the park, passed through this meadow-land; but, in place of the graceful little bridge which spanned it higher up, there was here only a simple plank, strong and safe enough, but so narrow as only to afford room for one passenger at a time. Arthur stepped on to it quickly, and had advanced a few steps, when he came suddenly to a stand before Ulric Hartmann, who appeared to recognise him at the same moment. Berkow stood still, supposing that the Deputy would retreat and allow him to pass; but the latter thought possibly the time had now arrived for that provocation to which the chief-engineer had alluded. Whether he really were trying to force on a conflict, or only obeying the instincts of his own rebellious nature, he stood motionless, and made no sign of giving way.

"Well, Hartmann, are we going to stand still like this?" said Arthur quietly, after he had waited a few seconds in vain. "The plank is too narrow for us both; one of us must go back."

"Must I be the one?" asked Ulric, sharply.

"I should think so."

Hartmann was about to answer in an aggressive spirit, but all at once a reflection struck him.

"Well, yes, we are upon your ground; I have forgotten that."

He went back, and let his employer cross over. Arthur stopped when he reached the opposite side.

"Hartmann!"

Ulric, who had already one foot on the plank, turned round at this address.

"I should have sent for you before this, if I had not feared my doing so might be wrongly interpreted. As we have met, I should like to speak to you."

A gleam of triumph shot over the other's face; but it passed quickly, and his features re-assumed the reserved look which was habitual to them.

"Here in the meadow?"

"The place does not signify; we are alone here."

Ulric approached slowly, and placed himself opposite his employer, who was leaning against one of the willows which bordered the water-course. The evening mists were beginning to rise, and yonder over the forest, where the sun had lately set, the whole sky was suffused with a deep crimson after-glow.

They were a strange contrast, these two. The slender, almost delicate figure of the high-bred man with his pale face in complete repose, his dark earnest eyes, whence that light had now vanished which gave to them at times so inexplicable a charm, and the giant frame of the miner, carrying his fair curly head so proudly, whose gaze, full of fire and a sort of savage satisfaction, never swerved from his adversary's pale countenance. The instinct of jealousy taught him to see and mark that which was observed by no one else, and, if all the world maintained that Arthur Berkow had passed by his beautiful wife unmoved, that he had never felt the slightest interest in her, Ulric knew well that no man could remain indifferent who called such a woman as Eugénie Windeg his own, knew too all that the loss of such a woman implied, since that morning when he had stood under the pines, watching her carriage as it rolled away.

But, through all the pain of the separation, there rang a note of triumph. A wife who loves her husband does not leave him at a time when all around him is reeling and falling, yet she had gone, gone to the safe protection of her father and brothers, and left him alone exposed to all and everything. That must have struck home to him, to this proud Berkow, whom neither hatred nor menace, neither fear of violence or revolt, or even of ruin itself, could touch, and though he should succeed in deceiving all about him with that calm brow of his, yet he could not deceive his enemy. That blow had surely gone to his heart.

"I need not tell you now of all that has occurred of late," began Arthur; "you must be as well acquainted with it as I am, perhaps even better. The other works have followed your example; we are entering upon a lengthened conflict. Can you answer for your comrades?"

Ulric started at this question.

"How do you mean, Herr Berkow?"

"I mean, shall we be able to settle this business ourselves without foreign interference? On the other works they have found it impossible to do this. Up at the forges they have already sent a request for help from the town. You are no stranger to the tumults there, and you best know whether this were necessary or not. I should assuredly only have recourse to such a measure in a case of extreme need, and in legitimate self-defence. But such a case may arise. Already several of my agents have been insulted, I myself was within an ace of meeting with insult in the woods. Do not build upon my patience or upon my weakness. However much I may desire to avoid all extreme measures, I warn you I shall oppose force to force."

At the first words Ulric had looked up in surprise. He had expected something other than this declaration, but the quiet manner in which it was made took from it all aggressive action and imposed a moderate tone on him, the adversary. There was but a slight scoff in his voice as he answered,

"That is nothing new to me. Force to force! I knew from the first we should come to that some day."

Arthur looked steadily at him.

"And whose fault is it, if we must come to that? Is it brought about by the resistance of the masses or by the obstinacy of one man?"

"By the obstinacy of one man, you are right there, Herr Berkow. You know it needs only one single word from you for us all to be at work again to-morrow."

"And you know that I cannot speak the word, because it involves that which is impossible. It is for you to concede something now. I propose it to you once again."

"Really?" said the miner, with an outburst of scorn. "No doubt, because the whole province is astir, and we have got our mates to help and back us."

Berkow drew himself up quickly, and his eyes flashed.

"Because we shall have to restore by force of arms that order and discipline you are now trampling under foot, and because I wish, if it be possible, to save my people from such a fate. Lay aside your scorn, Hartmann, you do not believe in it yourself. Whatever has happened, or may yet happen between us two, we may, I think, mutually absolve each other of cowardice."

Again there came the look and tone which had struck all dumb with astonishment that day in the committee-room. Ulric looked with mingled wrath and admiration at his employer, who dared so to speak to him at an hour like the present. The scene in the forest must have shown him what the possible consequences of these chance meetings might be, and yet he had himself sought an interview in this solitary place.

The park was quite empty; there was not a soul in sight across the fields, and the houses lay at some considerable distance. Not one of the officials would, under such circumstances, have stopped to hold converse with the dreaded Hartmann, no, not even the bold chief-engineer. It was only the once despised "milksop" who was ready so to face danger. Truly, his enemy had absolved him of cowardice long ago.

Arthur seemed conscious of the advantage he had gained. He came a step nearer.

"Can you not see, Hartmann, that with such behaviour as this you are making your future stay here quite impossible?" he asked gravely. "You think, perhaps, that when we come to negotiate, your friends will put pressure upon me. I shall yield to no constraint, I give you my word. Nevertheless, I can and do appreciate your valuable powers, misguided as they are. So far, they have been used to my injury alone, but, for that very reason, I can better estimate the services they might render, should you one day cease to be hostile to me. Listen now to the voice of reason. Be satisfied with the practical concessions you have obtained, and, of my own free will, I offer you to remain on the works with the usual chances of promotion. I know there is a certain risk in retaining an element of discord like yourself among my hands, but I am willing to run the risk, if my trust in you meets with similar confidence."

The offer in itself was somewhat hazardous perhaps, made, as it was, to a man who looked on all moderation as a proof of weakness. Berkow, however, had not altogether miscalculated his aim. Ulric did not answer, but, for a nature like his, it was much that the proposal was not at once repulsed with harsh distrust.

"So far I have asked for confidence in vain," continued Arthur. "Up to this time you have refused to trust me. I came here as a stranger, if not to the place itself, to you at least and to all that concerns the works. You met me with a declaration of war, without even inquiring what alterations and improvements I might be willing to make. You received and treated me as an enemy, and yet you could not know whether I were your enemy at heart or not."

"We are at war," said Ulric curtly. "Everything is fair at such times."

All around them as they stood blazed the reflection of the crimson sunset, and Arthur's face, as he raised it, was tinted with the bright warm colour.

"Must there be war between us? I do not mean the present strife, which must come to an end sooner or later. I mean that secret embittered warfare which hard treatment and oppression on the one side, and rancour and hatred on the other, feed and foster continually. It has been so all these years, I know, and it will be so again, if you submit only through compulsion. We ought to make peace before there is blood shed on either side. We can still do it. As yet, nothing has happened to make the breach irreparable; in a few days it may be too late."

With all its quietness there was something in the young master's voice which went home to the hearer's heart, and the emotion visible in Hartmann's face showed that he had not been insensible to it. Accustomed to rule over his equals, he was the more keenly alive to any supercilious treatment on the part of his superiors, and also to any evidence of an ill-concealed fear.

Now he found himself raised to a position which had never yet been assigned him. He knew well that Arthur would not have so spoken to any other of the men employed, perhaps not to any of the officials; he felt it was solely due to his own personal qualities that he was dealt with thus. The owner of the works spoke to him as man to man, on a matter upon which the ill or well being of both depended, and he would surely have carried the day had he been any other than Arthur Berkow. Ulric's nature was too untrained, too passionate, for him to do justice there where his hate was fully roused.

"Our confidence has cost us dearly," said he bitterly. "Your father made such a claim upon it during all those long years that we have none left now for his son. I believe you don't make the offer out of fear, Herr Berkow, I should not believe it of any one else, but I do of you. But, as we have set about helping ourselves, I think we had better fight it out to the last. Let it be decided this way or that. One of us must win in the end."

"And your comrades? Will you take upon yourself the responsibility of all the care, the want, the chances of defeat, which this 'fighting it out' may bring with it?"

"I can't help it. It is done for their sake."

"No, it is not done for their sake," said Arthur firmly; "but for the sake of their leader's ambition. He wishes to get the domination over them into his hands, and, were he to get it, he would prove a worse despot than their former masters ever were. If you still have faith left in your so-called mission, Hartmann, you can no longer impose on me with it; for I see that you throw aside as worthless all that I declare myself ready to do for the improvement of the people's condition, and you keep steadily the one aim and end in view, the true bearing of which I understand but too well. You wish to make me and my agents powerless for the future, helpless in face of any resolution you may be pleased to adopt, or any insurrection you may stir up. Now that you speak in the name of the masses, blindly obedient to your dictates, you wish to arrogate to yourself all the rights of a master, and, with the empty title, leave me nothing but the onus of the position. You do not wish for a recognition of your party; you wish for a subjugation of every other. That is why you stake all upon a throw, and, believe me, you will lose it."

This was a bold speech to be addressed to such a man; it stung Ulric to fury.

"Well, as you seem to know so much about it, Herr Berkow, you may know more for all I care! You are right. This is not a question of higher wages or of a trifle more safety in the mines. That may be enough for those who concern themselves only about their wives and children, and think of nothing else all their lives long; the men of spirit among us require more. We want to have the reins in our hands, to have our rights as equals acknowledged and respected. It may be a hard lesson to learn for those who have had unlimited authority up to this time, but they will have now to treat with us. We have begun to understand at last that it is we who toil and you who enjoy the fruits of our labour. You have made use of our arms for this slavish work long enough, now you shall learn to feel them."

He hurled forth these words with exceeding violence, as though each of them were a weapon with which he would strike down and slay his enemy. All his outrageous passion burst forth anew, and the rage, which included an entire class, concentrated itself for the time being on the individual member of it now before him. As he stood there with clenched fists, the veins in his forehead swelling, he seemed ready to follow up his words with deeds.

Arthur, however, did not move a muscle or attempt to retreat by so much as a step from the dangerous neighbourhood. He stood in that attitude of cold, proud repose peculiar to him, and looked his adversary steadfastly in the face, as if by the power of his eyes alone he could fascinate and tame him.

"I think, for the present, you will have to leave the reins in hands which are accustomed and able to hold them. That also must be learnt. You may rise in rebellion and destroy existing institutions by brute force, but you will never create new ones with it. Try to conduct these works by the strength of your arms alone, to the exclusion of that powerful element you hate so much, which directs your labour, gives impulse to the machinery, and lends mind to your work. As yet this guiding faculty belongs to us. Keep to your own sphere and rank in life, and the equality of your rights will no longer be disputed. At present you can only throw into the balance the weight of numbers, and that will not suffice to give you the mastery."

Ulric tried to answer, but his voice was choked by passion. Arthur cast one look over at the forest where the red glow grew ever deeper and deeper; then he turned to go.

"If I could have foreseen that all conciliating words would be unavailing, I should not have sought this interview. I have offered to make peace with you and to let you remain on the works. Hardly any other man would have made such a sacrifice, and it cost me an effort before I could bring myself to do it. You have rejected my proposal with scorn and hatred. You will be my enemy. Well, be it so then, but the whole responsibility of what may now happen must lie with you. I have striven in vain to stem the torrent of disaster. Whatever may be the issue of the strife between us, you and I have done with each other for ever."

So saying, he turned his back on the miner and left him.

"Success to you," cried out Hartmann after him ironically, but Arthur did not appear to hear. He was already at some little distance, and now struck off into the road which led towards the houses.

Ulric remained behind. Above his head the willow-branches swayed to and fro in the evening breeze; over the meadows floated and curled a soft white vapour, and up yonder over the tops of the pines there came once more a weird blood-red flush which paled gradually until it faded completely away. As the Deputy gazed at the flaming sky, his own face caught a tinge of that sanguinary hue.

"'We have done with each other.' No, no, Arthur Berkow, we are only beginning now. I would not own to myself the cowardly feeling which held me back, but I dared not attack him whilst she was by his side. Now the way is open; now the time for a reckoning has come."

CHAPTER XXII

In the capital there reigned all the busy movement of a summer afternoon. A many-coloured ever-changing crowd thronged the main streets, promenaders, people intent on business, and artisans succeeding each other in one unbroken stream. All around unceasing noise and the endless roll of carriages, great clouds of dust rising on every side, and overhead the hot rays of the afternoon sun, already falling obliquely, and lighting up the whole scene.

From the windows of the Windeg mansion, situated in one of the principal streets, a young lady was looking down on the hurry and bustle below which had grown almost strange to her in the solitude of her mountain home.

Eugénie had returned to her father's house, and the short interval of her married life seemed effaced and forgotten. In the family circle it was rarely adverted to, and never except when some allusion to the approaching separation had to be made. The sons followed in this their father's example, and he kept silence on the subject at home, hoping thereby to stifle every painful remembrance.

At the same time he busied himself with those preliminary steps necessary before entering on the judicial proceedings of the divorce. Until this stage should be reached, the matter was not to be made public. The servants and those few acquaintances, who were still in town, knew no more than that the young wife had come on a visit to her family, in consequence of some disturbances on her husband's estates.

Eugénie occupied the rooms which had been hers before her marriage. Nothing in them had been altered, and when, as in former days, she stood at her favourite window, which opened on to a balcony, and looked out, all the old well-known objects met her sight; she might never have been away at all.

The last three months could be nothing more to her than an ugly dream, from which she had now awakened to the old freedom of her maidenhood, and to a freedom far more complete than any she had known before, for now there was no spectre of care haunting each step made by herself and those dearest to her. Every new day would no longer bring fresh humiliations and fresh sacrifices, each hour of the family life need no longer be poisoned by the fear of what might happen on the morrow, of possible disgrace, of ruin with all its fearful consequences. The noble old race of the Windegs could now come forward once more with all the prestige of wealth and power, for the Lord of Rabenau was rich enough, when all former losses were covered, to make a splendid provision for himself and all belonging to him.

There was indeed one shadow still on all this new-born sunshine, and it was caused by that plebeian name so detested by the Baron, and, at one time, by Eugénie.

But even this need only be a question of time. The beautiful talented girl had formerly met with many admirers of her own rank, who would sooner or later have become suitors for her hand, in spite of her father's embarrassed circumstances; indeed, any man wedding Eugénie Windeg might well forget that he would be taking home as his bride the daughter of a poor and debt-laden house. Then the elder Berkow had stepped in, had roughly interfered with all these plans and projects, and destined the prize to his own son. He was able to demand that which others must sue for, and he knew how to use his power. But now Eugénie would be free, and her father could afford to give her a brilliant dowry. He knew more than one among his peers who was ready, and not from interested motives alone, to take up again the thread which had been so rudely severed; and so, with the name, the last remembrance of that former marriage would vanish for ever, and, by a union of suitable rank, the young Baroness would be placed in a position equal, if not superior, to that assigned to her by birth. Then the last spot on the Windeg shield would be effaced, and it would shine out once more with undiminished lustre.

But the young wife hardly looked as calm and full of joyous hope as the advent of so much good fortune might have led one to expect. She had now been some weeks in her father's house, and yet the colour had not returned to her cheeks, and her mouth had not learnt to smile again.

Here, surrounded by all the love and care of her own people, she continued pale and silent as she had been by the side of the husband who had been forced upon her, and now, as she looked down on the crowds below, there was not one in all that varying multitude who had power to fix her attention for an instant. She gazed down on them with that far-off dreamy look which sees nothing near at hand, but is intent on some very different object in some far distant place. "In that city of yours one loses everything, even one's love of solitude and the woods." These words hardly seemed applicable here. Eugénie looked as if quite a painful longing for them had taken possession of her.

The Baron was in the habit of coming to his daughter's rooms for half an hour before going for his afternoon ride. He came in now with a graver face than usual and holding a paper in his hand.

"I must trouble you with some business matters to-day, my dear," he began, after a few words of greeting. "I have just had an interview with our solicitor, which has proved more satisfactory than we could have expected. The representative of the other side is empowered to meet all our wishes, and the two have come to an agreement as to the necessary steps to be taken. The whole affair will probably be settled much more quickly and easily than we had dared to hope. I must ask you to sign this paper, please."

He held out the document to her. Eugénie stretched out her hand to take it, and then suddenly drew it back again.

"I am to"----

"Just to put your name here underneath, nothing more," said the Baron calmly, laying the paper on a writing-table and pushing forward a chair. Eugénie hesitated.

"It is a deed, I see. Ought I not to read it over first?"

Windeg smiled.

"If it were an important document, we should have given it to you to read, of course, but it has reference only to the proceedings in divorce. The demand will be made for you by counsel, but your signature is required. It is a mere formality at the opening of the suit, the details will follow later. If you would like to hear how it sounds, I"----

"No, no," interrupted she, "it is not necessary. I will sign, but it need not be done at once. I am not in the humour for it now."

The Baron looked at her in astonishment.

"Humour? but you have only to sign your name. It will be done in a minute, and I have promised your counsel to let him have it this evening; he intends to present the petition to-morrow morning."

"Well then, I will bring it to you this evening signed. Only not now, I cannot do it now."

Windeg shook his head and looked displeased.

"This is a very strange whim, Eugénie, and I do not understand it at all. Why cannot you make this simple stroke of your pen now in my presence? However, if you insist upon it .... I shall expect that you will give it to me this evening at tea, there will still be time to send it off."

He did not notice that his daughter breathed a sigh of relief at these words. Going up to the window, he too looked down into the street.

"Will not Conrad come to me?" asked Eugénie, after a moment's pause. "I have not seen him yet except at dinner."

"He is very likely tired after his journey, and may be taking a little rest. Oh, there you are, Conrad, we were just speaking of you."

The young Baron, who came in at this moment, must have counted on finding his sister alone, for he said with evident and not altogether pleased surprise,

"You here, sir? They told me you were having an interview with the solicitor in the library."

"It is over, as you see."

Conrad seemed to wish it had lasted a little longer. He made no answer, but went up to his sister and sat down comfortably by her side. He had only come up from the country that day at noon.

A strange, and, in the Baron's sight, highly untoward chance had willed that the regiment to which his eldest son belonged should be quartered in the town nearest to the Berkow estates. Now, of all times, when the connection had so entirely ceased! An extension of leave for the young officer could not be thought of, as the rising of the miners throughout the neighbourhood had produced much agitation in the province, and riots were expected which might call for an intervention of the military, so Conrad must return very shortly to the garrison-town, where Berkow had, of course, many intimate acquaintances.

He had already received strict injunctions from his father not to mention the intended separation just at present. The Baron kept to his original tactics; he would present the world with an accomplished fact. For the rest, he fondly imagined, though he did not say so, that his son would avoid all personal contact with his whilom relative.

This supposition appeared to be correct; at least Arthur's name was never mentioned in the young officer's letters, and the existing state of things on his works only casually alluded to. Conrad had been sent to the capital on some matter relating to his service. There had been no opportunity as yet of talking freely; he had only been at home a few hours, and, at dinner, the presence of guests had imposed some restraint upon the family.

Now, however, the objectionable subject having once been introduced in reference to Eugénie's signature, the Baron inquired in a tone of the utmost indifference, as if asking for news of a very slight and distant acquaintance, how things were going on the Berkow estates.

"Badly, sir, very badly," said Conrad, turning to his father, but keeping his place at his sister's side. "Arthur fights like a man against the misfortunes which are assailing him on all sides, but I am afraid he will succumb to them at last. He has ten times more to battle against than the proprietors of the other works. All his father's sins, during twenty years of tyranny and oppression, are visited now upon him, and he has to suffer, too, for all the reckless speculations of later times. I cannot make out how he manages to struggle on. Any one else would have given way long ago."

"If the movement is growing too strong for him, I am surprised he does not call in military aid," said the Baron coldly.

"That is just it, but on this subject he won't listen to reason. For my part," cried the young heir of the Windegs, with the characteristic inconsiderateness of his class, "for my part, I would have shot down the fellows long ago, and have forced them to leave me in peace. They have given him cause enough, and if their ringleader goes on exciting them, as he is now doing day by day, they will be burning his house over his head soon. But it is all of no use, you may argue and pray. 'No, and once again no; so long as I can defend myself, no stranger shall set his foot on my works!'

"And to be frank with you, sir, they will be very pleased in the regiment if our help is not required; we have had to give it too often already during the last few weeks. At the other places round, things were not half so bad as at the Berkow mines, yet the first thing the owners did was to cry out for troops to protect them, and thereby place themselves on a war-footing with their own people.

"There have been some ugly scenes, and at such times, it is we who always have to bear the brunt. We are not to proceed with harshness, if it can be avoided, yet we are to make our authority respected, and the whole responsibility of whatever may happen falls upon us. So the Colonel and all the officers take it very kindly of Arthur that he has held out, and still persists in holding out, against his rebels by himself."

Eugénie listened to her brother with breathless attention. He seemed to look upon her as quite uninterested in the matter, and addressed himself solely to his father. The Baron, who had noticed with rising displeasure the constant recurrence of the word "Arthur," now said in a tone of chilling reproof:

"You and your comrades appear to be very well acquainted with all that goes on at Herr Berkow's works."

"The whole town is talking of it," declared Conrad, quite unmoved. "As for me, I certainly have been out there pretty often."

At this avowal his father gave a start of surprise.

"You have been out to see him, and that frequently?"

Perhaps the young man had observed the emotion which at his last words had become visible in Eugénie's face. He took her hand in his now and held it fast as he continued in the same careless way:

"Well, yes, sir. You told me not to talk about that business, you know, and it would have looked odd if I had ignored my brother-in-law altogether, especially situated as he now is. You did not forbid my going out there."

"Because I imagined your own sense of propriety would have forbidden it," said Windeg, highly incensed. "I took it as a matter of course that you would avoid that connection, instead of which you appear to have sought it, and that without writing one word on the subject to me. Really, Conrad, this is too bad!"

If he had told the whole truth, Conrad must have confessed that he had feared to receive a direct prohibition, and so had prudently abstained from all mention of his proceedings in his letters. In a general way he stood in proper awe of his father's frown, but to-day Eugénie's presence seemed to counterbalance its effect. He looked in her eyes, and what he saw there must have made the paternal reproaches easy to bear, for he even smiled as he answered quite unconcernedly,

"Well, I can't help it if I have taken such a liking to Arthur. You would have done the same in my place. I assure you he can be perfectly charming if he likes, only he is always so awfully grave. To tell the truth, his gravity suits him very well, though. I said to him yesterday, when I was coming away, 'If I had known from the first what you were, Arthur'"----

"Arthur!" interrupted his father, with his severest intonation.

The son tossed his head rather defiantly.

"Well yes, we call each other Arthur and Con, now, that is, I asked him to. I don't see why we should not, he is my brother-in-law."

"He is your brother-in-law no longer," said the Baron coldly, pointing to the table. "There lies our petition for a divorce."

Conrad glanced, not over tenderly, at the document in question.

"Oh, the petition. Has Eugénie signed it?"

"She is about to do so."

He looked at his sister. Her hand trembled in his, and her lips quivered as if she could with difficulty repress her agitation.

"Well, it seems to me, sir, that precisely with regard to this matter of the divorce, Arthur has behaved in a way to make all reproachful and bitter feeling towards him out of the question. It would be mean not to do him full justice now. I never should have thought it possible that a man could so shake off his languor and rouse himself to such energy as I see in him.

"All that he has been doing during the last few weeks, choosing always exactly the right time and place to make his action felt, all the horrible scenes and conflicts he has prevented, he alone in the midst of those rebellious masses by the mere force of his presence and personal influence--all that must be seen to be believed. He has become a regular hero. That the Colonel and all the officers say; in fact the whole town says so. The officials have behaved remarkably well, because he is always at their head.

"Not one among them has left the works, but when I came away, they seemed to have reached the extreme limits of endurance. The misfortune is, Arthur has taken it into his head that no stranger shall come between him and his people, and he is carrying out his resolution with rare consistency. I think, if it comes to the worst, he is capable of barricading himself and his staff up in the house and of making them all defend themselves to the last man, rather than call for help. It would be just like him!"

Here Eugénie pulled her hand out of her brother's; she got up quickly and went to the window.

The Baron rose also with an expression of the most lively displeasure.

"I really do not know, Conrad, how it is you answer a simple question about the state of things on Herr Berkow's estate by so exaggerated a panegyric of him. It shows a want of consideration for your sister which I should not have expected from you, for you have always professed to regard her with special affection. You will find yourself in an awkward position when the divorce proceedings become known. What figure you will then make with your eccentric admiration for this man, which you appear to have paraded before the whole garrison, I leave you to reflect. But now I beg this conversation may cease, you see how painfully Eugénie is affected by it. Pray come with me."

"Leave Conrad with me just a few minutes, papa," said his daughter; "I should like to ask him something."

The Baron shrugged his shoulders impatiently.

"Well, be so good then as not to touch upon this subject again, and so agitate yourself still more. In ten minutes the horses will be below, Conrad. I shall expect you to be there. Good-bye for the present, Eugénie."

The door had hardly closed upon him, when the young officer rushed up to his sister at the window, and threw his arm round her with rough but unmistakable tenderness.

"Are you angry too, Eugénie?" he asked, "was I really unfeeling?"

Eugénie looked at him with passionate eagerness. "You have seen Arthur, have spoken to him frequently, yesterday even, when you were coming away. Did he send no message by you, absolutely none?"

Conrad looked down. "He desired to be remembered to you and my father," said he, rather crestfallen.

"How? In what words?"

"He called after me when I was in the carriage, 'Remember me to the Baron and to your sister.'"

"And that was all?"

"That was all."

Eugénie turned away. She wished to hide from her brother the bitter disappointment which was written in her face, but Conrad held her fast. He had her own beautiful dark eyes, but with him their expression was bolder, more full of vivacity. At this moment, however, as he bent over her, all his thoughtless gaiety had vanished, and given place to a most unaccustomed earnestness.

"You must have wounded him cruelly at some time, Eugénie, and in a way he cannot get over. I would so gladly have brought you a line or a word at parting, but it was not to be had from him. He would never talk about you, but each time I mentioned your name he went deadly pale and turned away, and then dragged in another subject by the ears, so as not to hear any more, just exactly as you do when I speak to you about him. By Jove! there must be a regular hatred between you two?"

Eugénie tore herself free from him.

"Leave me, Con, for Heaven's sake! leave me, I can bear it no longer."

A look almost of triumph passed over the young man's face, and there was a ring of repressed joy in voice.

"Well, I don't want to intrude upon your secrets. I must go now, or my father will be getting impatient, he is in such an awful temper to-day. I shall leave you alone now, Eugénie; there is that divorce petition to be signed, you know. It will be ready, no doubt, by the time we come home. Good-bye."

He hurried off. The horses were standing before the door, and the Baron was looking impatiently up at the windows above. The ride was not a particularly agreeable one, for not only the eldest, but the two younger sons, soon felt the effects of their father's ill-humour. Baron Windeg could not endure that any one bearing the name of Berkow should, in his presence, be spoken of in terms of praise; and, as he naturally supposed his daughter to have the same feeling, he considered that an offence had been offered both to her and to himself.

Conrad had to bear many allusions to his "want of tact" and his "want of consideration." He let it all pass very quietly, however; on the other hand, he showed the most lively interest in the ride, or rather in the duration of it. It was so long since he had been in town; the drive on the outskirts was so animated and diverted him so much, that he contrived to spin out the expedition to a considerable length, and it was growing quite dark when the four returned to the city.

In the meantime Eugénie had remained alone. Her door was locked, she could endure no one near her now. The walls of her room and the old family portraits which adorned them, had witnessed many a fit of weeping, many a bitter struggle when the girl's marriage had been under discussion, but none so cruel as the present, for now the battle was with herself, and the enemy was not easy to conquer.

There upon the writing-table lay the paper by which a wife prayed to be judicially parted from her husband; only the signature was wanting. When once that was affixed the divorce would really be gained, for the consent of her husband and the Baron's influential connections assured to the affair a speedy and favourable issue. She had refused to make that all-important stroke of her pen, but it must be made now. What had the one hour availed? It would be all the same whether the inevitable step were taken sooner or later! But just then Conrad had come in with his story, and had torn open afresh the wounds which had not yet ceased to bleed.

And yet her brother had brought her no message, not even a word of greeting. "Remember me to the Baron and to your sister," that was all! Why not rather "to Lady Eugénie," that would have been colder still and more fitting. Eugénie went up to the writing-table, and her eyes wandered over the words of the document. There too all was cold and formal, though the fate of two people was decided by it. But Arthur had willed it so. He it was who had first spoken the word of separation, who first and unhesitatingly agreed to hasten it on; and, when she had gone to him and declared herself ready to stay, he had turned from her and bade her go. The blood rushed to her temple again, and she stretched out her hand to take the pen.

She was woman enough to know that this signature of hers would be a blow to him, although he must be in a great measure prepared for it. She had been able to interpret looks, and had been conscious of unguarded moments in which he had betrayed himself; but, that he had mastered his weakness to the very last moment, that he would not understand when she hinted to him of the possibility of a reconciliation, that he was peremptory to her as she had been to him, that he opposed his pride to hers--these were offences for which he must now suffer, even though the cost to herself should be tenfold greater.

The demon of pride rose up within her again in all its fatal strength. How often had it successfully held the field against all better feelings, not always for her own good or for that of others! But to-day another voice made itself heard as well. "Arthur is fighting like a man against the misfortunes which are awaiting him on all sides, but he will succumb to them at last."

And when he should so succumb, he would be alone, alone in his defeat as he had been in the battle. He had no friend, no confidant, not one. The officials might serve him devotedly, strangers might admire him; but there was no one to cleave to, no one to feel for him, and the wife, whose place was at his side, was at this moment signing the paper by which she prayed for a separation with the briefest possible delay from the husband whom she had already abandoned, and who was now struggling day by day against imminent ruin.

Eugénie let fall the pen and stepped back from the writing-table. After all, what had been Arthur's crime? He had shown himself indifferent to a wife who, as he believed, had married him solely with a view to his wealth. When she had convinced him of his error, she had added contemptuous words such as no man will bear if he has a spark of honour in him. Here, too, his father's sins had been visited on him, and he had abundantly suffered for them during his short married life.

Since that first conversation no further trouble had come to her, except that her husband had held back from her in distant coldness, but he--what had he not endured? Eugénie best knew what the three months had really been, which to those about them had presented only the superficial calm of indifference, and which had held stings sharp enough to irritate a man beyond endurance.

It is possible to wound with every look, with every breath, and this had been done. Looking down on him from the elevation of her rank and position, she had tried to crush him into that pitiful nothingness which, in her opinion, was his proper condition. Day by day she had used her weapons, all the more ruthlessly when she found he was vulnerable. She had made of his home a place of torment, of his marriage a curse, and all this that she might revenge herself on him for his father's unscrupulous treatment of her family. With fullest intent she had driven him so far that he himself had proposed a separation, because he could no longer endure life at her side. If, at last, he drew himself up and pushed aside the hand which had so racked and tortured him, whose was the fault?

She sprang up from the seat on which she had thrown herself, and began to pace up and down in terrible agitation as though trying to escape from herself. She knew well what she was trying to obtain from herself, whither her efforts were tending.

There was but one thing now which could help and save, but that was impossible, that could not be! If she were to make the sacrifice of all her pride, and the sacrifice were not accepted frankly and freely as it was offered? Might she not have been mistaken, have read those eyes amiss; they had never been unveiled for more than an instant, and then only reluctantly. If he were again to meet her with that same freezing look, asking her by what right she was doing that which would have been any other woman's simple duty? If he were again to say that he would stand or fall alone, if he were to bid her go once more? No, never! better the separation, better a whole life of misery and regret, than incur the possibility of such humiliation.

The departing sun, tipping the trees out yonder with gold, had long since set and twilight had fallen, but it brought no quiet or coolness to the heated overcrowded streets. Without, the sultry evening air was full of the same hum and stir; the stream of people still passed and repassed unceasingly, and the sound of voices and of the rattle of carriages was still borne up confusedly to the windows above.

But, through it all, another sound was heard, faint at first as a mere whisper, but growing ever nearer, ever more distinct. Had it been wafted over from those green forest-heights and made its way through the great busy thoroughfares of the city up to the young wife's ears? What it was she hardly knew; it was like the soughing of the wind in the pine branches, and, through it, echoed once more all the old forest music with its mysterious chords.

There came back to her vividly that first glimpse of spring, those bitter-sweet moments passed under the shelter of the friendly woods. The mists rose up around her again, the storm howled, and the brooks tumbled tumultuously down into the valleys below. Out of the thick grey mist one figure stood out clear and definite--the one figure which since that time had never left her sleeping or waking--and looked at her reproachfully with its great brown eyes.

He who has passed through such a crisis as this, when all the powers of the soul are concentrated on the resolution shaping itself within, may have known these rapid flashes of memory, may have seen again old scenes in their fullest details rising up before the mind's eye, without visible or external cause, but with a force irresistible.

Eugénie felt that the air around her was full of these memories, felt that, one after the other, the weapons were falling from her hands, until at last there remained only the magic influence of that hour when she had made the discovery that her hate was at an end, and that, in its place, something else was springing up, something against which she had striven, as it were, to the death, but to which she must now make surrender.

It was soon over, that last short struggle between the old demon of unbending pride, unable to forgive the repulse it had once met with, and the woman's heart telling her that she was loved, spite of all.

This time the forest voices had not spoken in vain. They gained the victory at last. The paper, which was to divide two people who had sworn to be one for ever, lay torn upon the ground, and the young wife was on her knees, raising her beautiful face, down which the hot tears were streaming, and sobbing,

"I cannot--I cannot do him and myself this wrong. It would strike home to us both. Come what may, Arthur, I will stay by you."

"Where is your sister?" asked the Baron, when, an hour later, he entered the lighted drawing-room and found his sons there alone. "Has not Lady Eugénie been told that we are waiting for her?" he continued, turning to the servant who had been preparing the tea-table, and was about to leave the room.

Conrad forestalled the answer.

"Eugénie is not at home." said he, signing to the man to go.

"Not at home!" repeated the Baron, in astonishment. "Has she driven out so late as this? Where can she have gone?"

Conrad shrugged his shoulders.

"I don't know. Directly I came in I ran up to her rooms. She was not there, but I found this lying on the floor."

He drew out a paper, and an odd little twitch played about his lips as, seemingly with the utmost gravity, he pieced the two halves neatly together and laid them before his father. The Baron looked down at them, but could make nothing of it.

"Why, that is the petition drawn out by the proctor, which I gave to Eugénie to sign! I will have the servants up. If she has really gone out, they must know where the carriage was to take her."

He laid his hand on the bell, but Conrad stopped him, and said very quietly:

"I think, sir, she must have gone to her husband."

"Are you out of your senses, Conrad?" cried the Baron. "Eugénie gone to her husband!"

"Well, I only fancy so. We shall soon know for a certainty, for I found this note on her writing-table addressed to you. I brought it down, it is sure to give us some information."

Windeg tore open the envelope. In his hurry, he did not notice that Conrad so far transgressed all etiquette as to go behind him and read over his shoulder. There could be no mistake now about the triumphant expression of the young officer's face. It was so evident, that the two younger brothers, who understood nothing of what was going on, looked first at him and then at their father with anxious and inquiring looks.

The note contained only a few lines.

"I am going to my husband. Forgive me, papa, for leaving so suddenly, so secretly. I will not lose an hour, and I do not wish to encounter your opposition; I must have withstood it, for my resolution is taken. Do nothing more in the matter of the divorce, and recall that which has been done already. I do not give my consent to it, I will not leave Arthur.

"Eugénie."

"Was such a thing ever heard of?" the Baron broke out, letting the note fall from his hands. "A daughter of mine dares to change her mind in this way and to make a clandestine flight from my house. She withdraws herself from my protection, destroys all my hopes and plans for her future, and goes back to this Berkow, who is on the very brink of ruin, goes back among all those miners in revolt, when the whole neighbourhood is in a state of anarchy. This verges on madness. What has happened? I demand to be told, but first this senseless plan must be frustrated, while there is yet time. I will go immediately" ...

"The express train to M—— left half-an-hour ago," interrupted Conrad, "and the carriage is just coming back from the station. It is too late now, any way."

At this moment the carriage, which had, no doubt, been used by Eugénie, was heard coming in at the gates. The Baron began to see that it was too late, and now the vials of his wrath were turned upon his son.

He reproached him with being the sole cause of all. With his ridiculous laudation of his brother-in-law, with his exaggerated accounts of the man's situation, he had stung Eugénie's conscience, until a morbid sense of duty had driven her to her husband's side, for no other reason than because he was unhappy; and when once she was there, who could tell whether a complete reconciliation might not come about, if Berkow were selfish enough to accept the offered sacrifice?

But Windeg swore by all that was dear to him, that he would carry through the divorce in spite of all. The thing was set on foot, it was in the hands of counsel, and Eugénie must and should be brought to reason. He, the Baron, "would see whether he could not use his authority as a father, although two of his children"--with a crushing glance at poor Conrad, who, for the nonce, was the only criminal at hand, "although two of his children appeared to disregard it altogether."

Conrad let the storm pass over his head, and spoke no syllable in his own defence; he knew from experience that it was the best way. He sat with drooping head and downcast eyes, as if he were a prey to the most unmitigated remorse for the thoughtlessness of his conduct and the evil it had wrought.

But when the Baron, still furious, left the room and went to shut himself up in his private apartments, there further to ponder and growl over this incredible business, the young lieutenant sprang up with a bound, the roguish expression of his handsome face and the sparkle in his eye telling plainly how little the paternal anger had gone to his heart.

"To-morrow morning Eugénie will be with her husband," said he to his brothers who now assailed him with questions and reproaches, "and my father may try to come between them with his lawyers and paternal authority as much as he pleases. Arthur will take good care of his wife when once he knows she belongs to him; he has not known it so far. As for us," here he cast a very meaning glance at the door by which his father had disappeared, "we shall have stormy weather for the next week. The worst is yet to come, when my father finds out how things really are between those two, and that something else is in question here than mere conscience and a sense of duty.

"One comfort is, Arthur will have sunshine; with it and Eugénie at his side he will win through, never fear. Thank goodness, there is an end of the divorce suit, courts of justice and counsel included, and if one of you has a word to say against my brother-in-law, let him say it to me. I'll answer him."

CHAPTER XXIII

Early in the forenoon of the following day a postchaise, travelling along the road from M----, came to a halt at the entrance of the valley where lay the Berkow works, the first outlying buildings of which were already to be seen quite close at hand.

"Don't do it, my lady," said the driver, speaking to some one inside the carriage.

"You had far better turn back with me as I begged you to do at the last station; I heard of it there, and the peasants we just met on the road told us of it again. There are battle and murder up on the works to-day. Quite early this morning the men were pouring in from all the villages around, and there is the devil to pay now out yonder. With the best will in the world, I can't take you up to the house. I should be risking my horses and the chaise too. When these fellows are once in revolt, they spare neither friend nor foe. Must you go up there just to-day? Could you not wait until to-morrow?"

The young lady, who was the sole occupant of the carriage, made no reply, but opened the door and stepped out.

"I cannot wait," said she gravely, "but I will not endanger you or your property. It is not more than a mile, I can easily go there on foot. You can turn back."

The driver renewed his warnings and remonstrances. It seemed very strange to him that this unknown and elegant lady, who had paid him so liberally, urging him at the same time to use the utmost speed, should now venture alone into the tumult. He obtained nothing from her, however, by his entreaties. She impatiently signed to him to turn back, and at last, shrugging his shoulders at her persistency, he made up his mind to obey.

Eugénie took a footpath which did not lead direct to the works, but ran across the meadows towards the upper entrance to the park, and where she would in all probability be safe. If it came to the worst, she would, at all events, find protection and an escort in one of the officials' dwelling-houses, which lay in that direction. How necessary both might be, she certainly had not known when, yielding to a sudden impulse, she had set out on this journey alone, and even now she did not understand the full extent of the peril to which her present expedition exposed her.

It was not the possibility of danger which brought that heightened colour to her cheeks, that restless sparkle to her eye, which made her heart beat so violently that she was forced to stop every now and then to take breath. It was the fear she felt of the coming decision. That heavy dream-like feeling, which had come upon her on leaving her husband's home, had hung about her during all the weeks of the separation.

Neither the old home, nor her people's love, nor the bright and happy prospects opening out before them all, had sufficed to rouse her. That dreamy sense of unreality had clung to her with painful oppressiveness and with many a vague longing. Now the awakening had come, and all her thoughts were bent on the one question.

"How would he receive her?"

She had just reached a small solitary house, forming, as it were, the extreme outposts of the works, when she saw a man hurrying towards her. He started with·a look of terror as he recognised her.

"My lady! For Heaven's sake, how did you come here, and to-day of all days?"

"Oh, Manager Hartmann, is it you?" said Eugénie, going up to him. "Thank God I have met you! Troubles have broken out on the works, I hear. I had to leave my carriage out yonder, the driver dared not bring me on. I am going on foot up to the house."

The Manager shook his head, and replied hastily:

"You cannot, my lady, you cannot go up now. To-morrow perhaps, or perhaps towards evening, but not now."

"Why not?" cried Eugénie, turning very pale. "Is our house threatened? Is my husband" ...

"No, no, Herr Berkow is not mixed up in it today. He is up at the house with all the officials. This time the trouble is among themselves. Some of the men wanted to take to their work again this morning, and my son" ....

Here the old man's face worked with agitation.

"Well! you must know it before long! My son was furious about it. He and his party have driven them back, and set a guard round the shafts. The others won't put up with that, and now they are banding themselves together. The whole works are in revolt, every man against his neighbour. Merciful goodness! what will happen next?" cried the Manager, as, in spite of the distance, rumours of the wild clamour and uproar were borne distinctly over to them.

"But I intended to avoid the works," urged Eugénie. "I was going to try and gain the park by the path across the meadows, and so on to" ....

"For Heaven's sake, don't go there!" interrupted the old man. "Ulric and all his followers are holding a meeting out in the meadow yonder. I was on my way to try once more if I could not make him listen to reason, and induce him, at all events, to set the shafts free. We are going against our own flesh and blood now, but he has neither eyes nor ears for anything in his fury. Not that way, my lady, it is the most dangerous of all."

"I must go up to the house," Eugénie declared resolutely. "I must go, cost what it may. Come with me, Hartmann, only as far as the houses. In case of the worst, I can stay there until the road is clear again. At your side I shall be secure at least from open violence."

The old man shook his head sadly.

"I cannot help you, my lady. Now that we are all in arms, one against the other, my own life is hardly safe in the midst of this strife and turmoil, and if once they get to know who you are, my being at your side would be of very little use. There is only one man now they feel any respect for, who can make himself obeyed in case of need, and that is my Ulric. But he hates Herr Berkow mortally, and he hates you too because you are the master's wife. Good God!" broke off the old man suddenly, "here he comes! There has been mischief doing again, I can see it in his face. Go out of his sight just for the present, I implore you."

He pushed her through the half-opened door of the little cottage, and he had hardly done so, when steps and loud voices were heard approaching. Ulric was coming up the road followed by Lawrence and several other miners. His face was crimson, and on his brow lay a thunder-cloud ready at any moment to explode. He was talking excitedly as he came along, and he did not notice his father's presence.

"If they are our mates and our brothers, no matter! Down with them directly they turn traitors to us. We gave our word to stand by each other, and now they crawl up to the old collar like cowards and desert us and our cause. They shall be made to pay for it. Are the shafts well guarded?"

"Yes, but" ...

"I'll have no buts," cried the leader imperiously to the man who would have ventured to hazard an objection. "That was about the one thing wanting, treason in our own camp, just as we are on the eve of victory. They shall be driven back by force, I tell you, if they make the least attempt to go below. We will teach them their duty and their proper place, if they have to learn it at the cost of a few broken heads."

"But there are two hundred of them," said Lawrence gravely, "and to-morrow there may be four--and, if once the master steps in and begins to talk to them--you know how that tells! We have seen it often enough of late."

"If there were four hundred," shouted Ulric, "if half our people were on their side, we would fight them with the other half and beat them too. I'll see if I can't make myself obeyed! But now, forward, lads. Karl, you go over to the works and bring me word if Berkow is meddling in the matter and talking to the men in that cursed way of his, getting hundreds to desert from us again. You others, back to the shafts. See that the way to them is thoroughly blocked, I will come myself presently. Off with you!"

His command was at once obeyed. The miners hurried off in the prescribed directions, and Ulric, seeing now for the first time that his father was standing by, hurried up to him and said,

"You here, father? Why, you ought to be"----all at once he stopped, rooted to the ground; his face grew deadly white, every drop of blood slowly receding from it, and his eyes were fixed and dilated as though he had seen a ghost. Eugénie had come out of the house and was standing before him.

A sudden thought had flashed into the young wife's mind, and instantly she acted on it without staying to reflect on the boldness and the peril of her venture. She was bent on going to her husband at any cost, and now she must overcome the horror with which this man had inspired her ever since she had discovered the true reason of her power over him. She had often put this power to the proof; now the time had come to turn it to account.

"It is I, Hartmann," said she, mastering an involuntary shudder and appearing before him calm and composed. "Your father was just warning me not to go on my way alone, and yet I must go on."

At the sound of her voice, Ulric seemed first to realise that it was actually Eugénie Berkow who stood before him, and no mere vision of his heated fancy. He would have rushed up to her, but that look and tone still kept their old influence over him. As he listened, a calmer and milder expression came over his face.

"What are you doing here, my lady?" he asked uneasily, his rough imperious manner softening into one that was almost gentle. "There is ill work among us to-day, which is not for women to see, least of all for you. You must not stay here."

"I want to go to my husband," said Eugénie quickly.

Formerly she had almost invariably spoken of Arthur as "Heir Berkow;" now she called him her husband, in a tone which seemed to make Ulric understand all that was implied in that one word.

In the first moment of his surprise he had not reflected how or why she had come there so suddenly; now he glanced quickly, first at her travelling dress, and then around, as though in quest of her carriage and attendants.

"I am alone," said Eugénie, catching this glance, "and it is that which prevents my going on. I am not afraid of any actual danger, but of the insults I might be exposed to. You offered me your escort and protection once, Hartmann, when I did not need them. Now I mean to make a claim on both. Lead me over to the house. You can, if you will."

The Manager had stood by, anxiously looking on, expecting that at any moment his son might attack the wife of a master he so hated, and ready to rush in between them. He could not understand Eugénie's tone of quiet assurance towards a man whom she, like every one else, must know to be the real instigator of the whole rebellion. Now as she made this request wishing to entrust herself to the rebel leader's safe keeping, the old man's bewilderment knew no bounds. He looked at her in horrified amazement.

As to Ulric, he was roused to violent anger by the demand made upon him. That milder gleam had vanished, and the old imperious defiance had come back to him.

"I am to lead you over?" he said in a low hoarse voice. "And you ask that of me, my lady, of me?"

"I ask it of you." Eugénie kept her eyes steadily fixed on his face, feeling that so her power over him would be greater. It seemed now, however, to have reached its limits. He burst out like a madman.

"Never, never! I would rather see the house stormed, see it pulled to the ground, than take you there again. What? he up yonder is to have you at his side again, so that he shall take courage and resist to the last? He is to have the triumph of knowing that you have come away from the city by yourself and made your way through the whole place in revolt, just that he should not be left alone? But you may look for another guide for that, and if you find one"--with a threatening look at his father--"he shall not go far with you, I'll take care of that."

"Ulric, control yourself, you are speaking to a lady!" cried the Manager, stepping between them in mortal fear. He naturally saw nothing in this scene but an outbreak of that unrestrained enmity which his son had long cherished towards the whole Berkow family, and he took up a position before his master's wife, determined, come what might, to protect and shield her. She pressed by him, however, gently but resolutely.

"So you will not go with me, Hartmann?"

"No, a hundred times, no."

"Well then, I shall go alone."

She turned away in the direction of the park, but with two strides Ulric reached her and placed himself before her, barring the road.

"Back, my lady, you can't get through, I tell you, least of all, this way where my men are. Lady or not, it is all the same to them now. Your name is Berkow, and that is enough. As soon as they find out who you are, you will have them all upon you. You cannot and shall not go over there now. Stay here where you are."

These last words were spoken imperatively and in a tone of menace, but Eugénie was not accustomed to submit to orders, and the almost delirious violence with which he was striving to keep her from Arthur called up in her a vague anxiety and dread lest things should be worse with him than she had been led to believe.

"I shall go to my husband," she repeated very resolutely, "and I shall see whether on my way to him any one dares stop me by force. Let your friends assault a woman, give the signal for it yourself, if you care to take the credit of the heroic deed. I shall go."

And she went; darting by him and taking the path which led across the fields.

Hartmann stood gazing after her with eyes which glowed again, paying no heed to his father's prayers and remonstrances. He understood better than the old man what she intended by this venture, what she wished to compel him to. But this time he would not yield to her. She might perish on the threshold of her own house, in sight of her husband, before he would take her back to the arms of a man he hated, before he ...

At this moment a troop of miners made their appearance, excited and uproarious, coming from the place of meeting to rejoin their leader. The foremost of them was only some hundred paces off. They had already noticed the solitary female figure before them; in another minute she would be recognised, and he himself had, but half-an-hour ago, been goading on these men to blind fury against all that bore the name of Berkow.

Eugénie went forward to meet the danger, not attempting even to conceal her face. In his desperation Ulric stamped on the ground; then he tore himself free from his father, and in an instant was at her side.

"Put down your veil," he said, and grasped her hand with an iron grasp.

Eugénie obeyed, drawing a deep breath of relief. She was safe now; she knew he would not loose his hold on her hand again, if all the men on the works were to attack them at once. She had gone on deliberately to meet the danger, with full consciousness of what she was doing, but also with the conviction that nothing short of her visible and imminent peril would win for her that protection which had been refused.

They now came up to the troop of insurgents, who at once attempted to throng round their leader so as to place him in their midst, but he briefly and emphatically bade them make way, and ordered them over to the shafts without loss of time. They obeyed at once as their comrades had done previously, and Ulric, who had not halted for so much as a second, drew his companion on more rapidly than ever. She began to see plainly how impossible it would have been for her to force a passage through by herself, and how idle any other protection would have proved than that which was at her side.

This stretch of meadow-land, usually so peaceful, was to-day the scene of busy surging tumult, although the actual strife was confined to the neighbourhood of the shafts. Knots of miners were trooping about, or standing closely grouped together in noisy conference. Everywhere angry faces and threatening gestures were to be seen, everywhere turmoil and confusion reigned paramount, an object only seemed wanting for them to give vent to their wild excitement by some deed of violence.

Happily, the footpath skirted the edge of the fields where the tumult was relatively less, but even here Ulric no sooner showed himself than he became the centre of observation, and was greeted everywhere with loud shouts, in which there mingled a certain note of surprise. A host of astonished, distrustful, suspicious glances were levelled at the female figure by his side. No one guessed that, attired in that dark travelling-dress and thick veil, the master's wife was passing through their midst. Had any one fancied he recognised her gait and bearing, such a notion would have been scouted by the others.

Ulric Hartmann was protecting her, and he would most surely never have accorded his protection to any one connected with the house of Berkow; still it was a lady who was walking with him, the Manager's rough, uncourteous son, though he cared nothing for women generally, not even for Martha Ewers, who was cared for, in some degree, by almost every unmarried man in the place.

Ulric, who, at a time like the present, looked upon and treated his comrades' wives as an unnecessary burthen to be shaken off as much as possible, Ulric was now playing the guide to this stranger, and there was a look on his face as though he would strike down any one who ventured a step too near her. That short walk, which lasted barely ten minutes in all, was a bold experiment even for the young leader himself, but he showed that here, at least, he was master, and that he knew how to make use of his power.

Now, by a few imperious words, he dissolved a group which stood in his way; now, again, he issued orders and instructions to a troop of miners bearing down upon him, which took them off in another direction; to those who would have pressed round with questions and reports of what was going on he cried,

"By and by, I am coming back!" and all the time he never lost a moment, but drew his companion swiftly on, so as to prevent discovery or delay.

At last they reached the park, closed at this spot by a wooden gate only. Ulric pushed it open, and stepped inside with her under the sheltering trees.

"That is enough," he said, letting go her hand. "The park is safe still, and in five minutes you will be at the house."

Eugénie was still trembling at the danger they had passed through, and her hand ached from the iron pressure of his. She put back her veil slowly.

"Make haste," said he with bitter sarcasm. "I have honestly done my part towards helping you back to your husband. You will not keep him waiting now?"

Eugénie looked up at him. His face betrayed the torture she had inflicted, by placing before him the alternative of witnessing an attack upon her, or of himself leading her to her husband.

She had no courage to thank him, but she put out her hand in silence.

Ulric pushed it away.

"You asked much of me," he said. "So much that it was within a hair of miscarrying. Now you have your will. Do not attempt to compel me again as you did to-day, especially when he is by; for, if you do, I swear I will give you both up to your fate."

On the terrace before the house stood the two servants, Frank and Anthony, gazing over in the direction of the works with anxious yet curious looks. They started back no less affrighted than the old Manager had been, for, without the sound of carriage wheels to announce her coming, and unattended even by her maid, they suddenly saw standing before them their mistress, whom they supposed to be far away in the distant capital.

She could not possibly have come through the works, still less by way of the park, for out on the meadows at the back things were even worse--yet she was there! They were both so confounded, they could hardly answer her hasty question, but she managed to find out that Herr Berkow was at that moment at home, and hurried past them up the steps.

Frank, who followed her, had even more ground for astonishment, for she hardly allowed him to take her hat and shawl, and, when he would have hastened with the news of her arrival over to the wing occupied by his master, she bade him stay, and said she would go and announce herself. The man stood with the cloak in his hand, staring after her with open mouth. It had all passed like a whirlwind. What could have happened in the city?

Eugénie passed rapidly through the several rooms in succession, until all at once she stopped. Arthur's study was near at hand, and from it the sound of voices met her ear. She had so surely reckoned on finding her husband alone, had wished to come to him thus unexpected, unannounced, and now she found him in the company of a stranger!

Ah! she could not meet him in the presence of another! Eugénie stood undecided whether to stand back or to remain. At last she stepped noiselessly behind the heavy portière, the folds of which almost hid her from view.

"It is impossible, Herr Berkow," said the sharp clear voice of the chief-engineer, "If you push forbearance further, you will do it to the injury of those who are beginning to take to their work in an orderly manner. They beat a retreat on this occasion, because they were the weaker, but we shall have worse and bloodier scenes than what took place this morning. That was only a hand-to-hand skirmish. Hartmann has shown that he will not spare his own people if they rebel against his system of terrorism. Friend and foe may suffer alike, but his principles must be upheld."

Eugénie could see through the open door into the room. Just opposite her at the open window stood Arthur, the full light falling upon his face, which had grown so much more sombre since last she had seen it. Even then the shadow of care had lain on his brow; at that time, however, it had been new to him and had not marked itself there indelibly, but now two deep furrows were graven which probably would never again be effaced.

Each separate line in his face was sharper, more severely defined; the look of energy, which then had but newly dawned and was only distinctly visible in moments of excitement, had now become the dominant expression of his countenance even when at rest, and had altogether replaced the old dreamy air; his voice and manner were alike firm and decided. It was evident that he had learned in a few weeks that which it takes others years to acquire.

"I should certainly be the last to advise seeking help from without, if it could be avoided, but I do think that now we, and you in particular, have abstained from it long enough. There really can be no blame to us if, at length, we have recourse to measures which were employed on the neighbouring works long ago without any such pressing necessity as ours."

Arthur shook his head sadly.

"The other works can be no rule for us. A few arrests, a few slight wounds, and matters were settled there. Fifty men and three or four shots in the air were sufficient to quell the whole revolt. Here they have Hartmann at their head, and we all know what that means. He would not yield to a bayonet charge, and all his party are ready to stand or fall with him. They would challenge us to do our worst, and, to buy peace, we must sacrifice some lives."

The other was silent, but his significant shrug showed that he was of the same opinion.

"But if peace is to be had in no other way?"

"If it were to be had at all! but it is not, and the sacrifice of life will be made in vain. I can crush the rebellion for the time being, but in a year, in a few months perhaps, it will break out again, and you know as well as I do that the last chance of keeping on the works would be gone from me then. Elsewhere there are some signs of returning confidence and of a juster feeling; elsewhere the people seem to be coming to their senses again, but that is not to be hoped with us. The distrust sown during long years cannot be speedily overcome. Hatred and hostility was the watchword given out against me when I came here; it is the watchword still, and, if once I cause blood to be shed, all will be over for ever between us."

"Hartmann may venture to bring his recusant followers back to obedience by open combat and to impose his will on them by force, he will still remain their Messiah to whom they look for salvation. If I were to order one shot to be fired, if I take up arms in my own defence, I shall be called a tyrant, ready to murder them in cold blood, and taking delight in their destruction. The old Manager was right that day, when he said: 'If troubles break out here among our people, the Lord have mercy upon us!'"

There was no complaint, no dispirited lament in these words, only the bitterness of a man who finds himself at length borne to the very verge of that precipice to avoid which he has in vain been straining every nerve.

Probably the young master would have so spoken to no other. The chief-engineer was the only person who seemed to have drawn nearer him of late. He had stood by him so steadfastly through all the danger, helping so actively to carry out all the necessary measures, and he was the only one to whom Arthur would occasionally speak freely, passing beyond the mere instructions and encouraging speeches which were all the other officials ever heard from his lips.

"But some of the hands are willing to take to work again already," objected the elder man.

"And that is just what compels me to make war on the rest. There is no making terms with Hartmann. I have tried to do so and failed."

"With whom? You have tried what?" asked the other, with such a horrified expression that Arthur looked at him in surprise.

"To come to an understanding with Hartmann. It was not done officially, it is true, that might have been interpreted as a sign of weakness. It was when we met one day accidentally that I held out my hand to him once again."

"You should not have done it," interrupted the other almost passionately. "Held out your hand to that man! But I had forgotten, you know nothing as yet."

"I should not?" repeated Arthur sharply. "May I ask what you mean, sir? Be satisfied that I am well able to maintain the dignity of my position even on such an occasion as that."

The chief-engineer had already regained his composure.

"Excuse me, Herr Berkow, I intended in no way to criticise your conduct as master of the works, it was in your position as the son that I----but you are ignorant of the reports connected with your father's last moments. We agreed not to mention them before you; it was done with the best intention, but now I see that we were wrong, that you must be told. You would have offered Hartmann your hand, and that, I repeat, ought not to have been."

Arthur looked at him fixedly. His face had grown colourless and his lips quivered.

"You speak of Hartmann and of my father's death. Is there any connection between the two?"

"I fear so, we all fear so. General suspicion rests upon the Deputy, not among us alone, but among his fellow-miners."

"Down there in the shaft," cried Arthur terribly agitated. "A murderous assault on a defenceless man! I do not believe that of Hartmann."

"He hated the deceased," said the chief-engineer emphatically, "and he has never denied his hatred of him. Herr Berkow may have exasperated him by some word, some command. Whether the ropes really broke, and he seized the moment of danger to save himself and hurl the other down into the depths below, or whether the whole thing were premeditated, is all a dark mystery, but innocent he is not, that I'll answer for."

Arthur was evidently deeply moved by this disclosure; he leaned heavily on the table.

"At the inquest it was proved to be an accident," said he in an unsteady voice.

"Nothing at all was proved at the inquest, so they concluded it was an accident and let it pass as such. No one dared make an open accusation, proofs were wholly wanting, and there would have been endless conflicts with the miners if their leader had been taken up on suspicion and then discharged, as he, no doubt, would have been. We knew, Herr Berkow, that, under existing circumstances, a struggle was inevitable between you and him, and we wished to spare you the bitterness of knowing your adversary for what he is. That was why we kept silence."

Arthur passed his hand across his brow.

"I never dreamt of that, never! Even though it be nothing more than a suspicion, you are right, I should not offer that man my hand."

"That man," broke in the official, speaking with much energy, "that man, as leader of the rest, has brought the whole misfortune on us, that man has constantly heaped coals on the fire and kept up the strife, and now that he sees his power is on the decline he is doing all he can to make the breach irreparable, and a reconciliation impossible. Can you, will you, spare him still?"

"I spare him? No! I had done with him when he so roughly repulsed the overture I made him, but I cannot spare the others either after what has happened to-day. I am driven to take extreme measures. There were two hundred this morning who wanted to return to work, and they certainly have the right to require protection at their labour. The shafts must be secured at any cost, and I cannot do it alone, so"----

"So ...? We are waiting your orders, Herr Berkow?"

There was a pause of a minute, then the struggle visible in Arthur's face yielded to an expression of pained but firm resolve.

"I will write to M----. The letter shall go today. It must be."

"At last!" murmured the chief-engineer, half reproachfully. "It was high time!"

Arthur turned to his writing-table.

"Go over now and see that the Director and the other gentlemen remain at the posts I assigned them when I was at the works. It would have been useless to interfere in all the clamour this morning; perhaps now it may be possible. In half-an-hour I shall be with you. Should anything particular occur before send me word over at once."

Before leaving the room the official stepped up to his side again.

"I know what the resolution has cost you, Herr Berkow," he said earnestly, "and we none of us take the thing lightly, believe me, but we must not look on the dark side. Perhaps it may be settled without bloodshed after all."

He bowed and left the room, much too hurried and too preoccupied to notice Eugénie, who, at his approach, retreated still farther behind the sheltering curtain. Without looking to the right or the left, he passed rapidly through the adjoining room and closed the door after him. Husband and wife were alone together.

Arthur had only replied by a bitter smile to the chief-engineer's parting words.

"Too late!" he said to himself, "they will not yield until blood is shed. I must reap what my father has sown."

He threw himself down on a chair and leaned his head on his hands. Now that he had not to meet the eyes of strangers, now that he need no longer play the leader on whose resolution all depended, the look of energy faded from his face, and, in its place, came one of exhaustion, such as may overcome the strongest man when, for weeks at a stretch, his powers of mind and body have been overwrought and strained to the uttermost.

It was a moment of despairing dejection, coming naturally enough to one who had striven on and on, and all in vain, against the curse of a past in which he himself had not been to blame, except in so far as he had held himself aloof from the duties of it. Now the fatal inheritance was his alone, and the weight of it almost crushed him to the earth.

The accusing words against his father, which had escaped his lips, had been silenced in the self-same moment by the terrible suggestions he had listened to respecting the manner of that father's death. Yet to his predecessor was it solely due that he, the son, was now driven to the last terrible necessity, that, with ruin staring him in the face, deserted by his wife, forsaken by all his former friends, he was forced to resort to the only means which might yet save himself and all that he could still call his own from an enmity sown and nourished for many a long year, and whose fruits he was now compelled to taste. Arthur closed his eyes and leaned his head back on the arm-chair. He was worn out.

Eugénie had noiselessly left her hiding-place and had stepped on to the threshold. Forgotten now the peril she had passed through, forgotten the accusations she had heard with such feelings of horror, forgotten even the man on whom they rested and all that had reference to him.

Now that she was so near her husband, she saw and thought of nothing but him. The veil, which had so long divided them, would now be torn away. All would be made clear, and yet she hesitated and trembled at the coming decision as though sentence of death were about to be passed on her.

If she had been mistaken, if she were not received as she had hoped to be, as, after the sacrifice she had wrung from her pride, she felt she must be received .... The blood rushed violently to the young wife's heart, and it throbbed in an agony of suspense. Everything for her hung on the next minute.

"Arthur!" she said very softly.

He started up, as though he had heard a voice from the dead, and looked around him. There in the doorway, close to the spot where she had bade him farewell for ever, stood his wife.

In that first moment of recognition all consideration and reflection vanished; he rushed towards her and the cry of joy which was wrung from his lips, the radiant brightness of his eyes, revealed all that up to this hour had been disavowed by the self-restraint of months.

"Eugénie!"

She breathed freely, as though a mountain load had been lifted from her heart. The look, the tone with which he spoke her name gave her at last the long questioned certainty, and even though he stopped short in his hasty advance towards her, trying, as a protection against himself, it seemed, to take up the old mask once more and veiling that tell-tale glance, it was too late, she had seen too much!

"Where do you come from?" he asked at length, recovering himself with difficulty, "so suddenly, so unexpectedly, and how did you get up to the house? The works are in open revolt, you cannot possibly have passed by them."

Eugénie drew nearer slowly.

"I only arrived a few minutes ago. I had indeed to force my way through. Do not ask me how, at present, enough that I forced it. I wanted to be with you before danger reached you."

Arthur tried to turn from her.

"What does this mean, Eugénie? Why do you speak in that tone? Conrad has been making you anxious, though I entreated him not, though I expressly forbade him to do so. I want no sacrifice made from generosity or from a sense of duty. You know it."

"Yes, I know it," she returned steadily. "You sent me from you once before with those words. You could not forgive me that I had once done you a wrong, and in revenging yourself for it, you nearly sacrificed both yourself and me. Arthur, who was the hardest, the unkindest, of us two?"

"It was not revenge," he said in a low voice. "I set you free, you wished it yourself."

Eugénie was standing quite close to him now. The word, which once no consideration on earth would ever have forced from her lips, was so easy to speak now that she knew herself to be beloved. She raised full upon him her dark eyes, all dewy with tears.

"And if I tell my husband that I will have no freedom away from him, that I have come back to share with him whatever may befall us both, that I--that I have learnt to love him, will he once more tell me to go?"

She received no answer, at least not in words, but already she was in his arms, and they held her in an embrace so close and warm, it seemed as though they would never again give up the prize they had won at last.

As she lay there and felt the passionate caresses he showered upon her, she knew how cruel a blow her loss must have been, and all that her return was to him at a moment like the present. She saw a radiance in those great brown eyes, such as she had never before seen there, not even during those old bright lightning-like flashes.

The spell was broken. The world so long lying perdu had risen from its depths up to the broad light of day, and some instinct must have revealed to the young wife all the treasures that world held for her, for she laid her head upon her husband's breast, yielding herself up to him in fullest trust and confidence, as he bent over her whispering,

"My wife! my treasure!"

Through the open window came a breezy rustling greeting from the green wooded heights up yonder. Those forest-voices must have their say and mingle their whispers in the new-found bliss. Had they not helped to create it? Long ago they had understood, these two, before the two had learnt to understand themselves, at a time when they stood face to face in haughty contest, and spoke the word of separation in the very moment when their hearts were meeting.

But the contention and pride of the children of men avail but little when, with their loves and hopes, they come within the magic circle traced by the spirit of the mountains, as, amid the surging mists, he travels through his dominions in that first early hour of spring--and that which meets then, will cleave together for evermore!

CHAPTER XXIV

The day which had begun so stormily for the Berkow colony ended in comparative quiet, such as could hardly have been looked for after the scenes of the morning. Any one unacquainted with the situation might have taken the calm, which towards evening fell upon the works and their neighbourhood, for the most peaceful repose. But it was only a truce, and, after this pause of a moment, the storm would break forth again with redoubled fury.

In the Manager's dwelling there reigned a brooding, oppressive silence, covering so much that was disastrous. The old man sat dumb in his arm-chair by the stove. Martha went about the room, making work for herself and casting an occasional glance at Ulric, who, with folded arms, paced gloomily and silently up and down the little space. No one spoke to him, and he spoke to no one.

The old confidential footing, which, owing to the young Deputy's unmanageable conduct, had, it is true, often enough led to violent quarrels, but as often to reconciliation afterwards, had long ago ceased. Ulric ruled at home as absolutely as he ruled abroad among his partisans; even his father ventured no longer to oppose him, but, here as there, he governed only through fear. There was no talk now of love or confidence.

The silence had lasted long, and would probably have lasted longer if Lawrence had not come in. Martha, looking through the window, saw him approach and went to open the door for him.

The relations between these young engaged people seemed strangely cold. In spite of that day's grave work, which had little in common with tender passages, the girl's welcome might have been warmer; perhaps at so troubled a moment it ought to have been warmer, or so the young miner seemed to feel, for he looked hurt, and broke off in the middle of his cordial little speech. Martha did not notice it, however, and he turned hastily from her towards Ulric.

"Well?" asked the latter, pausing in his walk.

Lawrence shrugged his shoulders.

"Just as I told you. To-morrow four hundred of them will report themselves for work, and as many more are hesitating and balancing what to do. You are hardly sure of half now."

This time Ulric did not exclaim violently as was his custom on such occasions. The savage irritation he had shown in the morning about the desertion of a comparatively small number of his followers contrasted oddly with his present almost unnatural calm.

"Hardly half now," he repeated. "And how long will they hold out?"

Lawrence evaded an answer.

"All the younger men are with you. They have been on your side from the first, and they will stand by you still even if there should be trouble at the shafts again to-morrow. Ulric, will you really go such lengths as that?"

"He will go all lengths," said the Manager, standing up. "He will go on until they all drop off from him one by one and he remains quite alone. I told you before, you will never succeed with your senseless demands and your senseless hatred. It was fitting enough towards the father; but in truth and conscience the son has not deserved it. What he offered you was sufficient; I ought to know after all, for I have worked in the mines in my time, and I can feel for my fellows as well as another.

"Most of them would have gladly accepted it too, but they were cried down and threatened, until not a man among them dared move a finger, just because Ulric had set his mind on getting more than was possible. Now it has been going on for weeks, with all the misery and care and want, and it has all been in vain. There comes a day at last when the starving wife and children at home have to be thought of before everything, and that day we have reached now. You have brought us to it, Ulric, and nobody but you; now let there be an end of it." The old man had risen; as he spoke, he fixed on his son a look which had something of menace in it, but even this reproach, which at another time would have aroused Ulric to angry defiance, now failed to ruffle his gloomy composure.

"There is no arguing with you, father," he said coldly. "I have known that a long while. You are satisfied if you can eat your bit of dry bread in peace, and anything beyond that seems foolishness or a crime to you. I have staked everything on a throw. I thought to succeed, and I should have succeeded if that Berkow had not stood up all at once and shown us a front of iron. If we fail--well, Karl says, I am sure still of half the men, and with them I will let him see what it costs to get the better of us. He shall pay dearly enough for his victory."

The Manager looked at Lawrence, who was standing by with bowed head taking no part in the discussion, and then again at his son.

"Look to it first whether the half will remain true to you, if the master interferes in the matter again as he did this morning. That lost you the other half, Ulric. Do you think it has no effect upon them that he should behave as he has from the very first day you began to threaten him? Do you think they don't feel, all of them, that he is their match and yours too, and that he is able to hold them in hand himself, if ever it should chance that you cease to be their master? The first set took to work again this morning; they would have done it three weeks ago if they had dared. Now that they have made a beginning, there will be no stopping them any more."

"You may be right, father," said Ulric in a low hollow voice, "there may be no stopping them now. I have built on them as on a rock, and they are but thin sand running through my fingers. Berkow has learnt how to draw the cowards to him with his fine speeches and cursed way of stepping in among them, as if there were no stones to fly at his head and no mallets to be used, if necessary, on the person of our respected lord and master. That is just why they dare not attack him. I know why he carried his head so high to-day all of a sudden, why he came into the midst of all the uproar, looking as if success and happiness could never fail him more, and I know too that they are coming back to him. I myself guided them to his arms this morning."

The last words were lost in the banging to of the door which he had opened while speaking, and no one present understood them. Ulric stepped out into the open air and threw himself down on a bench.

The unnatural calm, which to-day pervaded his whole being, was almost alarming in a man accustomed to give the reins to his wild passionate nature. Whether the defection of his comrades had wounded him to the core, or whether some other feeling had been at work within him since the morning, it seemed that the proud certainty of victory, which he had shown even in those hours, was paralysed now, if not destroyed.

Past the little garden flowed the broad brook which, farther on in its course, served to turn the wheels now standing idle. It was a mischievous ill-regulated stream, this brook, it had nothing of the murmuring and silver-clear twinkling of its companions up in the hills, yet it too came from out of the mountain depths, close to where the shafts were situated. How often had it tried to draw harmless little children at play into its eddying course, so as, at least, to frighten and torment, though it dared not injure or kill, and so to revenge itself for having been made to lend its aid to man's machinery and labour.

The dark rapid flood looked weird in the last glimmer of the evening light, and still more uncanny was the brawling of its waters as it flowed by, hissing at times and babbling, full of scoff and of mischief, as though down below in the depths of the mountains it had learnt the tricks of the earth-gnome, how he weaves his toils round the men who are ever trying to drag his treasures from him, and how he has claimed as his due many a young warm life and buried it down in the regions of endless night.

There was nothing holy in its murmuring flow, and this was no holy hour in which its sound ascended to the young miner's ear as he sat there motionless, staring down before him as though harkening to some mysterious voice.

He had sat there for some time when he heard a step approaching, and directly afterwards Martha stood before him.

"What do you want?" asked Ulric, never turning his eyes from the stream.

"I wanted to see where you were staying all this while, Ulric," said she with repressed anxiety in her tone.

"Where I was staying? Your sweetheart is there within, keep your care for him. Let me be where I am."

"Karl has gone again," said Martha hastily, "and he knows well enough that it can do him no harm if I talk a bit with you."

Ulric turned round and looked at her. He seemed glad to tear himself from the thoughts which that brawling voice below had awakened in him.

"Listen, Martha; Karl puts up with more from you than any one else would stand. I would not suffer you to meet me in that manner. You should not have said 'yes,' if you had no heart for him."

The girl turned away almost angrily.

"He knows I have no heart for him. I told him so when we gave each other our word. He would have me consent. I can't alter it, at least not now; perhaps I shall learn to after the wedding."

"Perhaps!" said Ulric, with a sarcasm so deep and cutting as to seem inapplicable to the words he spoke. "Perhaps! So much is learnt after the wedding, with others at least, and why not with you?"

He looked down again at the dark flowing water, as if he could not tear himself away from it. There below was the same low plash and murmur, whispering to him only evil, evil thoughts.

Martha still stood a few paces off. That shyness and dread of him which, since the "accident," had been felt by all about him, had fettered her also. For weeks she had avoided every meeting, all contact with him, but to-day the old inclination had sprung up again strong within her, and had drawn her forcibly to the spot where he was. She was not deceived by that strange calm, she guessed what lay behind it.

"You cannot get over the desertion of the men?" she asked gently. "But half of them are with you still, and Karl will stand by you to the last minute."

Ulric smiled contemptuously.

"To-day there are still half, to-morrow there will be a quarter, and the day after---- Don't talk of it, Martha! As for Lawrence, he has never had more than half a heart for it. He has stood by me and not by the cause; by me, because I was his friend, and there will soon be an end of his friendship too. He cares far too much for you to have any very honest liking for me now."

The girl turned to him with a hasty gesture.

"Ulric!"

"Well, there is nothing in that to hurt your feelings. You would not have me when I asked you to be my wife. If you had, it would have been better in many ways."

"It would not have been better," said the girl decidedly. "I am not made of stuff to endure all that Karl puts up with so patiently from day to day, and things would have been between you and me much as they are now between me and him, only I should have been the one who had all to bear. I never had the least bit of your heart, your love was given elsewhere, in quite a different place."

There was bitter reproach in her words, but even this allusion could not rouse Ulric to-day. He was standing up now and gazing over towards the park as it lay shadowy in the distance, searching, as it were, for something between the trees.

"You mean I might have done better nearer at home, if I had sought for it, and you are right; but this is not a thing to be sought after, Martha. It seizes you all at once, and never looses you again while there is breath in your body. I have learnt to know it I have given you pain, my girl; now for the first time I know how much. But, believe me, no blessing comes with such love; it gives one more to suffer than the bitterest hate."

Words like these, nearly approaching to a prayer for forgiveness, sounded strangely from Ulric Hartmann's lips; he was little used to ask whether he gave pain or not. There was about him a sort of dull resignation quite foreign to his nature, and the grief which moved him now was all the more profound that it showed itself by no passionate outburst. Martha forgot her repugnance and her fear, and went close up to his side.

"What ails you, Ulric? You are so strange to-day. I have never seen you like this. What is the matter?"

He pushed the curly hair from his brow, and leaned up against the wooden gate.

"I don't know. Something has been weighing on me all day long. I can't shake it off, and it takes my strength from me. I want it for to-morrow, but directly I try to think, all grows black and dark before me, as if there lay nothing more beyond, as if to-morrow all would be at an end--all!"

Ulric started up suddenly with a dash of his old spirit.

"Absurd nonsense! I think the water down there has bewitched me with its confounded brawl. I have so much time just now to be listening to it, really! Good-bye."

He turned to go, but the girl held him back anxiously.

"Where are you going? To see the men?"

"No, I am going first on an errand of my own. Good-bye."

"Ulric, I implore you, stay!"

But the young miner's short-lived softened mood was over already. He tore himself free impatiently.

"Let me go. I have no time for talk--another time!"

He pushed open the garden gate, and, setting off in the direction of the park, soon disappeared in the growing darkness.

Martha stood with folded hands, looking after him. Wounded feeling and bitter pain strove together in her countenance, but the pain gained the upper hand.

"No blessing comes with such a love."

The words found an echo in her heart. She felt that there was no blessing on hers either.

Meanwhile Eugénie Berkow sat alone in her husband's study. There had been little opportunity as yet for these two to enjoy their newly-won felicity. Twice had Arthur been compelled to leave her; in the morning when he had thrown himself into the thick of the tumult and quelled it for the time being, and now again when he had been called away to a conference with the officials.

But, in spite of her anxiety about him and of the dangerous situation in which they were placed, the young wife's face beamed with a reflection of that deep inward happiness which, gained at the cost of many an arduous struggle, was no longer at the mercy of outward storms. She was with her husband, at his side, under his protection, and Arthur was, it seemed, a man able to make his wife forget all else in that one fact.

Suddenly a door was opened, and steps resounded in the adjoining room. Eugénie rose to meet the newcomer, whom she naturally took for her husband, but her first feeling of surprise at seeing a stranger gave way to one of terror as she recognised Ulric Hartmann.

He was startled too at seeing her, and stood still in some embarrassment.

"Ah, it is you, my lady! I was looking for Herr Berkow."

"He is not here, I am expecting him," she answered quickly, in a trembling voice.

She knew what a source of danger this man had been to Arthur, what a part he had played here on the works, yet she had not hesitated to trust herself to his protection, when that morning it had seemed her only chance of reaching the house. Between the morning and evening, however, had come the hour in which she had stood by and listened to the accusations brought against him by the chief-engineer.

They were based on suspicion alone, but even the suspicion of so dastardly and perfidious an act as the assassination of a defenceless man is something terrible, and she had shuddered with horror at the thought of it. She could trust herself to the openly-declared and ruthless enemy of her husband, but she shrank back from the hand which was possibly dyed with the blood of her husband's father.

Ulric noticed the movement only too plainly. He still stood on the threshold, but in his voice there was a tone of unmistakable scorn.

"I have alarmed you by coming. It was not my fault that I had not myself announced. You are ill served, my lady. Neither on the stairs nor in the corridors did I meet with one of your lacqueys. I should very likely have thrust them out of my way, if they had refused me admittance, but the noise of it would have been a sort of announcement in itself."

Eugénie knew that he could have come in without hindrance. The two servants were, by Arthur's express command, stationed in the ante-room leading to her own apartments. In the excited state of men's minds, now that every restraint was loosed and all order overthrown, it might be that some would so far profit by the general license, as to attack, or at least to force their way into, the house.

Anxiety and an uneasy restlessness had driven Eugénie over to her husband's rooms. They were situated in another wing, and from their windows she would see him come, but the entrance to them was unguarded and she was there quite alone.

"What do you want, Hartmann?" she asked, summoning up her courage. "After all that has happened, I did not think you would attempt to enter our house again and to gain access to Herr Berkow's private rooms. You know that he cannot receive you now."

"It was just on that account I was looking for him. I have a few words to say to him. I thought I should find him alone. It was not you I was seeking, my lady."

He stepped a little nearer to her as he said these words. Eugénie retreated involuntarily; he laughed out with a bitter laugh.

"What a change a few hours may make! This morning you were begging for my protection and leaning on my arm as I led you through all the noise out there. Now, you fly from me as if your life were not safe when I am by. Herr Berkow has used his time well, he has painted me in the colours of a robber and a murderer, has he not?"

The young wife's delicate eyebrows contracted angrily, as, mastering her agitation, she replied shortly and sternly,

"Leave me! my husband is not here, you see yourself, and if he were to come now, I should hardly leave you alone with him."

"Why not?" asked Ulric slowly, but lowering darkly at her. "Why not?" he repeated more vehemently as she remained silent.

Eugénie's fearless nature had often led her into acts of imprudence. She did not reflect now on the possible consequences of her words, as, returning his gaze steadfastly, she hazarded the dangerous answer,

"Because your company has been fatal to one Berkow already."

Hartmann started, and turned very pale. For one moment it seemed that he would break out with all his old violence, but no! his features still wore that rigid calm, and he spoke in the same dull under-tone he had used throughout the interview.

"So that was it? Truly, I might have known it would find its way to you at last."

Eugénie looked on in surprise. She had not expected such calmness as this, it struck her as unnatural, yet she was stimulated by it to a still greater venture. She had that morning tested her power and found it to be great.

If it were only for Arthur's sake she longed for a certainty as to this man who stood opposed to him in the fight, and she felt that though the truth should be denied to all the world beside, it would not be so to her.

"You know what I mean then?" she began again. "You understand to what I allude? Hartmann, can you solemnly declare the reports connected with that unhappy hour to be false?"

He crossed his arms on his breast, and looked moodily to the ground.

"If I were to do so would you believe me?"

Eugénie was silent

"Would you believe me?" he asked again, in a tone as though life or death hung on her answer.

She let her eyes rest for a moment on his face. It was fully turned towards her now, and she saw that it was ashy pale, and, like his voice, betrayed an agonised tension of feeling.

"You might be capable of a crime, I think, if you were stung to passion. I do not think you are capable of a lie."

Ulric's mighty chest heaved with a deep sigh of relief. As though completely to re-assure her, he stepped back again away from her.

"Ask me what you please, my lady, I will answer you."

She trembled a little and leaned against the back of the sofa. It was a dangerous colloquy, she felt, to hold with such a man, but still she put the all important question.

"They tell my husband that it was not by mere accident the ropes broke on that fatal day. How was it, Hartmann?"

"It was accident or something better, if you will, justice perhaps. Our employer had caused alterations to be made in the pumps and lifting-machine, just what was indispensable to keep them working, but nothing to ensure safety. It was the same in this as in everything else. What did it matter if a few hundred miners, constantly going up and down, were every day brought in danger of their lives? Double and treble the loads were lifted, the most outrageous weights were raised, and at last the weights did their work, only this time the victim was not one of the men, but the master himself. It was no man's hand, my lady, which severed the ropes just at the moment when they were bearing him up, and mine least of all. I saw the danger coming, we had just reached the last stage but one. I risked the leap and"----

"You thrust him?" said Eugénie breathlessly, as he paused.

"No, I only let him go. I could have saved him if I would. Half a minute would have been sufficient. I must have risked my own life, it is true; he might have dragged me down with him, but for any one among the men, for any of the officials even, I should have risked it; for that man I could not! In that instant the thought rushed through my head of all the evil he had done us, that the fate now threatening him was only what he had exposed us to, day by day, for nothing but to save money, and that I would not meddle in the matter if for once Providence chose to be just. I did not move a hand, in spite of his cries. Next minute it was too late; the cage had been dashed below and he with it."

Hartmann was silent. Eugénie looked up at him half in pity, half in horror. She knew well enough that the accusations he had heaped on the dead man were merited. Even she, however, would, in a moment of peril, have stretched forth her hand to save the hated Berkow, but the man opposite her had learnt neither to forgive nor forget. He stood quietly by, and saw his enemy perish before his eyes.

"You have told me the whole truth, Hartmann? On your word of honour?"

"On my word of honour."

His eyes met hers without flinching. There was no doubt now in her mind, and she answered reproachfully.

"And why did you not clear up the error? Why did you not speak to the others as you have done to me?"

A scornful look passed over his face.

"Because not one of them would have believed me. Not a single one, not even my own father. He is right. I have been wild and reckless all my life, flinging down everything that stood in my way, and not caring for what others said to me. I have had to pay for it now. They all knew that I hated the man, and the accident happened when I was by, so I must have been the cause of it, there could be no doubt as to that. My own father told me so to my face, just because I could not say 'yes' at once, when he asked me if I was in no way to blame for Berkow's death.

"I should only have had to stretch out my arm to save him and I had not done it--because I could not say yes at once, he would not listen to me any more. He would not have believed me, if I had sworn it to him. Then I tried here and there among my mates. They did not contradict me, but I saw in their faces that they took me for a liar. I was not going to beg and pray them to believe me, so I let the thing go as it would. I had had enough of their friendship and companionship. If I had been brought into court and had found that matters were going against me, I should have spoken out, but it is a question if any one there would have believed what I said."

Eugénie shook her head.

"You should have made them believe you, Hartmann; you could have done it, if you had tried in earnest, but your pride would not suffer it. You met suspicion with contempt, and that was the very way to strengthen it. Now you have an ill name on all the works, with the officials and with my husband."

"What do I care for Herr Berkow?" he broke in roughly, "what do I care for any of them? It is all the same to me whether they condemn me or not, but I could not bear that you should turn from me in loathing, and you believe me now, I see it in your eyes. The rest is all one to me."

"I do believe you," said Eugénie earnestly, "and my husband's mind, at least, shall be cleared of those worst suspicions. If you failed to save, where rescue was possible, it is not for us to judge you. You must answer for it to your own conscience, but Arthur shall not think that it is his father's murderer who stands opposed to him. It is too late now for a reconciliation, you have gone too far for that. It is only within the last few hours that I have learnt all that has happened, all that yet may happen, if the attack on the shafts is renewed to-morrow. Hartmann," she was imprudent enough to go right up to him and to lay her hand on his arm. "Hartmann, we are on the verge of a frightful catastrophe. You have compelled my husband to protect himself and those belonging to him, to prepare himself for whatever may befall, and he is determined to do it. If blood is shed, must needs be shed, to-morrow, think on whose head it will be?"

Her close vicinity, the touch of her hand on his arm, were not without effect on Ulric, but this time they worked no good. The dull quiet tone in which he had spoken hitherto was changed now; his voice grew sharper and louder, as he replied:

"On mine, you mean? Take care, my lady, you may have to suffer too, if for instance, some one you are very fond of should be made to answer for it. Herr Berkow will not stay securely here at home when there is fighting going on outside. I know that, and I know too whom I shall seek out first when once the battle is fairly on."

Eugénie had long ago withdrawn her hand, now she moved away from him, warned by that tone and look. He was still but as a half-tamed tiger, obeying her voice one minute, but ready perhaps the next to rise up against her with all the old fury of his savage nature. That minute seemed to be at hand. His look had menace in it even to her.

"Hartmann, you are speaking to your employer's wife," she said, making a vain attempt to recall him to his senses.

"My employer!" cried he in scorn. "There is no question of my employer here. I have only to do with him when I am at the head of my men. It is Arthur Berkow I hate, because you are his wife, because you love him, and I ... I love you, Eugénie more than any one in the whole wide world. Do not shrink from me so in horror. You must have known it long ago.

"It has mastered me each time I have come near you. I have kept it down and tried to crush it by force, but it was of no use. It is of no use now either, though to-day again I have had to learn the old lesson that like cleaves to like, and that nothing is left for such as we are but disdain and just a haughty shrug of contempt, even though we should have risked our lives in your service. But next time there is a life to be lost, I shall not be the one to offer myself up madly, as I did on the day of your home-coming, by rushing under your horses' hoofs. Next time the peril shall be another's, not mine. I have hated one Berkow to the death already; it seemed to me then I never could hate any one worse, but I know better now. He did not make a murderer of me; but there is one man, and only one in the world, who could! I did the father no hurt, but, if ever I find myself so, man to man, with the son, then it shall be he or I ... or, if it must be, both!"

It was a terrible moment. The man's frenzied passion had burst all bounds and broken loose in a wild torrent which nothing now could stem or stay. Eugénie saw that no words would avail her at the present crisis, she understood that her power was at an end. She could not escape, he had placed himself between her and the door, but she ran to the bell and pulled it with all the force at her command. The servants were upstairs at the other side of the house, still it was just possible the sound might reach their ears.

Hartmann had followed her; seizing her hand, he would have dragged it from the bell rope, but at that moment he was himself thrust back by an arm to which indignation lent such strength that it flung his giant form aside as though he had been a child. Arthur stood between them. With a cry of joy and yet of mortal fear, Eugénie rushed to her husband; she knew what would come now.

Ulric recovered himself quickly and no sound passed his lips, but his face was so distorted by rage as to be hardly recognisable. There came a look in his eye, as he turned and faced his enemy, which foreboded that enemy's immediate destruction; but Arthur, with quick presence of mind, tore down one of the pistols which hung over his writing-table, and throwing his left arm round his wife, he levelled the weapon at the intruder.

"Back, Hartmann! Do not dare to come nearer. One step forwards towards my wife, one single step, and I stretch you on the ground."

The threat took effect. Almost blinded by passion as he was, Ulric saw the barrel pointed at him with a firm and sure aim, saw too that the hand which held it did not tremble; at the second step he took forward the bullet would strike him, and his foe would remain victor. He clenched his fist and gnashed his teeth in his rage that a like weapon was wanting to him.

"I have no pistols," said he, "or we should meet here on equal terms, as we never have met yet. You are better provided than I. I have nothing but my fists to set against your bullets, it is easy to see who would get the best of it."

Arthur kept his eyes steadily fixed upon him. "You have taken care, Hartmann, that we should always have at hand arms ready for use. I shall protect my house and my wife even at the cost of a bullet. Back, I repeat."

For one second the two looked each other full in the face, as on that first occasion, so pregnant with consequences, when they had measured each other's strength: now, as then, victory declared itself for the young master, though, in the pass they had now reached, other means of coercion had been needed than the look of his undaunted eyes. He stood motionless, his finger ready to press the trigger, following every movement of his foe, until the latter receded.

"I have never set much store by my life," said Ulric. "I should have thought you both might have known that, but I am not going to let myself be shot down at your door. I have accounts to settle with you. You need not tremble so, my lady, you are in his arms, and he is safe, for the present at least, though we have not finished with each other yet. You stand there together as if nothing could tear you apart, as if you were bound one to the other for ever and ever; but my time will come yet, and then you shall have cause to remember me."

So saying, he went; his departing steps echoing through the adjoining room, then more faintly in the ante-chamber, until at last they died away outside.

Eugénie nestled more closely in her husband's arms; she had learned to know now how well they could protect her.

"You came at the right moment, Arthur," said she, trembling still. "I had left my rooms in spite of your warning. It was very imprudent, I know, but I wanted to wait for you here, and I thought in the house I should be sure to be safe."

Arthur lowered the pistol, and drew her nearer to him.

"But you were not, we have gained that experience. What was Hartmann doing here in my study?"

"I do not know. He was looking for you, and certainly with no good intent."

"I am prepared for anything from that quarter," he answered quietly, as he laid the pistol on the table. "You see, I had provided for any such emergency, but I greatly fear it was only the prelude to what will take place to-morrow, when the real drama begins. Does it frighten you, Eugénie? The help we have sent for cannot be here before evening; we shall have to hold out alone all day against the rebels."

"Nothing frightens me when I am with you. But, Arthur," she pleaded anxiously, "do not go out by yourself again into the midst of all that tumult, as you did this morning. He will be there, and he has sworn to take your life."

He raised her head gently and looked into her eyes.

"Life and death are not in Hartmann's hands alone; their decision rests with another. Make your mind easy, Eugénie; I will do my duty, but I will do it in a different way than in the days gone by. I know now that my wife is anxious about me; that is not a thing one forgets so easily!"

On the terrace outside stood Ulric Hartmann. Darkness had fallen now, and the expression of his features was no longer discernible as he gazed up at the windows of the house he had just left, but his voice was low and hoarse with emotion as he repeated the threat he had before used with reference to Arthur Berkow,

"He or I, or, if it must be, both!"

CHAPTER XXV

Next morning! The thought of it had filled not only Arthur and his wife, but every one connected with the Berkow establishment, with grave and anxious care. It had come now, that dreaded morning, and all the apprehensions which had been felt respecting it seemed likely to be realised.

At a very early hour the whole staff of officials was assembled at the great house. They had either come to hold counsel or had taken refuge there; it almost seemed the latter, for the men's faces were pale, haggard, excited, and there was a great buzz of talk going on among them, much anxious discussion pro and con, proposals rejected as soon as made, and many fears expressed as to coming events.

"I am still of opinion that it was a mistake to arrest those men," Schäffer declared, speaking to the Director. "It might have been risked if the soldiers had been on the spot, but it should never have been attempted by us, while we are unsupported. They will storm the house to set the prisoners free, and we shall be obliged to give them up."

"Excuse me, we shall do nothing of the kind," cried the chief-engineer, in complete opposition to his two colleagues as usual. "We shall let them storm, and we shall hold out and defend ourselves here in the house if necessary. Herr Berkow is determined to do it."

"Well, you ought to know best what he has decided on doing; you are his only adviser," said the Director, rather piqued. He could boast of no such intimacy with the proprietor, although his position would rather have entitled him to it.

"Herr Berkow is in the habit of deciding for himself," replied the chief-engineer, drily. "Only it happens this time as usual that I fully agree with him. It would be contrary to all right and justice, it would be nothing better than mere paltry cowardice, to let these miscreants go. Why! they had avowed an intention of destroying the engines for us."

"By Hartmann's order," interposed Schäffer.

"It does not signify who gave the order. Their master arrived just in time to hinder them from performing their rascally trick, and I should like to see the man who would calmly have let the offenders go. He had them arrested, and he was right. Hartmann was not by, he was still down at the shafts in the thick of the row, but he could not prevent the others going below after all; his own father went and stood up against him."

"Yes, it was a good thing the Manager came to our aid," said the Director. "He must have seen there was no other way of averting the worst, for he came to us of his own free will this morning and offered to take the lead of the men going on shift, though it is no part of his business. He knew his son would not venture to attack him, and not one of the others lifted a hand against their mates when they saw their leader held back. If the descent was made, we have only the old man to thank for it."

"I tell you this," maintained Schäffer, "the descent had been accomplished, more than half the miners had stood by neutral, and if they had not been exasperated by the arrest of their comrades, the whole business might have been settled peaceably and quietly."

"Peaceably and quietly, while Hartmann is in command?" the chief-engineer laughed outright. "There you are quite mistaken. He was looking for a pretext, no matter what, to attack us, and, if he had found none, he would have attacked us all the same without. This morning's work must have shown him that his power is rapidly drawing to an end, that perhaps after to-day he may not be able to count on his partisans, so he will risk his last throw. The fellow knows he is lost, and he will drag down with him recklessly all who obey him still through habit or through fear. He will stand at nothing now, and least of all at injuring us."

Here they were interrupted by Herr Wilberg, who left the window where he had been posted for the last ten minutes and came back to them with a very white face.

"The noise gets worse and worse," said he timorously; "there can be no doubt that they mean to besiege the house, if Herr Berkow does not give way. The park-gates are down already, all the beds are trampled up. Oh! and all those lovely roses blooming on the terrace"----

"Don't come bothering us with your sentimental nonsense," cried the chief-engineer, as the Director and Schäffer hurried to the window. "Now when the rebels are storming the house about our heads, you are thinking of your trampled-down rose-trees. Why don't you go and sit down and put your lamentation over them into verse? I should think it would be just the theme to inspire a poet."

"I have been so unfortunate for some time as to excite your displeasure by everything I say or do, sir," returned Herr Wilberg, offended, but not without a sort of secret self-satisfaction which seemed to increase the other's ill-humour.

"Because you never say or do anything sensible," he growled, turning his back on the young man and going up to his colleagues, who were still looking out at the ever-growing tumult.

"We shall have it in earnest now," said the Director uneasily. "They are threatening to force an entrance. Herr Berkow ought to be told."

"Let him have a minute's peace," interposed the chief-engineer. "He has been at his post ever since daybreak. I think you might let him have five minutes with his wife now. All the necessary measures are taken, and when danger is really at hand, he will not be wanting, as you well know."

He was right. Ever since the dawn Arthur had been actively occupied, giving orders and instructions, and personally superintending all that was being done. He had hardly seen Eugénie until now, when he had gone with her for a few minutes into one of the adjoining rooms.

During this short interview he must have made her fully acquainted with the situation, for her arms were clasped round his neck, and she was clinging to him in the greatest agitation.

"You must not go out, Arthur. It would be a mad, a desperate venture. What can you do, one against so many? Yesterday, when you interfered, they were fighting among themselves, but to-day they will all turn against you. You will pay the penalty for your rashness. I will not let you go."

Arthur freed himself gently but firmly from her embrace.

"I must, Eugénie! It is the only possible way to avert the attack, and it is not the first time I have had to face such scenes. Why, what did you yourself do yesterday when you arrived?"

"I was coming to you," said she, in a tone which implied that any venture would so have been justified. "But you want to tear yourself from me and wildly expose yourself to the blind fury of this Hartmann. Think of what happened yesterday evening, think of his threats. If you must go, if there is no choice left, let me go with you at least. I am not afraid, I only tremble when I know you are in danger and alone."

He bent down to her gravely but lovingly.

"I know that you are brave, my Eugénie, but I should be a coward myself before those crowds, if I knew that a stone from their midst might strike you too. I want all my courage to-day, and I should not have it if I saw you in peril and felt I could not protect you. I know why you wish to go with me. You think I shall be safe from that one arm while you are at my side. Do not deceive yourself, that is all over and past since yesterday evening. You share the hatred now with which he has persecuted me, and if it were not so"--here his voice lost its soft inflection and his brow grew dark--"I would not owe my safety to a feeling which is alike an offence to you and to me, and which would in itself be sufficient to call for the man's dismissal, if his conduct in other respects did not make it necessary."

She must have felt the justice of his words, for she drooped her head in silent resignation.

Arthur started.

"The clamour is breaking out again, I must go. We shall only see each other for a few brief minutes at a time to-day, and even they will be anxious minutes for you, my poor wife. You could hardly have come back at a worse time."

"Would you rather have held out against them without me?" she asked in a low voice.

His face brightened, and there came into it an expression of passionate tenderness.

"Without you? I have gone on so far like the soldier of a forlorn hope. I only found out yesterday how one can fight with a will when the prosperity of a lifetime and all one's future are dependent on the result. You brought back to me the desire for both, and now they may assail us on all sides as they like. I believe in success now that I have you at my side once more!"

The officials hushed their noisy debatings as Berkow and his wife entered, and the impression produced on all hands by their appearance was due to something more than mere respect for the master. All eyes were at once fixed upon him, as though they could read in his face what was to be hoped or feared; they all pressed round him, as round a centre where support was to be found, and every one breathed more freely when he came in, as if the danger were half conjured already. This movement, involuntary as it was, showed Eugénie sufficiently the position her husband had conquered for himself, and the way in which he stepped in among them proved too that he well knew how to maintain it. His face, which she had seen but a few seconds before heavily clouded over by care, bore, now that it had to meet all those anxious enquiring looks, no other expression than that of a calm gravity, and there was an assurance in his bearing which would have instilled confidence into the faintest heart.

"Well, gentlemen, things look rather hostile and threatening outside. We must hold ourselves prepared for a sort of siege, perhaps even for an attack; does it not appear so to you?"

"They want to have the prisoners set free," said the Director, with a glance at Schäffer, inviting his support.

"Yes," said the latter, coming forwards, "and I fear we shall not be able to hold our own against all this uproar. The arrest of the three miners is their sole motive or pretext at present; if that were taken from them"...

"They would find another," interrupted Arthur, "and the weakness we should have betrayed would remove from them the last restraint. We must show neither hesitation nor fear now, or we shall lose the game at the last moment. I foresaw what would happen when I had those mischievous fellows arrested, but in the face of such a criminal attempt as that there was no choice but to proceed with the utmost severity. The prisoners will remain in custody until the troops arrive."

The Director beat a retreat, and Schäffer shrugged his shoulders. They had learnt to know that this tone of his would brook no contradiction.

"I do not see Hartmann in the crowd," continued Arthur, turning to the chief-engineer; "he is generally first wherever there are noise and tumult. To-day he seems only to have urged the others on, and then to have left them. He is nowhere visible."

"I have missed him for the last quarter of an hour," answered the other gravely. "I hope he is not up to fresh mischief elsewhere. You ordered back the men posted about the engine-houses, Herr Berkow?"

"Certainly. The few men we can dispose of are even more necessary here in the house, and, since the descent has been effected, the shafts and engines must be perfectly safe. They could not meddle with them without endangering their comrades down below."

"With such a leader, they may even be meaning that," said the official reflectively.

Arthur's brow grew dark, "Nonsense! Hartmann is an unruly fellow, a furious madman even, when he is irritated, but he is not a scoundrel, and that would be a scoundrelly act. He would have injured the engines to prevent the descent being made, but when he found he could no longer prevent it, why do you suppose he rushed off to the sheds? Certainly not to see that his father and comrades were given up to destruction; he wanted to recall his former orders, and it was only when he saw we had been beforehand with him that he broke out against us in his wrath at the failure of his plans. The engines are secured to us by the fact of the men being below. Not a hand will be raised to injure them while the Manager and the rest are in the mine, and so the storm is now turned against the house. I shall go out and make an attempt to calm them."

During the last few weeks the officials had been accustomed to see their leader act on similar occasions with resolute boldness and without regard to his own personal safety, but this time entreaties and remonstrances resounded on all sides; even the chief-engineer joined in to dissuade him, and Schäffer, knowing from what quarter opposition would alone avail, turned to Eugénie, still standing at her husband's side.

"Do not allow it, your ladyship. Not to-day, it is much more dangerous to-day than it has ever been before. The men are horribly excited, and Hartmann is staking his last throw. Keep Herr Berkow back."

At this warning, which did but confirm her own fears, she grew deadly pale, but she retained her composure; something of Arthur's calm seemed to have been communicated to her.

"My husband has told me he must make the attempt," she answered steadily, "he shall not say that I kept him back with tears and lamentations from what he holds to be his duty. Let him go."

Arthur held her hand clasped in his. He only thanked her by a look.

"Now, gentlemen, take example by my wife's courage. She has most cause to tremble. I repeat it, the attempt must be made. Let the hall-door be opened."

"We will all go with you," said the chief-engineer. "Fear nothing, my lady, I will not stir from his side."

Arthur put him aside quietly, but firmly.

"I thank you, but you must remain here with the other gentlemen. In such a case one man alone is generally safe against a crowd. If you were all to appear, they might take it for a challenge. Hold yourselves in readiness to cover my retreat into the house, if it comes to the worst. Farewell, Eugénie."

He went, accompanied as far as the stairs by the chief-engineer and several of the officials. No one attempted to stay him now. They all knew that in his appearance outside lay the only chance of averting a danger which it would be hard, if not impossible, for them to withstand for hours together here shut up in the house.

Eugénie rushed to one of the windows. She did not notice how all present were anxiously pressing round the others, did not hear the remarks exchanged in an undertone by the Director and Schäffer who were standing close behind her; she only saw that wild rebellious crowd, that sea of heads so densely packed together surging round the house, only heard those fierce cries demanding the surrender of the prisoners.

To this crowd her husband was about to expose himself alone; in the very next instant his life might be menaced by it. The iron gates of the park, more elegant than strong, had already yielded to the battery; they lay broken to pieces on the ground; the beautiful, carefully kept gardens, trodden under foot by hundreds, were nothing now but a desolate chaos of earth, remnants of flowers and plants, and trampled-down bushes.

Already the foremost men among the rebels had all but reached the terrace, and so were drawing very near the house itself; already here and there clenched fists could be seen, armed with stones and ready to hurl them at the windows. There was a confused rumour of shouts, threats and cries of all descriptions; every minute the clamour waxed louder and louder, until now and again it would rise for a second to a howl which was almost unearthly.

Suddenly there came a deep breathless silence. The uproar ceased abruptly, as though by an order from on high; the agitated groups paused in their restless movement, the great masses fell back, as if they had all at once encountered an obstacle, and all eyes, all faces, were turned in one direction. The hall-door had been opened, and the young master stepped out on to the terrace.

The lull lasted a few seconds, then the momentary surprise gave place to a fresh and more terrible outburst of fury which no longer lacked an aim. Those fierce yells, those faces distorted by passion, those threatening upraised arms, were all directed against one man; but that man was their master, the proprietor of the works, and that which the father, with all his industrial genius, his tenacity of purpose and arbitrary will, had failed to acquire during twenty years and more, the son had won for himself in a few weeks: the authority of his own personal influence; it worked even now when all the customary restraints of order were loosed.

He let the storm take its course. With his slight figure well erect, his steady eyes fixed on the multitude before him, every individual of which was superior to himself in strength, he stood facing them, alone and unarmed, with no protection save that which his authority gave him, waiting, as though the breakers of revolution, beating idly against him, must spend themselves in vain.

And they spent themselves. The general clamour gradually subsided into distinct and separate cries, then into a sullen murmur. At last even this was hushed, and Berkow's voice was raised, unintelligible at first through the movement surging round him, interrupted often by the tumult, which at intervals would break out afresh, then sink powerless again, until finally it died out altogether. Then the master's voice was heard, loud, clear and distinct, reaching the ears even of those who were farthest from him.

"Thank God!" muttered Schäffer, passing his handkerchief across his brow, "he has got them in hand now; they may be restive and struggle, but they will obey. See, my lady, how they are quieting down, how they recoil before him. They are actually retreating from the terrace and letting the stones drop from their hands. If Providence will only keep Hartmann out of the way, the danger is over."

He little knew with what intensity Eugénie reechoed the wish in her own mind. Up to this time she had sought in vain for that one dreaded figure; so long as it was not visible her courage did not fail her, so long she believed Arthur might yet be safe; but now security and hope were over. Whether the sudden lull in the uproar he had busied himself to raise had summoned the missing man to the spot, or whether a suspicion of what was taking place drew him thither at that critical moment, Ulric Hartmann, risen, as it were, from the ground, appeared suddenly at the park entrance behind them. One look sufficed to show him how matters stood.

"Cowards that you are!" he thundered to his comrades, as, followed by Lawrence and Deputy Wilms, he forced his way through the dense masses. "I thought as much almost, I thought you would be getting yourselves caught in his nets again while we were seeking information as to what they had done with the prisoners. We know now where they are, there at the balcony to the right, on the ground-floor, just at the back of the dining-room; that is where the attack must be made. Break in the plate-glass, it will save forcing open the door."

No one obeyed the injunction as yet, but it had its effect. Nothing is more vacillating, more unstable of purpose, than an excited crowd, accustomed to bow to the will of one resolute man.

In all the previous clamour and disturbance there had been an absence of any fixed plan, an indecision which had kept the rebels from any positive action; the eye, the arm, of the leader had been wanting. He was there now, and, as he grasped the reins, he gave them an aim and sure direction. They knew now where the prisoners were lodged, and knew how to get to them, and thus the danger, which had so nearly been conjured, was kindled afresh.

Ulric cared little at that moment whether his order were obeyed or not. He had forced a passage for himself through to the terrace, and stood confronting the master with all the defiant hostility of his rebellious nature, his gigantic form towering nearly a head above his fellows. He was a born leader of the masses; his fierce energy and despotic will carried them with him in blind obedience, and, spite of all that had happened, that might happen yet, his command over them was still for the time being unlimited. All the advantage which Arthur had obtained was called into question, if not wholly destroyed, by the mere appearance on the scene of this man whose influence worked at least as powerfully as his own.

"Where are our mates?" asked Hartmann in a tone of menace, and stepping up still closer. "We want them out at once! We will have no violence used to any of us."

"And I will not have my machinery destroyed," answered Arthur coldly and calmly. "I had the men arrested, though they were only the tools in another's hand. Who ordered that attempt upon the engines?"

There was a triumphant gleam in Ulric's eye; he had foreseen this firmness and built his plan upon it. He himself needed no pretext; he was bent on satisfying his hatred at any cost, but his partisans, wavering and ready to desert their flag, were in want of some provocation to urge them forward; it was necessary now to goad them on, and the adversary was bold and proud enough to offer them an incentive.

"I owe you no answers," he said disdainfully, "and I shall not allow myself to be questioned in that dictatorial way. Give up the prisoners, all the men on the works demand it, or" .... and his look completed the threat.

"The prisoners will be detained," declared Arthur unmoved, "and you, Hartmann, have no longer the right to speak in the name of all the men employed on the works; half of them have seceded from you already. I have nothing more to say to you."

"But I have something to say to you," shouted Ulric, desperate with rage. "Forwards," he cried, turning to the rebel masses, "forwards, on to our mates, strike down all that comes in your way!"

He would have rushed upon Berkow, thereby giving the signal for a general onset, but, before he could do so, before it could be determined whether the crowd behind him would render or refuse obedience, there boomed suddenly through the air a strange and terrible sound, making all the ground around them tremble.

The leader stopped electrified, and all present stood spell-bound, listening breathlessly for what would follow. It had been like the reverberation of a dull and distant shock, coming, as it seemed, from the very bowels of the earth, and was succeeded by a low rumble under ground which lasted a few seconds; then all was still as death, and hundreds of scared faces were turned in the direction of the works.

"Good God! that came from the mine; something has happened there!" cried Lawrence, with a great start of alarm.

"That was an explosion!" said the voice of the chief-engineer; during the last few critical minutes he had been on guard in the great hall at the head of the younger officials and all the available servants, ready to hasten to Arthur's assistance. "An accident has happened in the mine, Herr Berkow, we must go over."

For one moment horror seemed to paralyse every limb. No one moved; the warning was all too terrible. At the very moment when one party was rushing forward bent on the other's annihilation, destruction of another kind had reached their brothers down below. Now they were imperatively called on to abandon the attack and hurry to the rescue. Arthur was the first to recover himself.

"To the shafts!" he cried to the other officials, who by this time had come out of the house and were pressing round him, and, so saying, he set the example by himself speeding off before them all in the direction of the works.

"To the shafts!" shouted Ulric, turning to the miners.

The command was unnecessary; in an instant the crowd was rushing in wild haste, their leader at their head, to the scene of the disaster. He and Arthur reached the works first, and almost simultaneously.

Nothing was to be seen as yet of the effects of the destroying element; the thick column of smoke issuing from the shafts alone bore witness to what had happened, but it was eloquent enough. In less than ten minutes the whole surrounding space was crowded with human beings, who, now that their first mute horror was over, broke out loudly into lamentations and cries of fear and despair.

There is something appalling and yet elevating about a great misfortune which is not due to the hand of man, for it almost invariably brings into play the better side of human nature, saving its honour, and cleansing it from those evil passions which at other times disfigure and obscure it. The revolution in the general feeling was so sudden, so instantaneous, it hardly seemed to be the same multitude which, but a few minutes before, had clamoured round the house, menacing destruction if not murder, because their wild demands were not conceded. Strife, enmity, the hatred of long months, all gave way now to the one thought of rescuing those below.

To this rescue, miners and officials, friends and foes, pressed forward indiscriminately, and foremost among them were they who had been most ardent in rebellion. An hour before they had threatened their comrades, and would have attacked and beaten them down if their leader's own father had not led the gang, and now that the self-same comrades were in peril of their lives, each man would have risked his own to have succoured them. The awful message had borne fruit.

"Back!" cried Arthur, stepping forward to meet them, as, without any definite plan, they pressed blindly forward. "You cannot help now, you will only hinder the officials' approach. We must first ascertain how and where it is possible to penetrate into the shaft. Make way for the engineers."

"Make way for the engineers!" repeated those nearest him. The cry resounded through the ranks, and a narrow passage was at once formed for the chief-engineer and his staff, who now came up from an opposite direction.

"There is no possibility of forcing our way in over there yonder," said he to Arthur, pointing towards the lower shaft which was in connection with the upper one, and from which mighty columns of smoke and thick vapour were issuing. "We have not even made the attempt, for no human being could breathe in that infernal steaming cauldron. Hartmann tried it, but when he had gone five or six steps, he was forced to beat a retreat half stifled, and he was just able to drag out Lawrence, who had followed him, but had fallen at the entrance. Our only hope lies in the upper drawing-shaft; perhaps they may have taken refuge there. Set the engines going, we must make the descent that way."

The man in charge of the machinery, to whom these words were addressed, stood by pale and agitated without preparing to obey.

"The engines have refused service for the last hour," he reported in a tone of distress. "I wanted to send word of it, for all the gentlemen were up at the house, but my messenger could not get through on account of the row there was up there, and I thought, at all events, the gang at work could ascend by the lower shaft which remained free. We have been trying hard to work them, but we can't make them move."

"Heavens and earth! that about finishes us," cried the chief-engineer, rushing by into the shed.

"But by the ladder-way?" Arthur turned hastily to the Director. "Cannot we get down there?"

The other shook his head.

"The ladder-way has not been available since the morning. You know, Herr Berkow, Hartmann had all the upper ladders destroyed, so as to prevent the descent at all hazards. He did not succeed; the men went down by the drawing-shaft, and that is the only access left us now to the mine."

Ulric appeared at this moment with Wilms and several of his usual companions.

"Down there it can't be done," cried he to the miners, while he pushed his way through their ranks. "We should sacrifice our lives all for no use, and they are needed just now to help. Perhaps up here it may be possible, we must go down with the drawing-cage."

He was pressing hurriedly on to the engine-shed, when he was suddenly confronted by Arthur Berkow, who looked sternly at him and said in a loud sharp tone:

"The engines have refused service for the last hour, and it is only ten minutes since the accident happened; there can be no connection between the two. It is just an hour since your three delegates were taken up. What had happened before that, Hartmann?"

Ulric fell back as if he had received a blow.

"I recalled the order," he gasped, "the moment my father and the rest went down. I came myself to stop it, but they had done it already. I would not have had that, I swear, I would not!"

Arthur turned from him to one of the engineers who now came out.

"Well, how goes it?" he asked, hastily.

The official shook his head.

"The engine does not act. We have not been able to find out the cause, it is certainly not the explosion, for that happened nearly an hour later, and had no effect whatever on the buildings about the shafts. This injury has been done wittingly. We must have overlooked something this morning when we examined the machinery. If we do not manage to get it into working order all access to the mine is cut off from us, and the men below are hopelessly lost, Manager Hartmann with the rest."

He had raised his voice as he spoke the last words and fixed his eyes on Ulric, who, with a deadly pallor on his face, was standing by dumb and motionless; but now he started violently and made a hasty movement forward. Arthur barred the way.

"Where are you going?"

"I must be up and doing!" groaned the young Deputy. "I must help, let me go, Herr Berkow; I must, I tell you."

"You cannot help," interrupted Arthur bitterly. "There is nothing to be done now by the sheer strength of a man's arms. You could destroy and increase the danger tenfold, leave the repairs to those who understand them. They alone can make it possible for us to come to the rescue, and they must not be hindered or interfered with at their work. Keep the space round the house clear. Director, and you, Herr Wilberg, fetch down the prisoners immediately. They must know where their hands have been busy, perhaps they can put the engineers in the right way. Be quick."

Wilberg obeyed, and the Director prepared to carry out his instructions. He found no difficulty in so doing; the crowd around knew that everything now depended upon the activity of their superiors. All felt something of that truth which Arthur had once expressed in answer to their leader's challenge.

"Try," he had said, "try to do without that powerful element you hate so much, which directs your labour, gives impulse to the machinery, and lends mind to your work."

Here were hundreds of arms, hundreds of strong men ready to help, and not one could raise his hand, not one knew how to employ his strength; the whole power to save, the whole possibility of coming to the rescue, lay now with the few, who here again must set their minds to work to discover means of even yet affording help, while the many, together with their leader, could do nothing but hurry blindly on to certain death. Those detested, much contemned officials! Every look now hung on them; directly one of them appeared, he was surrounded by an eager throng, and they and their work would at this juncture have been protected at any cost, had such protection been needed.

Minute after minute went by in anxious, torturing suspense. Wilberg had long ago come back with the three prisoners who had been confined in one of the rooms on the ground-floor of the great house. The men knew what had happened; like all the rest they came in breathless haste, to stand by, like them helpless and despairing. They were no longer wanted, for the cause of the stoppage in the engines had already been found; the injury proved to be trifling, and might be quickly repaired. The engineers, under their principal's superintendence, worked with might and main, while out of doors a plan for the rescue was being drawn up, and preparations set on foot for carrying it out.

Continued attempts were made to effect an entrance into the mine by the other shaft, but they were always made in vain. The danger had knitted together again the loosened bonds of discipline; every one obeyed orders, and obeyed more quickly, with greater alacrity, than even in former days, before the strike had broken out.

But most active and ardent of all was the master himself. His eye, his voice, were everywhere, assisting and encouraging. Arthur possessed little or nothing of the special knowledge and experience required by the occasion. The young heir to the works had been brought up in total ignorance of all that it would have been most necessary for him to know, but one thing he did possess, which no teaching could have given him, and that was the gift of command. This was exactly what was wanting now, for the only really energetic official, the chief-engineer, was detained near the engines, and the Director and the rest, half stunned by the rapid succession of events, and by the catastrophe itself, seemed, in spite of their knowledge, experience and ability, to have lost all presence of mind.

It was Arthur who gave them back composure, who, at a glance, found the right place for every man, and urged him on to do his utmost in it; Arthur who carried all with him by the fervour of his zeal. The young man's character, so long misunderstood by those about him, and most of all by himself, had never so brilliantly proved its worth as in this hour of danger.

At last the heavy creaking sound was heard of the machinery being set in motion; then followed a snorting and groaning, spasmodically at first and at intervals, then in regular cadence; the pistons rose and sank again obediently as ever. The chief-engineer came out to Berkow, but his face had not cleared.

"The engine is at work, but I am afraid it is either too early or too late to make the descent. The smoke is pouring out here now, the fire-damp must have extended. We shall have to wait."

"Wait!" said Arthur, with a hasty movement of impatience. "We have waited a full hour, and the lives of the unfortunate men may hang on each minute. Do you think it is possible to get down the drawing-shaft?"

"It may perhaps be possible. It seems to be only smoke that is coming up, but any one who goes down now will risk his life. I would not venture on it."

"But I will!" broke in Ulric's voice, speaking with great decision. As soon as the machinery had begun to move he had pushed forward, and he was now standing by the great iron cage in which the ore was lifted.

"I shall go down," he repeated, "but one man is of no use below, I must have help. Who will go with me?"

Nobody answered. All present recoiled before a journey down that steaming gulf; they had seen how the brave fellows, who had tried to force an entrance through the other shaft, had stumbled back or fallen. Lawrence still lay unconscious; he had succumbed to a venture from which his stronger companion had escaped scathless, and not one among them had the temerity to follow that companion in an expedition where return or retreat seemed almost hopeless.

"No one?" asked Ulric after a pause. "Well then, I will go by myself. Give the signal."

He sprang into the cage, but suddenly a slender white hand was laid on its grimy edge, and a clear voice said:

"Wait a moment, Hartmann, I am coming with you."

A cry of horror broke from the lips of all the officials standing round; on all sides a loud opposition was set up.

"For God's sake, do not, Herr Berkow! You will sacrifice your life uselessly. You can give no help." And so on, in every tone and alarm of anxiety.

Arthur drew himself up, looking every inch the master as he replied,

"I do not go to help but to set an example. If I start first, they will all follow. Make every arrangement in your power up here to ensure our safety; the Director will keep order outside. At this moment I can do nothing but try and give the people courage, and that I mean to do."

"But not alone and not with Hartmann," cried the chief-engineer, almost dragging him back. "Beware, Herr Berkow, it is the same situation and the same company which proved fatal to your father. You too might meet with other perils down below than any caused by an explosion of fire-damp."

It was the first time the accusation had been openly launched before witnesses; though none dared to echo it, their faces showed how fully the suspicion and fear were shared by them. Ulric still stood in his place; he neither spoke nor moved, neither contradicted nor attempted to defend himself, he only turned his eyes full upon the young proprietor, as though awaiting from his mouth an acquittal or condemnation.

Arthur's look met his; only for a second, then he freed himself from the strong arms which would have held him back.

"Below in the mine are more than a hundred lives which must be lost if we cannot come to the rescue, and there, I think, no hand will be raised except to save. Give the signal. Your arm. Hartmann, you must help me."

Ulric stretched out his arm with convulsive eagerness to give the required help. Next minute Arthur stood by his side.

"As soon as we are safely down, send after us any who can and will follow. God grant us good speed!"

"God grant us good speed!" repeated Ulric in a low voice, but with equal firmness. The words had a solemn sound; both men, as they uttered them, turned to brave the depths which were yawning to receive them. The engine was set in motion and the cage sank slowly. Those who stood above could only see how the young master, giddy with the unaccustomed journey, confused by the smoke which, happily, was now rising only in thin clouds, reeled to one side, and how Hartmann threw his arm quickly round him and supported him. They then disappeared into the reeking gulf.

Arthur was right. His example was decisive while Ulric's would have been quite ineffectual. The people were accustomed to see Deputy Hartmann set his life at stake for a much less cause and always escape uninjured, so that a sort of superstitious belief had spread among his companions that no danger could touch him.

It was he who had made the ladder-way inaccessible, who had caused the machinery to be tampered with, so that all help had been delayed for more than an hour; his father was below with the rest, lost, perhaps, through his doing--it was a thing of course that he would rush unhesitatingly forwards to face a risk which none would willingly share with him. But when the master led the way, the proud, delicately-nurtured man, who had never set foot in his own mines while they were comparatively safe, when, now that destruction impended, he pressed forward, all were ready to follow.

The next to volunteer were the three miners who had meddled with the machinery in the morning; they went down under the conduct of an engineer. Then more and more helpers came forward; there was no need to appeal for, no need to require, assistance. Soon the chief-engineer was obliged to turn back applicants, as only a certain number could admitted to the work of deliverance.

Hour after hour passed by, the sun had long since reached its meridian, had long since sunk below it, and still, down below in the very bowels of the earth, the mind of man and the will of man were struggling to snatch their prey from the revolted elements. It was a more terrible fight than any fought in the light of day. In order to advance at all, every foot of earth had to be conquered, every step forward to be painfully won at the risk of their lives, yet they did advance; and it seemed as if such incredible exertions would be rewarded by results equally incredible.

Communication with the unfortunate prisoners had been established; it was hoped they might yet be saved, now that it was found they, or at least some of them, were still living. A happy chance, the finding of two lanterns which had been lost thrown away in the hurried flight, had led to the right track. The explosion seemed to have only partially destroyed the upper shaft, and the miners had apparently had time to take refuge in the side-galleries, where the fire-damp had not reached them, but where they were blocked up and completely walled in by a fall of earth in the outer chambers.

The question was how to work a way through to them, how to find a passage in which the liberating party would at least be able to draw breath, and so to carry out the prompt and efficient plan which had been conceived for their rescue.

"If the whole earth lay on them we must get through!" Ulric had cried when the first traces were found, and that had become the rallying word repeated by every man to his fellow.

Not one fell back, not one tried to evade the perilous duty of his post, yet the strength of many among them could not keep pace with their zeal, and, to avoid increasing the number of sacrifices, several of the workers had to be sent to the surface and their places filled by fresh volunteers.

Two only of the party never flagged and never wearied; Ulric Hartmann with his iron frame, and Arthur Berkow with his iron will, which steeled the nerves of the delicate, slightly-built man, and gave him power to endure on under circumstances, and in the midst of dangers, to which so many stronger than he succumbed. These two held on; side by side they pressed forward, and always in the van.

Ulric's giant strength worked marvels and overcame obstacles which seemed too great to be conquered by human hands: as for the master, it was sufficient that he should be there at their head, that he should be there at all. He could, indeed, do no more than encourage the others in their labours, but in doing this, he rendered better service than by toiling with his arms.

Three times already the hand of his more experienced companion had pulled him back, when, unacquainted with the dangers of the mine, he had exposed himself imprudently; already the engineers had entreated him to turn back, now that there were workers enough and officials enough to lead and direct. Arthur refused each time most resolutely. He felt how much depended upon his remaining among these men who had so suddenly turned from open, violent revolt, to aid and succour in the present distress.

Now all looks were on the master, who, since he had reached independence, had ever stood opposed to them, who, now for the first time, was in their midst, facing danger and death, ready to expose his life like the least among them, and, like them too, leaving above ground a young wife in the throes of a horrible suspense.

In these hours of a common work and common peril he won for himself at last that which had so long and so persistently been refused to the son and heir of a Berkow, their full trust and confidence. There, in the rocky mine below, the old hatred and the old discord were buried, there the strife came to an end.

Arthur knew that for him more was involved than a mere temporary risk, which any one in his place might have run; he knew that, by staying on to the last, he was assuring the future of his works and a future for himself, and the thought of this induced him still to leave Eugénie alone in her anxiety, and to remain at his post.

So they worked on with unabated activity and endurance, advancing slowly, it is true, and step by step, but still advancing, until at last the malevolent powers which dwell below yielded to man's potent will, and a path was opened down to the fellow-men beneath.

As the sun up above sank to its setting, the way to them was found, the rescued miners were lifted to the light of day, injured, half suffocated, stupified by fright and by the fear of death, but still living, and following them came the deliverers, worn out in their turn and half dead with exhaustion. The two who had been first in the bold undertaking were also the last to leave the field of action. They would not stir until every man was in safety.

"I can't think what is the reason that Herr Berkow and Hartmann are delaying so down below," said the chief-engineer, uneasily, to the officials round him. "They were close to the opening of the shaft when the last of the men came up, and Hartmann knows the dangers of the mines well enough not to wait a minute longer than is necessary. The cage is still below, they have given no signal, and they do not reply to ours. What can it mean?"

"I trust no misfortune has happened at the last moment," said Wilberg anxiously. "There was such a strange noise down in the shaft just as the last load came up. The distance was too great, and the noise of the engines too loud, for me to distinguish clearly what it was, but the whole ground seemed to tremble. Suppose there should have been an afterfall."

"God forbid! but you may be right," cried the chief-engineer. "Give the signal once more as loudly as possible. If that is not answered, we must make the descent again and see what is the cause of it."

But before he or the others could carry out this resolution the signal for drawing up was given below sharply and quickly. The men above ground breathed more freely and drew near to the shaft's mouth.

After a few minutes' waiting the cage appeared. Ulric stood in it, his face disfigured and blackened by perspiration and dust, his clothes torn to rags, and covered with earth and fragments of rock and stone, while blood poured from his brow and temples. As at the time of the descent, he was supporting the young master, but now Arthur was not merely staggering; his head rested on his companion's shoulder, his eyes were closed, and he lay motionless and deadly pale in Hartmann's arms, which seemed to be exerting all their strength to hold him upright.

A cry of fear resounded on all sides. Before the engine had well come to a stop, twenty arms were outstretched to receive the unconscious man and to carry him to his wife, who, like all the rest, had never once stirred from the scene of the calamity. Every one pressed round the two, help was called for, the doctor summoned, and in the general confusion no one paid attention to Ulric, who had stood strangely quiet and passive, and suffered his burthen to be taken from him.

He did not spring out of the cage with his usual rapid movement; slowly, painfully he got out, catching twice at the chains to keep himself from falling. No sound escaped him, but his teeth were tightly set as in an extremity of pain, and the blood gushed forth more violently from his wound; under that thick layer of dust it could not be seen that his face rivalled that of the master in pallor. He advanced a few paces with an unsteady gait, then he stopped all at once; grasping convulsively with both hands at the pillars before the engine-house, he managed to support himself by them.

"Make your mind easy, my lady," consolingly said the doctor, who had been in attendance on the sufferers, and had at once hastened to the spot. "I do not find that Herr Berkow has sustained the slightest injury. He will recover."

Eugénie took no comfort from his words. She only saw that white face with its closed lids, that prone inanimate form. There had been a time when, as a bride, but a few hours after her wedding, she had been snatched from peril by the hand of a stranger, and, being in uncertainty as to her husband's fate, she had coolly and quietly turned to her deliverer and said, "Pray look to Herr Berkow!"

For such cold disdain as this she had more than atoned by the torture of the last few hours. They had taught her what it is to tremble for a loved, one without having power to help, without even being near and sharing the danger. Now she would have no one at his side but herself, now, like any other wife in her anguish and distress, she was on her knees beside her husband, calling piteously on his name,

"Arthur!"

At the sound of this passionate despairing cry a great quiver passed through the miner's frame as he still stood leaning against the pillars, and he drew himself up erect. He turned his mournful blue eyes once more on those two, but there was nothing of the old defiance and hatred in his look, nothing but a dumb profound sorrow. Then all grew cloudy before him, he raised his hand, not to his bleeding brow, but to his breast where no external hurt was to be seen, as though the greater pain were there, and at the very moment that Arthur, still supported by his wife's arms, re-opened his eyes, Ulric fell heavily to the ground behind them.

Though the last man had now been brought to the surface, an uneasy silence still reigned among the assembled crowd. There were no demonstrations of joy; the sight of the sufferers forbade all rejoicing, for as yet it could not be told whether life was really saved, or whether Death would not after all come in and claim the victims who had been snatched from him at the cost of so much toil and labour.

The master had recovered from his fainting fit more quickly than had been expected. He and his companion had really been overtaken by an afterfall of earth, rudely shaken and dislodged by the recent explosion, but, marvellous to say, Arthur had escaped unhurt. Supported by his wife's arm he could stand up already, though wan still and weak, and he was trying to collect his thoughts so as to answer Eugénie's questions.

"We were close to the opening of the shaft. Hartmann was on in advance and in perfect safety. Something must have shown him what was coming. I saw him suddenly rush back to me, he seized my arm, but it was too late; all was giving way around us. I only felt that he pulled me with him to the ground, felt that with his own body he shielded me from the avalanche which was coming down upon us, then I lost consciousness."

Eugénie made no answer. She had feared this man so intensely, had been a prey to such unutterable alarm ever since she heard that Arthur had undertaken the dangerous task in his company, and now it was to this man's presence alone she owed her husband's life and rescue.

The chief-engineer came up to them. His face was very grave and his voice sounded almost solemn as he said:

"The doctor says they will all be saved, all but one; for Hartmann no help can avail! The efforts he made down in the mine to-day were too much even for his strength, and the wound has done the rest. How, in such a state as that he could possibly have worked a way for himself and you through the ruins, have raised you into the cage and held you until you were in safety, is almost incomprehensible. No one but himself could have done it; he has succeeded, but he will pay for it with his life."

Arthur looked at his wife. Their eyes met, and they understood each other. In spite of his exhaustion, he shook himself together, took

Eugénie's hand and drew her with him to the spot where prompt aid and attention were being lavished on the sufferers. Only one, the last, had been carried to one side. Ulric lay stretched on the ground; his father was still unconscious and knew nothing of his son's state, but he was not therefore left alone or altogether dependent on the help of strangers.

At his side a girl was kneeling, holding the dying man's head in her arms, and gazing into his face with a look of heart-breaking anguish: she paid no heed to her lover, who was standing on the other side holding his friend's hand, now rapidly growing cold Ulric saw neither of them, perhaps no longer knew that they were there. His eyes were wide open and fixed on the flaming sky, on the setting sun, as if he would drink in one last ray of the external light and carry it with him down into the shades of the long dark night.

Arthur put a question in an undertone to the doctor standing by; he answered with a silent shake of the head. The master knew enough. He left his wife's hand free, whispered a few words in her ear, and then stepped back, while Eugénie bent over Ulric and spoke his name.

Then life leapt up within him again, flashing one last gleam through the mists of death. Perfectly conscious now, he turned upon her a look in which all the glow and passion of former days were for one moment concentrated. She put a timid low question.

"Hartmann, are you badly wounded?"

His face quivered with the old pain, and he answered in low broken tones, but quietly,

"Why do you ask about me? You have him, why should I live on? I told you before, it should be he or I.... I meant it differently, but that was what came into my head when the wall fell in. I thought of you and your grief .... I remembered that he had held out his hand to me when no one else would .... and then .... then I threw myself over him."

He sank back, that last bright spark quenched in the effort of speaking; the life, which had been so full of fire and of wild restlessness, now ebbed gently away without struggle or pain; the man, whose whole existence had been passed in hatred of and rebellion against those set over him by fate, had come to his death in the act of rescuing his enemy.

So was the presentiment fulfilled, which had been borne in upon him yesterday as he listened to the murmuring water; from the inner depths of the earth the stream had brought Death's greeting to his victim. Ulric, truly, had no need to look beyond the morrow, shrouded from him by the impenetrable veil; all had indeed come to an end for him with that "morrow"--all and everything!

From the high-road out yonder sounded the regular march of an advancing troop, with now and again a word of command or the clashing of arms; the help, which had been requested and expected from the town, had arrived. As soon as he reached the first outlying houses of the settlement the officer in command learned what had happened. Drawing up his men in the road, he himself, accompanied by a slight escort, went over to the scene of the accident, and asked to speak to the proprietor.

Arthur went forward to meet him.

"I thank you, Captain," he said quietly and gravely, "but you have come too late. I do not need your help now. For the last ten hours we have fought together, my people and I, for the lives of some of us who were in danger, and during that time we have made peace--I trust for ever."

CHAPTER XXVI

Summer had come again. Once more mountains and valleys lay bathed in sunshine and verdant with beauty, and down in the Berkow settlement there was busy life and movement as in the old days, only freer and more cheerful than it had ever been before. There was an atmosphere of liberty and happy contentedness about the works now; extensive as ever, they had gained all that had previously been wanting, but this had not come about in weeks or even in months. Years had been needed, and those following the catastrophe had not been years of ease. When work had been resumed, a heavy load still rested on the young master's shoulders. He had, it is true, made peace with his people, but he stood on the brink of ruin. The crisis was past, the moment of danger when personal courage and personal sacrifices could suffice to restrain the excesses of a rebellious multitude; but now came a time harder to bear, a time of constant arduous toil, of struggling, often desperate, against the force of circumstances by which Arthur was well nigh crushed. But in the first trial he had learnt to test his strength, in the second he knew how to use it.

For more than a year it remained doubtful whether the works could be kept on under their then owner, and even when this critical period had been tided over, there were still dangers and losses enough to be faced. Even during the last years of the elder Berkow's lifetime the position had been seriously shaken, the fortune impaired by his wild speculation, his lavish expenditure, and, above all, by that unscrupulous system of working which only aimed at great and immediate profits and eventually recoiled on the employer himself.

Then came the interruption of all business, which had lasted nearly a month, the accident in the shafts, requiring most important repairs; all this combined threatened completely to overwhelm a situation already greatly imperilled. More than once it seemed impossible the works could be preserved, more than once it seemed as though the memory of past wounds, caused by harsh treatment and by the late open strife, rankled too deeply ever to be allayed; but Arthur's character, aroused so late, steeled itself and grew to fuller development in this school of incessant and strenuous activity.

All the foundations were shaken and the edifice tottering to its fall when, years before, Arthur had undertaken the difficult task of bringing order out of the chaos of debts, engagements and claims upon him, which had to be met first of all, and of establishing a perfectly new system. But he had learnt confidence in himself; his wife was at his side, and on his exertions depended Eugénie's future prosperity and his own. That thought gave him courage to withstand, where any other would have yielded in despair; supported him even in moments when the task seemed beyond his strength, and obtained for him the victory at last. Now every lingering ill effect of the catastrophe had been overcome; the name of Berkow, stripped of all the evil which had attached to it, had won back for itself the old luck, and stood pure and honourable before the world.

The works, more extensive and on a greater scale than ever, were prosperous and safely established as they had never been before, and their owner's wealth now rested on a strong and sure basis. This wealth, which at one time had threatened to be, and nearly became, fatal to the young heir, accustomed to treat the gifts of fortune with contemptuous indifference because they lay ready at his feet, grew precious in his eyes now that he had reconquered it by the striving of years, and that in his hands it had become a blessing to so many.

It was getting towards noon as the Director and the chief-engineer walked home together on their way from the works. They had both grown older in the course of years, but, in other respects, they were unchanged. The one was good-natured, the other sardonic as ever; there was the old malicious ring in the latter's voice as he went on with his conversation.

"Baron von Windeg's eldest son has announced his father's intention of paying us another visit again already. It appears that our relationship may be boasted of now, though it was condescended to at first with so much repugnance. Since the government has accorded us such flattering attention and, even in higher quarters, interest has been shown in our organisation and the industry of the place, the works have become 'presentable at court' in the old aristocrat's opinion. His son-in-law has been so a long time, and I rather think we are at least on a level with the Windegs now. All the grandeur of the Rabenau property does not amount to half the value of the Berkow estates, or give its owner a tithe of our influence. The Baron is beginning to find out that with all his possessions he is lost in the crowd of wealthy men, while we have grown to be a power in the province and are recognised as such by every one."

"Greater progress has been made here than elsewhere," said the Director. "All around they are studying our improvements and our system, but as yet no one has imitated us."

"Yes, if we go on like this, we shall reach the 'philanthropic model establishment' which the late Herr Berkow used to protest against so vigorously. Well, thank God,"--the chief-engineer raised his head with self-satisfaction--"we can afford it. We are in a position to expend sums for our people's benefit which other folk would have to stow away carefully in their pockets, and certainly the sums are not small. Yet it is not so very long since we were fighting, not for influence or fortune, but for the existence of the works, and we should not have succeeded in saving that but for a few lucky chances which came to us just in the nick of time."

"Or but for the admirable way in which out people behaved," added the Director. "It was no trifle for them to remain quiet while agitation and a regular ferment were going on all around them. The accident in the mine cost money enough just at a time when every hundred was hard to spare, but I think Herr Berkow did not pay too dearly for what he gained with his people. They had not forgotten the hours of suspense and danger he shared with them down below, and they will not forget them. Such a thing as that binds men together for a lifetime. Ever since that time they have trusted him, and when he gave them his word that he would set matters straight if they would only give him a little breathing time, they waited loyally, so it is no wonder if he does more than he promised."

"Well, so far as I am concerned, he can indulge himself in the luxury for the future," said his colleague. "Besides, it is satisfactory to see that, under given conditions, philanthropy may be compatible with a good business. Our yearly balance is more considerable than under the old régime, which, certainly, could not be accused of undue tenderness; all was squeezed out of the works then that was there to squeeze."

"You are an incorrigible joker!" said the Director, "no one knows better than you do that Herr Berkow is guided by no such considerations."

"No, he is too much of an idealist for that," returned the chief-engineer, accepting the reproach with great equanimity. "Luckily, he can be practical at the same time, and he has been through too hard a school not to know that to be practical is the first condition of success in such a case as ours. I have not much opinion of the ideal myself, as you know."

The other smiled rather slily. "Yes, we all know that, but you will modify your thinking, won't you, when you get such a purely imaginative element in your family as Herr Wilberg. The time is drawing near, is it not?"

This little thrust of the Director's seemed to have told, for his colleague made a wry face, and replied angrily:

"Don't talk to me about it, I hear enough of it at home. To think that such a thing should happen to me! to me who hate nothing so much as your sentimental romantic nonsense. To think that fate should have reserved for me, of all people, a son-in-law who writes verses and plays the guitar. There is no getting rid of the fellow with his sighs and his love-making, and Mélanie will not listen to reason. But I have not given my consent yet, and I am not at all sure that I shall."

"Well, we will leave that to Fräulein Mélanie," said the Director laughing. "She has got a bit of her father in her, she knows how to have her own way. I can assure you that Wilberg goes about with the mien of a conqueror, and answers all congratulations with the words, 'No, not yet!' in a way which is exceedingly eloquent. The two young people must be pretty sure of their affair. Good-bye. Mind, I am to be told first of the happy event."

This time it was the Director's turn to be mischievous, and not without result, for the chief-engineer looked greatly put out as he went up the steps to his house.

Fräulein Mélanie came out to meet him, and was unusually tender in her attentions. She gave him a kiss, took his hat and gloves, coaxed him a little, and, after these preliminaries, considered that the time had now come to proffer a petition.

"Papa, there is somebody here who wants to speak to you at once, and on important business. He is in there with mamma, may I bring him to you?"

"I can't be spoken to now," growled her father, guessing what was before him, but the young lady took not the smallest notice of the refusal. She disappeared into the next room, and next minute pushed out the somebody who was there, whispering at the same time a few encouraging words in his ear.

They appeared to be much wanted, for Herr Wilberg, his hair carefully parted, dressed in a frockcoat and presenting the general appearance of an official suitor, stood rooted to the spot, as though he had fallen unawares into a lion's den. He had prepared a neat little speech for the important occasion, but his superior's grim looks and very forbidding manner as he inquired "What he wanted?" were altogether disconcerting to him.

"My hopes and wishes"--stammered the lover, "encouraged by Fräulein Mélanie's favour--the bliss of calling her my own."

"I thought as much! The fellow can't even make his offer in a rational manner!" grumbled the chief-engineer, not reflecting that his reception was of a nature to discompose any suitor; as the young man stumbled on, getting more and more confused in his speech, he cut him short.

"Well, there, that's enough. What you hope and desire can be no secret from me now. You want to have me for your father-in-law?"

Wilberg looked as if this additional blessing, so inseparable from his future marriage, did not afford him any special delight. "I beg your pardon, sir, what I want is to have Fräulein Mélanie for my wife," he replied shyly.

"Oh! and you will reluctantly take me into the bargain?" asked the irritated father-in-law in spe. "I really don't know how you dare come to me with such a proposal. Have you not been in love with Lady Eugénie Berkow? Have you not filled reams of paper with verses addressed to her? Why don't you go on still with your platonic affection?"

"Oh, that was years ago!" pleaded the lover in his defence. "Mélanie has known that for a long time, indeed that was the very thing which brought us together. There are two sorts of love, sir: the romance of youth, which seeks its ideal in a higher sphere far removed and beyond its reach, and another more durable affection, which finds its happiness on earth."

"Oh! and for this second matter-of-fact sort of sentiment my daughter is good enough? Deuce take you!" cried the chief-engineer, furious.

"You will not understand me," said Wilberg, deeply hurt, but still with some consciousness of the advantage of his position; he knew what a powerful reserve he had in the next room. "Mélanie understands me, she has given me her hand and heart"----

"Well, this is a very pretty business," growled the exasperated parent. "If daughters can bestow their hands and hearts in this manner without more ado, I should like to know what fathers are here for! Wilberg,"--here his face and manner became somewhat milder--"Wilberg, I must do you the justice to say that you have become more rational during the last few years, but you are far from being rational enough. You have not left off versifying for one thing. I would wager you have got some sonnets about you now."

He glanced suspiciously at the young man's frock-coat. Wilberg reddened a little.

"As an affianced husband I should be quite justified in writing them?" said be, with a sort of timid enquiry.

"Yes, and in giving serenades! We shall have a nice time of it this summer," groaned the chief-engineer, in despair. "Look you, Wilberg, if I did not know that Mélanie has got something of her father in her, and that she will soon drive out all your romantic nonsense out of your head, I would say no, once for all. But it seems to me you want a sensible wife, and more particularly a sensible father-in-law who will give you good advice from time to time, and as it appears it can't be helped--well, you shall have both!"

Whether the last-named advantage appeared as great in Herr Wilberg's eyes must remain undecided; in delight at obtaining the first he forgot everything else, and rushed up to embrace his new father-in-law, who made short work of the ceremony.

"There, don't let us have a scene," said he decidedly. "I can't stand it, and we have not time for it now. Come along to Mélanie. You two have plotted the whole matter together behind my back, but I tell you, if ever I find you at your verse-making and my girl unhappy and with red eyes, may the Lord help you!"

While the chief-engineer thus resigned himself to an inevitable fate, Arthur Berkow and Conrad von Windeg were standing together on the terrace before the château, waiting for the latter's horse to be brought round.

The thorough metamorphosis which Arthur's inner man had undergone was partly discernible in his outward appearance. He was no longer the slender pale young dandy, the strength and bloom of whose youth had nearly been destroyed by the life of the great city, but was now in all respects such as one would picture the head and administrator of so vast an undertaking. The lines, which long ago had been graven on his brow, and which years of care and hard work had furrowed there more deeply, could not be effaced by the present prosperous security. Such marks, once made, do not again disappear, but they did not ill become the manliness of his features.

Conrad was still the high-spirited young officer whose bright eyes and rosy lips had lost none of their gaiety and freshness, and for whom life was enjoyable and charming as ever.

"And I tell you, Arthur," he was asserting vehemently, "you do my father injustice if you suppose he still feels any prejudice against you. I wish you could have heard how he answered old Prince Waldstein when he said that the gentlemen up in the hill-districts could not have a very enviable time of it in the present troubled state of the working-classes.

"'That does not apply to my son-in-law, your Highness,' said my father with great aplomb. 'His position is too well assured and the authority he possesses over his people too complete for that; they are quite enthusiastic in their devotion to him, and, besides, my son-in-law is equal to any emergency.' But he has never forgiven you yet for refusing that peerage; he can't forget that his grandson will be only plain Berkow."

Arthur smiled rather ironically.

"Well, I trust the name will be no disgrace to him when he has to bear it before the world, and it is to be hoped your father may live long enough to see a Windeg at his side. How about your engagement, Conrad?"

The young officer drew a wry face. "Well, it will be coming off soon," he replied, rather slowly, "when we go back to Rabenau, probably. Count Berning's estates join ours and the Countess Alma was eighteen last spring. My father is of opinion that, as heir to the family, it is time I should be seriously thinking of getting married. I am under orders to make a declaration to the Countess this summer."

"Orders!" said Arthur, laughing. "You are going to marry by order?"

"Well, what did you do?" asked Conrad, rather piqued.

"Indeed yes, you are right But ours was an exceptional case."

"Mine is not," returned Conrad indifferently. "The thing is generally managed so in our set. My father will have it that I shall marry early and suitably, and he will stand no contradiction, except perhaps from you. You have impressed him so deeply that he will put up with absolutely anything it may please you to say or do. After all, I have nothing particular to urge against the marriage, except that I should have liked to be free a little longer."

Berkow shook his head. "I think, Con, you will do well to carry out your father's plan in this. So far as I could see during our last visit to Rabenau, Alma Berning is a charming girl, and it really is time for you to show more of the future peer and less of the wild lieutenant in your proceedings. He has got himself into some pretty scrapes, my young lieutenant!"

Conrad tossed his head.

"Yes, and on each occasion he has had to listen to a paternal lecture in which his brother-in-law has been held up as a pattern and extolled to the skies. I declare it has needed all my predilection for the model to keep me from detesting you! In fact, the whole marriage project dates from that. In one of these judicial encounters, I made the mistake of saying 'Arthur did much worse in his time; it is only since he has been married that he has become so remarkable for his excellence,' and then it immediately occurred to my father to have me married too.

"Well, I don't care! I have no objection to make to Alma, and besides I shall take example by you and Eugénie. You began your wedded life with the utmost indifference, if not with downright aversion, to one another, and you have ended by turning it into a perfect romance which has not spun itself out yet. Perhaps it will be the same with us."

A very sceptical smile played round Arthur's lips.

"I doubt it, my dear Con; you hardly seem to me to be cut out for a romance, and remember, every woman is not a Eugénie."

The young Baron laughed out loud.

"I declare, I thought something of that sort would come out. Just the same tone in which Eugénie said to me this morning, when we were talking of this: 'You cannot think of placing Arthur on a level with other men!' I must say you are stretching out your honeymoon to a good length."

"We had to do without it at first, and one is generally inclined to take double of a thing one has waited for. So you really cannot stay?"

"No, my leave is out this evening. I came over principally to tell you my father and brothers would soon be here. Good-bye for the present, Arthur."

His horse having been brought round while they were talking, he swung himself into the saddle, waved an adieu to his brother-in-law and galloped off. Arthur was about to return to the house, when an old miner appeared on the terrace and took off his hat to the master.

"Ah, Manager Hartmann!" said Berkow in a friendly tone. "Were you coming to me?"

The Manager came up with a respectful, but at the same time confidential, manner.

"Yes, if you will excuse it, Herr Berkow. I was out there yonder giving the orders, and I saw you come out with the young Baron. I thought I should like to thank you at once for having appointed Lawrence to be Deputy. It has brought great gladness to our house."

"Lawrence has shown himself so clever and capable during the last few years, he deserved the post, and he may want it with his ever-increasing family."

"Well, he has enough for his wife and children, I take care of that," replied the Manager good-naturedly. "It was a right good thought of Martha's to make it a condition that he should come and live in my house. I am not left quite alone in my old age so, and I can take some pleasure in their children. I have nothing else left me in all the world."

"Cannot you get over the old grief yet, Hartmann?"

The Manager shook his head.

"I cannot, Herr Berkow. He was my only son, and though he oftener gave me pain than joy, though at last he had got far beyond all control of mine with his wild ways, still I cannot forget my Ulric. Ah, well-a-day! why was an old man like me saved just for that? With him everything went down into the grave for me."

The old man wiped the bitter tears from his eyes as he took the hand Berkow held out to him in silent sympathy, and then went quietly away, Eugénie had been standing in the doorway during the last few minutes; she had paused there, not wishing to disturb the conversation. Now she came up to her husband.

"Cannot Hartmann feel resigned even yet?" she asked in a low voice. "I never thought he cared so deeply, so passionately, for his son."

"I can understand it," he said gravely, "as I could understand formerly the blind attachment of his comrades. There was something about that man which exercised a most powerful influence on all around him. If I felt this, I who was fighting for my life against him, how much more they for whom he fought! What might that Ulric not have achieved for him and his, if he had had a truer notion of the task before him, and had taken it up in another spirit than that of hatred, bent only on overturning all existing things."

His wife looked up at him half reproachfully.

"He showed us that he was capable of something better than hate. He was your enemy, but when it came to be a question of saving one of you, he snatched you from the danger and freely encountered death himself."

At the remembrance of that time a shade fell on Arthur's face.

"I, of all men, have least the right to bring accusations against him, and I never have done so since his hand rescued me from destruction. But believe me, Eugénie, a complete reconciliation would never have been possible with such a nature as his. He would always have been an element of danger, disturbing the peace between me and the people, and striving with me for the dominion over them. Things had gone so far, he could not have been allowed to go quite unpunished. If I had not accused and passed judgment on him, others would have done so. All that has been spared both him and us."

Eugénie leaned her head on her husband's shoulder. It was the same fair beautiful head, with the dark, dark eyes, but her face was fresher and rosier than of old. The former paleness and marble stillness had given way to that expression which happiness alone can bring.

"That was a bad time, Arthur, which came after the catastrophe," said she with a slight tremor in her voice. "You had hard work to fight through, so hard that at times my courage nearly failed me when I saw the cloud growing darker and darker on your brow, your eyes more and more troubled, and I could do nothing but just stay at your side!"

He bent over her with infinite tenderness.

"And was not that enough? in that long struggle I learned all the power of those two words which brace a man to exertion and make it sweet. I used to repeat them whenever the waves threatened to close over me, and they helped me to success at last: my wife and my child."

The sun stood high in the heavens, shining down brightly from the clear summer sky and pouring its rays on the château with its gardens and flowery terraces; on the works out yonder, teeming with life and manifold movement, which made it seem not a small thing to be ruler over such a world; on the mountains ranged around, forest-crowns on their lofty heads, and within, hiding far below in their depths, a mysterious busy kingdom of their own. This sombre region, which the great rocky arms would fain have shut for ever from mortal eye, has yielded to the might of man's mighty intellect, and opened to admit those forces which press ever onwards, pioneering their way despite of clefts and precipices. So the earth has been robbed of the treasures she held imprisoned in endless night, and they are borne up to the light of day, freed by the magic of human skill and industry.